The Healing Flow: Artistic Expression in Therapy

of related interest

Studio Art Therapy
Cultivating the Artist Identity in the Art Therapist
Catherine Hyland Moon
ISBN 1 85302 814 2

Art-Based Research
Shaun McNiff
ISBN 1 85302 621 2 pb
ISBN 1 85302 620 4 hb

The Expressive Body in Life, Art and Therapy
Working with Movement, Metaphor and Meaning
Daria Halprin
Foreword by Jack S. Weller
ISBN 1 84310 737 6

Contemporary Art Therapy with Adolescents
Shirley Riley
Forewords by Gerald D. Oster and Cathy Malchiodi
ISBN 1 85302 637 9 pb
ISBN 1 85302 636 0 hb

A Practical Art Therapy
Susan I. Buchalter
ISBN 1 84310 769 4

The Healing Flow: Artistic Expression in Therapy

Creative Arts and the Process of Healing: An Image/Word Approach Inquiry

Martina Schnetz

Forewords by Vivian Darroch-Lozowski and David C. Wright

Jessica Kingsley Publishers
London and Philadelphia

First published in 2005
by Jessica Kingsley Publishers
116 Pentonville Road
London N1 9JB, UK
and
400 Market Street, Suite 400
Philadelphia, PA 19106, USA

www.jkp.com

Library of Congress Cataloging in Publication Data

Schnetz, Martina.

The healing flow : artistic expression in therapy : creative arts and the process of healing : an image/word approach inquiry / Martina Schnetz ; foreword by V. Darroch-Lozowski ; foreword by David C. Wright.-- 1st American pbk. ed.

p. cm.

Includes bibliographical references and index.

ISBN 1-84310-205-6 (pbk.)

1. Art therapy. 2. Imagery (Psychology)--Therapeutic use. 3. Healing. I. Title.

RC489.A7S365 2004

616.89'1656--dc22

2004011515

British Library Cataloguing in Publication Data

A CIP catalogue record for this book is available from the British Library

ISBN-13: 978 1 84310 205 2
ISBN-10: 1 84310 205 6

Printed and Bound in Great Britain by
Athenaeum Press, Gateshead, Tyne and Wear

Contents

List of Figures

Acknowledgments

The Healing Flow: Artistic Expression in Therapy matured into a book through the support and inspiration of all those who influenced and shaped my doctoral dissertation, on which this book is based. I would like to acknowledge OISE/University of Toronto for giving me permission to use parts of my doctoral thesis. I also would like to thank my thesis committee Dr. Vivian Darroch-Lozowski, Dr. Ron Silvers, Dr. Niva Piran and Dr. David Rehorick, who were instrumental in shaping my understanding and development of my work as a researcher, therapist and artist. I owe a special thanks to Dr. Vivian Darroch-Lozowski, my thesis supervisor and great friend, for her continuous support, encouragement and sensitive and creative guidance and knowledge. The Foreword that she has written to this book reflects the depth of her understanding and close connection to this work. I would also like to thank Dr. Ron Silvers for his artistic and thoughtful input as a thesis committee member as well as a photographer, and as a friend. Both Dr. Vivian Darroch-Lozowski and Dr. Ron Silvers' works have helped to shape and inspire what I have come to comprehend in this book. I furthermore would like to acknowledge Dianne Brassolotto for her skillful editorial responses to the manuscript that I think made the doctoral thesis more accessible. I would like to thank Dr. Helen Ball, a good friend, fellow researcher, therapist and writer, for her support and insight. Her work and the many conversations that we had over the years have helped to shape my thoughts and to refine my work.

I would like to thank Dr. David C. Wright, Director of Specialized Psychiatry Division and Psychiatrist at Homewood Health Centre, for his input as a colleague working on a multidisciplinary team for the Program for Post Traumatic Stress Recovery, and his insightful feedback on the manuscript that helped refine the work as well as his insights that he has summarized so well in his Foreword. I am especially grateful to the following colleagues for their input into the clinical dimension of this work: Sue Wilson and Mary Ellen Brown, who co-facilitated the creative arts group with me during the research phase and who helped me reflect on the therapeutic work by using different research tools described in my doctoral thesis. Dr. Dennis Hopkins, who was the Medical Director when I began as a therapist at the Homewood Health Centre, was instrumental in helping me to get the art therapy groups started. I greatly appreciated his input as a clinician and co-facilitator of one of the art therapy groups. I would also like to thank Dr. Edgardo Pérez, CEO and chief of staff at the Homewood Health Centre, for giving administrative support and permission for my doctoral research to be conducted at the Homewood Health Centre and for the art therapy component to continue to flourish over the years. I would especially like to thank Gillian Templeton, the program coordinator of the Program for Post Traumatic Stress Recovery, for her continuous support as a colleague and friend. Her feedback on the chapter describing the Program for Post Traumatic Stress Recovery was very helpful in getting another perspective on how the creative art therapy component had developed over the years and became integrated into the overall program.

The many voices represented in this work gave rise to the themes explored in this book and my understanding of the dialogical image word process within an art-based therapy context. I would like to thank all the patients that I have worked with over the years and whose experiences and images have helped to inform my understanding of the process of art toward healing. I would like more than ever to thank all the patients who have given their consent for their pictures to be included in the visual database at the Homewood Health Centre for educational and research purposes. Although only a few images from this visual database were used in this book many of these works were instrumental to my understanding as a therapist, and researcher. I furthermore would like to especially acknowledge those patients whose images were used in this book for helping in building an understanding of the process of art toward healing and for communicating the dialogical image–word process through their works. Given the organic nature of this book and the intuitive, embodied knowledge that was the foundation for what shaped its final form, I furthermore would like to acknowledge the many artists, authors, teachers, and co-workers who have informed this work more implicitly rather than explicitly. They are too numerous to list here; however, over the years many have helped me to reflect on how I see, conceptualize, and represent knowledge.

This work is also grounded in my own historicity and, therefore, I would like to acknowledge here the influences that have shaped my work more informally. I would like to particularly give a special thanks to my father, whose continuous support and encouragement to take risks have helped me not to lose sight of my roots in the arts. I also would like to thank my mother for her encouragement and for providing a view into a more cautious and reflective stance of the world. I would like to also acknowledge my closest family and friends for their support and for keeping me firmly grounded in life's everyday reality. This allowed me to explore theoretical and artistic adventures, which led me to travel into many uncharted territories. Both my children have played a big part in keeping me grounded in this everyday reality. I hope that this book may inspire them in turn to follow their own path and to find confidence, to learn to take risks through being inquisitive and to continue to grow through creative expressions in a sensitive and life-enriching manner.

Foreword

by Vivian Darroch-Lozowski

What is it to "make art" when one wants to heal? The art therapy discussed in this book is painting therapy. That one risks picking up a brush and expressing gestures of color and shape whose origins are deep within one's past can flounder us as much as it can heal us. We know this risk before we even begin. Yet, after the first and the often unsure lines are painted, there is a nameless need within us that captures us, that compels us to continue. This happens when we recognize that what is being formed on the paper is something we have never seen before and, yet, is something with which our body-psyche is intimate.

Wisely, in her therapeutic practice and writings about "healing flow," Martina Schnetz does not place symbols and interpretation at therapy's center. Her sight and the sight of the patients, who are "art-makers" in a group together, stay with the moving and actual reality of what is represented in the images being painted by them. A healing flow depends upon accepting the reality of any images we might make. It also depends on accepting our responses to an image-reality as it transforms itself before our eyes when we change it with our painting hands. Art supports us toward healing even when the "meaning" of the image, as it is being made, is yet out-of-consciousness and only within the body's sensorial gestures.

Art eases us into healing through a process that is alchemical in its subtlety. In creating a visual world on paper we are self-creating, too. We are self-creating by dialoguing between our eyes and our psyche without handling language. Art serves the healing of the psyche through the material substances of what is used in the making of an image. Here, it is the tactile sensuality of undiluted paint, the flowing rivers of water colors, the messiness of charcoals and graphite, and the dirty-ness of our hands and brushes and paint on the floor, the textures of paper and linens and walls upon which we can smudge and make marks. The unarticulated words that appear on paper as weeping selves, or burning houses, or fields of green wildflowers, or black and red raging or peaceful blue waves coagulate, here and there, in our psyche and as we work the painting marks of the image re-pattern us and our thoughts.

To show us this, Martina's descriptions of the patients' images in the context of the work itself and the group discussions afterward are exact. She fully and creatively illustrates how the images, through dialogue with them, become what she calls "embodied iconic abstractions." She also makes for us, the readers, a re-patterned patch-work quilt of her work with her patients that includes her process of writing this work. In the context of her reasons for working interpretatively as she does, the quilt-figure becomes a tangible sharing that explains how the healing flow model developed for her.

Just as gesture and texture in painting shows us how we bind and free our different energies, color also is an integral part of painting. We resonate differently with different colors' rays. Each of us will have a different color palette through which we can come to an understanding of what is inside us or outside ourselves. For example, red grounds us in a powerful and unambiguous shade that we know is the color of living; yellow invites us to shine and flow outward; blue is laden with spaciousness, perhaps quietude and, perhaps, a yearning. What is being yearned for in healing? This is "what" we may discover in therapy. And the white spaces on paper or on wall that we might let remain – are these not mysterious spaces unconsciously left for ourselves to dwell within at another time? The sequencing within each of the cases described by Martina document the step-less evolution of what happens during the wavering yet ever surfacing and evolving flow of healing while painting. The sequencing as she discusses it shows clearly patients' beings moving in and out of the being of the world.

Paintings that are made while healing contain shadows of our histories. They, too, fix in paint shadows of our memories, shadows of our thoughts, and shadows of the light into which our souls are evolving. When we paint we need to become attentive to how textures and substances and colors are occupying our minds. We need to become attentive to the marks we make as we work. It is these kinds of details and their relationships that Martina has elucidated meticulously as she writes about her practical experiences with others. We read, and as we come to appreciate her healing-flow model we recognize within it meaning for our own therapeutic artwork with others.

Vivian Darroch-Lozowski, Ph.D., C. Psych.
Professor, University of Toronto

Foreword

by David C. Wright

The world lived in by traumatized people is a world that has been shrunken. What is left is often only fear and isolation. These people suffer from re-experiencing images of their destructive past. Their worldview no longer contains the possibility of happiness and success. Filled with guilt and shame, for having survived, or falsely believing they could have prevented the traumatic experience, they repeat behaviors that keep the trauma alive. This permits their broken worldview to be reinforced as their future. As Dr. Martina Schnetz has described in this book they also have a broken image system leading to dissociation. The dissociation of the traumatized person, she states, is a dissociation that stretches beyond the individual into the rest of our culture.

Over ten years ago, Martina, myself, and a dedicated group of colleagues began a therapeutic journey together to try and treat, in a new way, patients who had experienced trauma, particularly during childhood. As colleagues, we have participated in an ongoing dialogue within the treatment team about how we can help traumatized patients heal and feel safe in a present-day world. Martina had already begun, and has continued to the present, a significant process of reflection. Examining herself and her therapeutic activities were key elements leading to the writing of this book. I wish to congratulate her on creating such a thoughtful book on the therapeutic process as it has matured within her.

However, at first many of us on the team were concerned that art therapy would allow patients to access previously unknown horrific images. We feared that the subsequent interpretations would be overwhelming and detrimental to the patients. Dr. Darroch-Lozowski has already mentioned Martina's wisdom in focusing on the "healing flow" rather than symbols and their interpretation. As a psychiatrist, a verbally trained therapist without any talent with brush, my own suspicions and reservations of art therapy were allayed. I have come to understand the very appropriate use of these techniques as described by Martina, in helping the patients to realize their own broken image systems and install healing processes to support the goal of creating safety in the present. As someone who has participated with Martina in numerous discussions over process and individual patient care, I value her insights and the impact that art therapy has.

New information gathered from brain imagery is showing that many people's stories of trauma are stored in fragmentary processes on their right side of the brain, and they are not connected to language centers on the left side of the brain. How then can people truly appreciate their own place in space and time if they cannot put words to their past experiences? Indeed, developments in neurobiology supports using therapeutic imagery as the basis for accessing and linking emotions with narrative, and ultimately developing understanding and meaning.

The metaphor of the Interpretative Quilt is very powerful. There is no videotape to be discovered. Instead images, once tolerated, can be rearranged in numerous ways, to create more than a linear story. Martina has embedded her experience of image-making within a therapeutic space, into a much larger theory of epistemology and theory of living. For Martina, she asks that we become participatory scientists, that we explore how we have let dissociation into our daily lives. I hope the readers of this book will engage and wrestle with the important questions and challenges she raises.

David C. Wright, MD, FRCPC
Director, Specialized Psychiatry Division, Homewood Health Centre

Part 1

Interpretative Quilting: A Qualitative Art-Based Approach to Inquiry

CHAPTER I

Introduction to the Healing Flow

An Image Oriented Approach to Inquiry and Psychotherapy

As she walked along the edge of the rocky seashore, her gaze fell upon a beautiful picture that had formed in the layers of mud. She could not quite comprehend how this had been possible. She knelt down to examine it more closely. There appeared to be little physical substance to the picture and its surface was almost water-like in nature. She hesitated for a moment before touching this mysterious image. Small patterns started to emerge where her fingers had made contact with the surface. She became fascinated with the configurations that were created by her touch of this liquid-like substance. The colors and shapes that emerged were so beautiful. After some time of quiet exploration she started to wonder how this strange phenomenon had evolved. She tried to feel if there was a structure that contained this mysterious, ever-changing image. She paused for a moment and then took both hands and reached into the depth of the liquid-like substance. As her hands penetrated into the depth beneath the shiny surface, the image changed once again to create even more beautiful patterns, shapes, and colors that formed powerful images.

She had lost a sense of time while she was exploring this mysterious phenomenon. She was strangely suspended in the action of play and meditation where rational thought had momentarily faded into the background.

The world of symbols and play allowed her to become differently connected to her sense of self and her relationship to the world. This transitional space allowed her to become aware of a force greater than her. Within the symbolic realm of this mysterious picture she was able to momentarily discover herself and the mysteries of being in the world. She was also able to make a deep connection with the universe. Her physical surroundings – the sounds of the roaring sea, the waves crashing against the rocky cliffs, and the wind in the trees – all faded into the background as she became more deeply absorbed by the immediacy of the images.

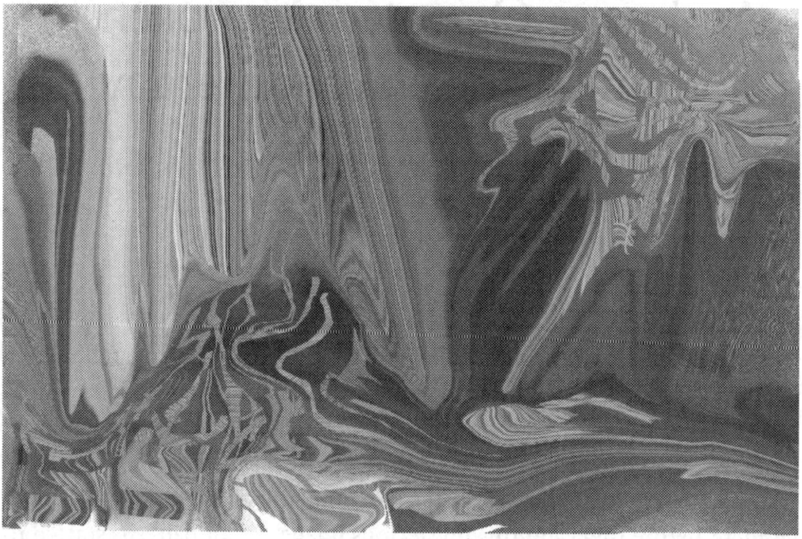

Figure 1.1: The first opening: Reconnecting with immemorial imagery (completed in 1999)

She reached once again into the liquid-like substance in order to create more images. The experience was like diving into the depths of a colored sea that reflected the endless possibilities of the universe. It was a beautiful and fascinating experience. As she let her hands sink deeper into the painting the colors became even richer and more beautiful. At the same time the ocean's waves became stronger and dangerously close. The sounds of the sea, the voices of her family and the connection to her community had now almost completely drifted out of her awareness. She had become fully absorbed by the exploration of this mysterious, ever-changing image that had brought her closer to her own creative force. She felt empowered by the pictures that she was able to create.

There seemed no limit to the pictures she could form. The deeper she reached beneath the surface, the more wonderful and powerful the images became. This playful exchange between the liquid substance, the image, and her actions set off a dialogical process that resonated deep within her soul. It seemed to feed the emptiness inside and it nurtured the core of her being. She felt so alive yet strangely dislodged from the world she knew. She realized that in order to harness the power of this creative energy without being overwhelmed by the waves she needed to bring it alive within the context and social structure of her physical world and within her community. Then she awoke.

Over the years she had learned to embrace the common myth of her times. The myth that claimed that science and technology, with their endless data and facts, would meet all our needs. She realized that technology and data did not nourish her soul. She realized that living is about experiencing. We affirm ourselves through our actions, our voice, and the quality of our dialogue between the world and ourselves. There are many forces that shape how we interact with and affect the world around us. Some of these forces flow underneath the level of our conscious awareness, yet they still affect us in many ways. The dialogical process between being (mind, body, and soul) and the world continuously redefines our boundaries and who we are able to be.

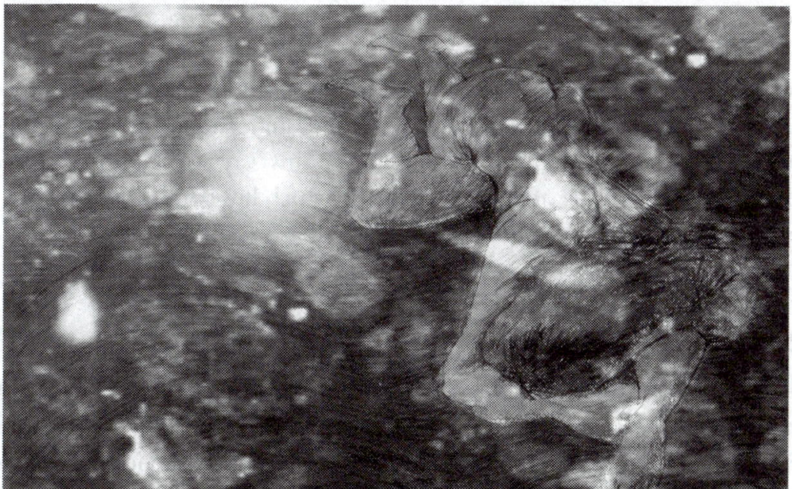

Figure 1.2: Dreaming and the healing flow of images (completed in 1999)

We are mind, body, and spirit and the songs of our being need to resonate with the physical, social, psychological, and spiritual realm in order for us to create the rich fabric of life. Each part needs to be in a continuous dialogical process with the other parts and with the greater whole. The waves of life must flow together to create the complex and beautiful tapestry of life. Balance and harmony include light and dark, the stormy sea and the peaceful waters. All are part of the greater web of being. The contemplative, interpretative dialogical process that art can provide is one way we may connect with and validate this healing, self-creating force within us. The languages of the arts need to have an equal voice in our life as they can link us with different aspects of existential and ontological reality. The symbolic realm of the image-making process can provide avenues through which we can get in touch with the greater whole and restore internal and external balance. This dialogical process with the creative forces is not without its own risks. There is a risk of being swept away by the process if the experience becomes disconnected from the other life forces, the physical reality of the world, and the community that one inhabits.

This creative energy needs to be grounded in one's existential and ontological reality. It is dangerous to enter the process in isolation or in order to lose oneself. We need a larger supportive context to affirm the voices of our being. We need to resonate with the world we live in. We connect with the world through our bodies, mind, and spirit. The soul is like the wind that moves through our being. Our dreams are shaped by the filter of our consciousness as well as by our thoughts and feelings. Within the safety of the community we can hold, learn to understand, and transform what we learned through this experience. In this way, we can find a voice through which we are able to express that which lies beneath the surface of reason. We begin to quilt a tapestry of life.

The Healing-Flow Model and its Implications

The arts are ubiquitous. They have been part of human development throughout time and are present in one form or another in all cultures (Dissanayake, 1988). They are a container for creative energies and behaviors that help to provide order, create rituals that are transformational, and give voice to aspects of being that are beyond reason and logic. They are the essence from which humanity creates a shared understanding of the world. The arts can be the

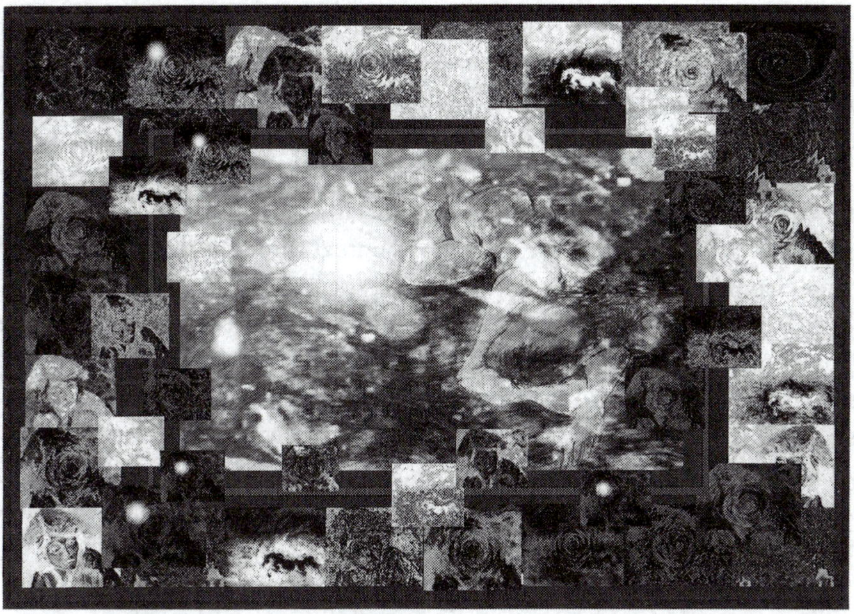

Figure 1.3: Quilted images as a residue of experience (completed in 2001)

vessels for strong emotions, and they require enactment that brings about awareness and compassion.

This book was an inquiry that explored the possibility of using an integrated approch to examining the process of art toward healing within a therapy context. The dissociated part that the arts played and continue to play on the cultural level perhaps parallels what has been discovered. If one draws a parallel between the microcosms that unfold within the art therapy context and the creative, cultural context one may wonder what would happen if the arts once again become more integrated in a meaningful and soul-enriching manner. Writers such as Adamson (1990), Bachelard (1969), Ball (1999), Barthes (1981), Berger and Mohr (1982), Caiserman-Roth and Cohen (1993), Cameron (1992), Darroch-Lozowski (1999, 1989), Darroch-Lozowski and Silvers (1982), Dissanayake (1988, 2000), Gadamer (1985, 1986), E. Levine (1995), S.K. Levine (1992), McNiff (1992, 1998), Silvers (1988,1993a,b), and Wilber (1995) make us further aware of the limitations of the current ways of studying and representing human experiences. They encourage us to go beyond current methods and to create a greater balance and respect between the arts, and the sciences.

For me as a researcher, therapist, and artist, the images in the imagistic pauses[1] of this book telegraph what has been comprehended in this work. The meaning of the metaphor of the Healing-Flow Model itself has significance for my work as a therapist, researcher, and artist as it embodies the complexities that underlie the work in these areas. In this book the personal and objective dimensions of my being were included when I was engaged in the practice of art within the psychotherapy context through using the dialogical image/word approach. It became clear that the personal dimension could not be separated from the objective narrative without going through an embodied, transformative process that transcended the narrative into the more universal realm of being. In this process I needed to recognize my historicity in my work as a therapist, an artist, and as a researcher. The professional aspects of all three cannot be separated from the subjective realm of the human condition. It was necessary to find new ways of representing human experience in an integrated and truthful manner.

The context and specific conditions in which the process of art toward healing evolved set up dynamics for possibilities that shaped the essential creative energies and transformed them into actions guided by practices. Within the social context of the environment that was grounded in a practice, actions could be given form through the symbolic space of the art in order to integrate them and to create a balance between the endless webs of part/whole relationships. In turn these actions became entry points that shaped and resonated with what was emerging through a dialogical process with a given context. They were emerging from my personally lived experiences, while at the same time speaking in more universal terms. In this book some of the complexities involved related to the phenomenon of art toward healing within the therapy context were explored. These complexities were impelled by the duality and complexity of mind, body, and spirit relationships. These complex relationships were examined within the microcosm of art therapy and my experience with the image-making process.

The pictures in the images contained in this book are their own record of the process of art toward healing. They show the possibilities they can offer to the patient, artist, viewer, therapist, or reader. All readings are context bound and the dialogical process between the reader and the images is grounded in the reader's historicity. Some renderings or ways of illustrating phenomena may be more easily recognizable as they perhaps follow more established ways of representation, and they may, at first, appear more realistic and true to their subjects.

> A story is told by a French railroad passenger who, upon learning that his neighbour on the next seat was Picasso, began to grouse and grumble about modern art, saying that it is not a faithful representation of reality. Picasso demanded to know what was a faithful representation of reality. The man produced a wallet-sized photo and said, "There! That's a real picture – that's what my wife really looks like." Picasso looked at it carefully from several angles, turning it up and down and sideways, and said, "She's awfully small. And flat." (Nachmanovitch, 1990, p.117)

A photograph or a snapshot of a person may, at first, appear as a more faithful representation of reality than perhaps a more abstract rendering. Whether we look at portraits done by Picasso with his numerous styles of representation (Rubin, 1980), or by other artists or photographers, each will bring us in touch with a different way of connecting with being-in-this-world. The following works speak to this and illustrate the complex nature of representation through art and photography: Berger and Mohr (1982); Gadamer (1986); and Silvers (1988). Besides the physical qualities and painting styles of a portrait, the viewers bring their own experiences, hopes, goal, and fantasies to the picture. The depth of the dialogical process that can unfold between image and viewer, as well as the connection the viewer is able to form with his or her own world, will determine what aspects of human experiences are brought into awareness.

To the man showing the photograph to Picasso, the picture embodied more than what was visible in the actual image. The photograph of the man's wife was an embodiment of his experiences. The image had become a symbol of the man's internal reality and experiences that were unique to him and his relationship to his wife. His experience of the photograph would be filled with memories, emotions, and thoughts that were specific to his experience. Another person looking at this photograph, in this case Picasso, would engage very differently with the image. He started by observing only the physical qualities of the picture and he chose not to bring his personal history or sentiment into the dialogical process. In his response Picasso stripped his experience of the photograph of its personal, symbolic, and aesthetic dimensions.

What Wilber calls *the descended worldview* is a world "...where there are no depths to be interpreted, only surfaces to be seen. Thus, no inner transformation required, only exterior and empirical mapping" (Wilber, 1995, p.430).

In this world the main forces that drive inquiry are pleasure and survival. In this book I have attempted to go beyond the functional aspects and to reintegrate the arts and internal truths with the more external objective truths of the sciences.

The description in the former passages speaks to the fact that each interpretation has its own strength and weakness with its own bias and systems or schools of interpretation. What is important to note here is that in the dialogical image/word approach, an embodied knowledge is gained through a continuous, dialogical process that is practice-based with what one sees or experiences, how it is represented, and how it resonates within one's being and the world. Thus, interpretations are limited. They can perpetuate fragmentation if they are not grounded in an understanding that is based on our minds', bodies', and spirits' knowledge. There must also be an acknowledgment of the limitations that each rendering can provide. This is true in inquiry as well as in art.

From my own experience of drawing or painting from life, I have become aware of how, during the process of painting, many layers become embodied as I am trying to give a rendering of the person or subject. My experiences of the person and the objects that surround the figure create an opening for many possible dialogical processes to unfold. "The Seated Woman" in the next imagistic pause (Figure 1.4) that was the source image for the quilt of the Healing-Flow Model was a rendering of a young woman that I had painted during a class at Art College in my last year of study.

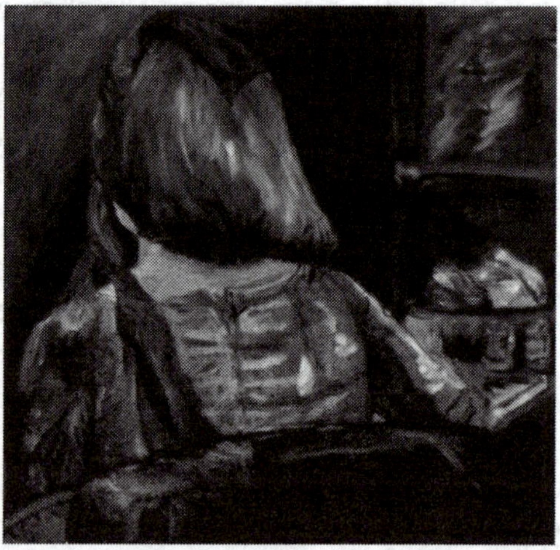

Figure 1.4: The Seated Woman (completed in 1983)

The painting was done in a realistic and representational style. In this painting I attempted to render what I was seeing in a truthful manner. This included the color of her hair, the clothing that she was wearing, and the objects that were on the table next to her. I had no knowledge of the model as a person, and I did not have a verbal dialogue with her that could have informed me about her as a person. In painting this picture I had no responsibility, as such, to the model to create a rendering of her that would please her and that would embody her life experiences, emotions, and thoughts. However, I did have a responsibility to my own internal truth, my perception and experiences, and my technical skills as a painter. These factors shaped how the visual narrative would unfold.

Before painting this portrait, I had to choose a vantage point from which I could start the picture. This presented a challenge, as I had to share the studio with many other students. In order to find a perspective that I could relate to, I walked around the model and finally I found a place that appeared to invite a painting. I chose a perspective that gave me a view of the woman's back. This viewpoint echoed the void of my personal history with the model and the absence of a personal relationship with her. As I was working with the physical qualities of what I was able to see, I gradually became drawn into a dialogical process that was based, in part, in my experiences of the world and the possibilities that could be. This gave rise to a visual narrative that began to take shape through the forms, textures, and colors that I shaped on the canvas. The painting started to take on a mood. This mood led to the formation of possible hypotheses that became embodied in the painting.

While focusing on the subject matter and engaging in a dialogical process on a mainly non-verbal level, I was able to gain a deeper understanding that resonated from within my being. The final image was created out of a blend of being attentive to the physical qualities of my subject, my level of technical skills or experiences, my internal world and reality, as well as the possibilities that I was able to envision. The portrait of the young woman was done over a number of sessions and the physical details, such as the lighting, the placement of the objects, and the model's posture, would change slightly during each session. This gave further layers of experiences that were captured in the final image, in some way. It is this that creates the richness and depth of a rendering and which opened my understanding of the subject more deeply and expanded my internal truth and understanding of the world with its possibilities.

The quilt in Figure 1.5 symbolizes the processing of an image, a memory, and an experience in a way that visually parallels what has been comprehended in this work and in the metaphor of the Healing-Flow Model. The different experiences described in this book needed to be rendered in various representational styles in order to create a whole. The interpretations of the phenomena under investigation needed to encompass all dimensions including the objective and the subjective sides of being with its endless part/whole relationships or *holon.* "Arthur Koestler coined the term *holon* to refer to that which, being a *whole* in one context, is simultaneously a *part* in another" (Wilber, 1995, p.18). Wilber (1995) writes: "My position is that every holon has these four aspects or four dimensions (or four 'quadrants') of its existence, and thus it can (and must) be studied in its intentional, behavioural, cultural, and social settings" (p.129). In Wilber's view a phenomenon needs to be examined in a way that reintegrates the "dissociation of the Big Three that, more than anything else, allowed the sweeping advances of the natural sciences (the it-domain), to overwhelm the interior, subjective, moral, and cultural domains (I and we)" (Wilber, 1995, p.416). Scientific methodologies and intellectually based interpretations can offer us maps of the exterior of phenomena but, if we do not risk finding ways that equally explore the interior with its subjective, affective, and intuitive side of our being, we may become trapped in a very small and flat understanding of what it means to be human in this world. This understanding has little room for our creativity and spirit to develop. Also, it devalues the languages of the arts and renders their potential healing powers impotent.

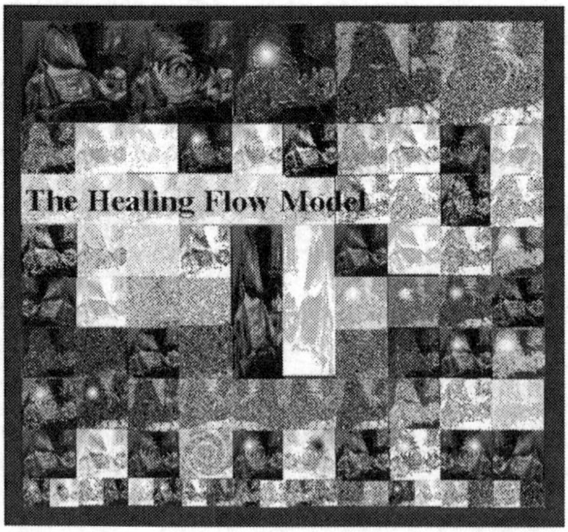

Figure 1.5: Healing flow quilt of the Seated Woman (completed in 2001)

The narrative of this book will show that creativity and our ability to deal with traumatic experiences in a transformative manner are perhaps vital to our ability to survive in a very complex world. Fragmentation and dissociation within an individual, as well as on a cultural level, are not sustainable in the long run. This work is an attempt to raise our awareness of this and to show how vital it is to take an integrated approach that includes the interior and subjective aspects of being in studying therapy and the arts. As it becomes more apparent that the experience of observing plays an important part in what we observe, the role of science and its focus needs also to shift from the more objective approach to a more participatory one. Writers such as Wolf (1994), Wilber (1995, 1996), and Talbot (1991) have explored this issue in their works. Talbot (1991) reasoned that scientists would begin to see themselves less as an observer and more as a participant. "As Harman states, 'A willingness to be transformed is an essential characteristic of the participatory scientist'" (Talbot, 1991, p.298). In this book I have taken a participatory as well as a reflective stance, and I have included the voices of the arts and the sciences. I have been transformed by the phenomena that I was studying.

When I create an image, the dialogical process between what I see and what I am creating through the art materials becomes continuously reorganized. For me it is a mainly non-verbal activity that suspends me in time and engages me in a play with the world. On reflection this also holds true in art therapy and as Levine (1995) phrases it: "What is interesting in expressive arts therapy work is that we can create a form for this experience to take place which is neither real nor un-real but exists in a play-space which is in-between and thereby protected and safe" (p.103). In this sense, engaging in play or art has a certain therapeutic aspect that can be enhanced and channeled through the therapy and the dialogical image/word process described in this book.

> Dialoguing with images is a method for expanding ego's singular vision. In opening to others, we do not have to give away our place within the interaction. Others have an experience of us that may be quite different from our experience of ourselves. All of these perspectives are elements in the psychic stew. Reality is an ever changing interplay and never a single, fixed position. (McNiff, 1992, p.2)

This does not mean that we have to take a relativistic view in which everything is equal. In his work Wilber (1995, 1996) describes natural hierarchies, which may be different from power-related hierarchies created by society. According to Wilber (1995, 1996) these hierarchies need to be respected, otherwise the part/whole relationships become disrupted when different holons either blend in too much and lose their distinction or when one becomes too dominant. If the natural orders are out of balance and are not respected, then pathology will develop. Therefore, within each approach to recording, analyzing, and interpreting phenomena, we are able to make distinctions between the balances that need to be maintained, the things that need to be challenged, and what to base our judgment on in order to determine good and truthful interpretations.

The Healing-Flow Model, with its dialogical image/word approach, offers a way in which we can engage in an honest dialogical process that involves all of our being including our mind, our body, and our spirit. It also is an approach in which an attempt has been made to reduce the risk of creating an inauthentic picture or misrepresentation. When using this process there will be no representations or interpretations that are true to the original image or phenomena. There will simply be different resonances that are truthful to an experience. If we follow an authentic dialogical process rather than rigidly clinging to a system of representations or methodology I feel we have a better chance of discovering truths in a more integrated manner.

> Dialogue assumes interaction between differences. It permits contradictions, conflicts, sudden shifts, vital exchanges, and there is no need to follow a single thesis. As the basis of psychotherapy, dialogue becomes a spontaneous and lively drama corresponding to the movements of psyche. (McNiff, 1992, p.69)

The images, with their symbolic and playful dimensions, verbalize an understanding of the world we live in that is based in the body, the mind, and the spirit with their endless part/whole relationships and possibilities. Within this space of dialogue and play, boundaries are created and worldviews and identities are able to develop.

In the imagistic pauses, the reader is invited to examine the images from a wider perspective and to recognize the many levels that these images can awaken. The pictures speak in their unique voices of the process of art toward healing. They speak about worlds that we can enter and resonate with from various perspectives, and they convey themes of what it means to be human in this world. The pictures inform us in a different way about the process of art toward healing as they speak of the artist who has created them, the group/social context they were created in, and its members who were part of the process. The image itself is part of a process as well as it is becoming an object with recognizable qualities that one can reflect upon.

Theoretical Considerations of the Healing-Flow Model and Interpretative Quilting

In the metaphor at the beginning of this chapter, theory and text are like rock and water. The rock contains and gives structure to the water. Yet the water has the power to change and move the rocks and sand that contain it. In a picture, it is the lines that define the shapes and that give form to colors. Colors influence our perception of lines. In a quilt, a border contains each quilt block. The border holds and brings forward the richness of the quilt blocks. The metaphor for this book is one of interpretative quilting – where each part of the quilt is a coagulated aspect of the healing flow. Within this quilt, the interpretative border provides a container for the phenomena under investigation. Through the descriptive and interpretative border, the different colors and themes represented in the different quilt blocks are clarified. Thus, the border and the organizational structure of the quilt freeze the continuous flow of lived experience and, in doing so, filter out some of the details and noise of the phenomena the quilt depicts. The following pages will introduce the reader to some of the important observations identified through this work.

The metaphor of the image of the earlier-mentioned water dream played an important part in this work and took the role of what Darroch-Lozowski (1993) has named *immemorial images.* According to Darroch-Lozowski, immemorial images go beyond our past and connect us with the larger web of life and energy. According to her it is this aspect that makes them immemorial – beyond memory and out of mind. It is this aspect that takes them beyond the personal realm.

> These pure "recollections" condense more than one's own story or the identity of one's own self; they hold every possible path which we might have taken or will take. I've come to accept that it is these images (not our remembered "memories") which are the pure images of our lives. (Darroch-Lozowski, 1993, p.25)

The images of the water dream are based on my experience of the world and are grounded in my dreams and my lived experiences as a woman living in the current North American culture and times. Yet, I feel that these images of the water dream and the Interpretative Quilt with its imagistic pauses go beyond that personal experience and allow me to connect more with social and universal themes. This connection acknowledges my belonging to a larger web of life, with its endless possibilities in time and space. Wolf (1994) writes: "In cyberspace we place ourselves inside of any representation we wish to explore. It allows us to explore symbols not only by interpreting them as we normally do, but by actually getting inside of them and thereby experiencing them" (p.342). When I began working with the images on my computer I began to explore new possibilities that would have not been possible in any other way. This new media mediated a dialogical process; it opened new possibilities for representing and expanding on lived experience. Out of this dialogical process the Interpretative Quilt gradually emerged. Working with the Interpretative Quilt affirmed my intuitive sense that, as Wolf stated in his writings, "Reality is not made of stuff, but it is made of possibilities that can be coherent so that possibility forms into solid matter" (p.344). Through the engagement with the material world, life's energy or creative energy becomes shaped and externally expressed. When an image emerges on a surface it reflects the outer reality of the material world and the inner processes of the person who creates it or views it.

Küchler and Melion (1991) write of the important role that images appear to play in memory, in remembering, and in the representation of lived experience. The authors speak to the notion that memory is not simply the result of neurological traces of past experiences. They argue that memory is an active construction that uses images as an essential part of this process. They examine this issue from a psychological perspective, through human cognition, and through exploring different artists and cultural, representational styles. These writings further support the notion of the importance of an image and the different functions it can play for us in our understanding of the world. The following four themes emerged in their work:

> First, memory is socially and culturally constructed, and recourse to the processes of construction must mediate the understanding of memory, especially the understanding of its embeddedness in active processes of cognition and image production. Second, memory operates through representation. Images do not simply encode prior mnemonic functions, but rather posit a dynamic of mnemonic processes. Images engender modes of recollection as much as they are determined by them. Third, modalities of recollection are historically based, and the project of understanding is

> a historical one. Fourth, forgetting and recollecting are allied mnemonic functioning. Forgetting can be the selective process through which memory achieves social and cultural definition. (Küchler and Melion, 1991, p.7)

Johnson (1991) writes along the same lines that all the "life-sustaining" and "self-enhancing" activities are dependent on the general cognitive capacity to use images and to create metaphors. His hypothesis is that images are central and that a link between

> our bodily experience, perceptual processes, and these linguistic and more abstractive cognitive constructions is provided by structures of imagination that emerge in our bodily interactions and are metaphorically extended to form our understanding of abstract concepts and patterns of thoughts. (Johnson, 1991, p.74)

In various activities such as the arts, metaphors and linguistic representations can become integrated with other daily activities. Imaginative patterns and processes evolve individually as well as collectively. Johnson (1991) continues by saying: "... that image schemata are also the basis for our shared, constructive, historically situated, and culturally articulated memories, which are the crucial means whereby we are able to inhabit a shared, meaningful world" (Johnson, 1991, p.86). He states that there are links between bodily experiences, perceptual processes, linguistic and more abstract cognitions, and imagination and the imaging system "that emerge in our bodily interactions and are metaphorically extended to form our understanding of abstract concepts and patterns of products" (p.74). Thus, a healthy imaging system is essential to processing lived experience, metabolizing traumatic events, and being able to be mindfully present, as well as being able to envision a future. Internal images, symbolic representations, and metaphors allow us to connect with the world. Through the imaging system we are able to translate creative energy and to express it through gestures, words, art, and rituals so that these things can be shared with others. Internal images, symbolic representations, and metaphors make us more aware and allow us to be able to dream and to create a future that has new possibilities, creativity, and spiritual connections.

Images and art go beyond the personal into the social and universal realms, as they are constructed through a continuous, dialogical process between lived experience and the world. They give us insights into our own functioning on an individual as well as on a cultural level. "It seems that we dream in images and not in words because images are a basic or perhaps primitive way of dealing with the outside world. I would also suggest that images are strongly connected with feelings" (Wolf, 1994, p.45). He further argues that emotions are vital to having memories. As well, images are also portals that open the door on new experiences, as in the case of the immemorial images described earlier.

What do we do with images that are frightening in nature, such as dreams that are filled with monsters or images of terror and abuse? Cohen (1996) explores the theoretical relationships between traumatic experiences and the internal world of people who are suffering from Complex Post Traumatic Stress Disorders and Dissociative Identity Disorder (DID) (formerly known as multiple personality disorder) with the visual arts and the images created in therapeutic-art making. Through an exploration of the works of artists such as M.C. Escher and the German expressionist artist Max Beckman, he states that: "Because visual and sensorimotor functions are critical in the storage, coding, and recall of traumatic events, one must be willing to learn about the impact of trauma on imagery and how they manifest through art making" (Cohen, 1996, p.527). He continues by saying that: "When experiences are found to be overwhelming, unexpected, or undesirable, they cannot be adequately processed" (p.528). Because the experiences that are overwhelming tend to be incongruent with our existing patterns, memories and understandings of the world, Cohen explains by drawing on Horowitz's work on congruent and incongruent schemas and memory. He says that incongruent patterns cannot be translated into verbal language patterns and that these "disrupted schemas are stored in short-term memory, primarily on an iconic (visual) and sensorimotor (body) level" (p.528), where they make up the basis of traumatic memories that tend to be wordless and de-contextualized, meaningless patterns.

Writings on sleep disorders, nightmares, and dreaming further indicate that images play an essential role in processing lived experiences and in restoring equilibrium. A healthy imaging system helps with how we as humans are able to adapt and develop and how we will function and make meaning of the world. Experiences, particularly those of a traumatic nature, can only be transformed by engaging them in an imaging system. Krakow, in his writings as well as in his presentation at the Homewood Health Centre in 2002, indicates that internal images can be worked with through "image rehearsal techniques" where nightmare images can actively be changed during the waking state. In his research he found that by using his image rehearsal techniques he had been able to help in the treatment of sleep disorders by facilitating nightmare reduction (Krakow *et al.*, 2001). Through working with internal images, the flow between images, feelings, and thoughts can be mediated until images of a traumatic nature can be gradually transformed from the original image, which is literal in nature, to increasingly more abstract and symbolic representations. Metaphors that are embedded and mediated by images, feelings, and thoughts offer opportunities for transformation and for breaking the cycle of abuse by working with what earlier has been referred to as immemorial images.

According to Wolf (1994), the pervasive prevalence of nightmare images is "evident if we just look around us. We might call it the nightmare of abuse that indicates that we are becoming aware of something beyond our material existence" (p.265). He continues by pointing out that: "We are aware that we humans not only abuse ourselves, in war and peace and in selfish forms of conflict, we abuse our children and our planet" (Wolf, 1994, p.265). In this book, I have made an attempt to explore ways of working with images in psychotherapy that facilitate a transformative process. The process of art toward healing explored here allows us to become more aware of the cycle of abuse. It shows how we can break the patterns of abuse by allowing our aggressive energies to be transformed and guided by explorations with immemorial images and by the revitalization of the arts.

Traumatic experiences, such as the ones described in this book, can deeply affect and disrupt an individual's internal balance and well-being. They can also damage an individual's ability to process and transform experiences. Traumatic experiences can rupture the healing flow between internal images, feelings, and thoughts. They can also lead to a sense of isolation and an inability to dream and to transform fragments of lived experiences from their literal form into gradually more symbolic and metaphorical types of images that could allow the individual to reconnect with the world in a balanced and reality-oriented manner. In his writing, Wolf (1994) indicates "that dreams are indeed necessary for creating the images of our daily life. Without those images we would get lost and possibly ill" (p.209). The internal imaging system and the overall functioning of a person can be damaged in many different ways, but art can play an essential part in healing that damage.

Over the centuries, dream images, poetry, painting, and sculptural images have allowed us to evolve and transform old patterns. In his book, Wolf (1994) pointed out that dreaming may play an important part in the process of developing a self and creating the necessary self/other separation that is so much a part of our understanding of who we are. According to Wolf, the mind, "like the matter it observes, also has structures that arise through self-reflection, a process that arises in the dreaming brain in its attempts to integrate, learn, remember, and forget all that is necessary for self-awareness" (p.341). This is to say that "Without the ability to dream, there may not be any ability to become self-aware" (Wolf, 1994, p.341). The languages of the arts, with their metaphors, symbols, rituals, and play, are all essential to our comprehension of the world and to our overall well-being as individuals and as a larger community. The languages of the arts resonate deep within our being. They are primal in nature and they have the potential for making us aware that we are a part of a greater whole of being while allowing us to celebrate our uniqueness.

All images, whether we view them alone or with others, are received within the social context of a community. Within the culture of this community the images resonate on many levels and make visible to each member the many threads that weave our perceptions into ever-changing, evolving wholes. The sense of wholeness is a temporary pause that is compelled by our need for closure and harmony. The breaking down and the analysis of our perceptions create a sense of clarity, yet also of fragmentation. The oscillation between looking at the part and perceiving the whole image weaves the tapestry of our evolution to an ever-higher complexity of awareness and understanding (Wilber, 1995, 1996). As will be shown in this book, it is necessary at times to unravel the tapestry or quilt that we have created. We need to pause and then reassess the trajectory of our life's journey through our immemorial images.

In this chapter, I speak of ideas that are relevant to understanding the function or life of visual images, creativity, illness, and existential and ontological realities as they relate to the dialogical process of being. I have already touched on the nature of images as they relate to dreams, memories, and the development of metaphors. The next section will explore the effect of the arts on the development of human beings on a personal, cultural, and collective level.

When examining the different functions of images and the quality of the dialogical image/word process, I would like to make a distinction between spontaneous expressions that reflect a snapshot or moment of expression compared with more sustained, carefully constructed images that were created outside the context of psychotherapy. Very different images emerge and the dialogical process that unfolds between the person who creates the image, the image itself, and the role it may play in the social context is very different in the spontaneous expression from that of a more carefully constructed image inside of the context of psychotherapy and outside of that context. The images that were created during the different creative arts therapy sessions that were explored in this book are qualitatively different from those created by individuals who worked on the survivor's monument (Irving, 1996) or who expressed some of their existential pain and experiences through art that is shown in public forums such as galleries and books. Authors such as Harris (1993) and Wisechild (1991) and many other artists have worked with images of abuse. There may be many similarities between the functions these images had for them both as individuals and socially and the function of the images that were explored in this book. However, in this work I have focused my attention on the function of the images as they related to the context of psychotherapy and the process of art toward healing.

The following different types of images were identified in this work. They will be explored throughout this book as they pertain to a research approach, an image-oriented psychotherapy, and the metaphor of the Healing-Flow Model.

1. Transitional images that allow emerging themes to become crystallized over time.
2. Images that provide clarity about one's existential or ontological reality.
3. Images that are attempts to escape from what is experienced in this world.
4. Images that are created to gain attention and thus become substitutes for one's sense of self.
5. Images that seem to come from some place beyond the existential self.
6. Images that reflect one's existential struggle.
7. Images that clutter up one's perception and that are related to internal and external overload or noise and image pollution.
8. Images of desire, which distort one's perception.
9. Grounding images that connect one more deeply with one's environment.

10. Images of acceptance that allow one to let go and accept that which has been given rather than using all of one's energy to create images that uphold an illusion.

The images in this book may not only have different functions for the person who created them and for the viewer, but they also differ in the amount of time spent on the images and the subsequent dialogical process within the social context of an inpatient-milieu treatment program. In spite of this qualitative difference in the time, nature, and quality of the dialogical process between the person who created an image, the image itself, and the social/interpersonal context in which the image was created and shaped, the images can still tell us about the process of art toward healing and about how we may be able to utilize it outside of this context. The images created by the patients in the creative arts therapy sessions explored in this book potentially illustrate a transformative process that may be ontic in nature. They may also illustrate how the transformative process of the healing flow can be propelled by the immemorial images discussed earlier.

Within the context of psychotherapy, Wright (1996) states that: "Visual images often escape the mind's censor more readily than words. Therefore, when the drawn image precedes the words, a deeper level of meaning can be achieved" (p.193). Creative arts therapy can provide a container, a space, or a process for expressing, contemplating, integrating, and transcending existential and ontological realities in a safe and culturally integrated manner (E. Levine, 1995; S.K. Levine, 1992; McNiff, 1992). "When patients are encouraged to use creativity, to turn to imagination, to symbolize, they reconnect with the healthiest and strongest parts of themselves" (Wright, 1996, p.217). The question then arises: How can we connect with our creativity in a way that is integrated and harmonious with our daily activities and on a cultural level?

In this book, the phenomenon of art toward healing was explored within the clinical context of different, interactive art-psychotherapy groups. But, the goal of this book was not to focus on a particular treatment approach and to evaluate its effectiveness but instead it was to uncover a broader understanding of the role of creativity and the image-making process on our well-being within this microcosm. The psychotherapy groups that were explored in this book provided opportunities for insight. As already stated, the metaphor of the Healing-Flow Model provided a focal point through which the multimodal experiences and interdisciplinary elements could be evaluated and synthesized. This dynamic was explored in this book within the microcosm of an image-oriented psychotherapy. Dissanayake's work (1988, 1995, 2000), as well as those of others such as E. Levine (1995), S.K. Levine (1992), McNiff (1992), Wilber (1995, 1996), and Wolf (1994), would indicate that this may also be true beyond this context of psychotherapy and may be the core of human development and well-being. If the arts, as will be explored in the last chapter of this book, could become once again more integrated and valued on a social, cultural level, only then could they fulfill their vital part in the growth and healing of individuals and their communities.

Note

1 The word "imagistic," according to *Random House Webster's Dictionary* (1991), refers to "a style of poetry that employs free verse, precise imagery, and the patterns and rhythms of common speech." The term "imagistic pause" as used in the creation of an Interpretative Quilt as a tool of conducting qualitative research is described in greater detail in Schnetz (2003).

CHAPTER 2

Interpretative Quilting as a Qualitative Approach to Inquiry

Over the years that it took to complete this work, many theories and approaches continued to shape the development of the Interpretative Quilt. Interpretative Quilting has grown out of the dialogical image/word approach and out of lived experience with the image-making process within a social context. The creative processes of play and art are essential parts of Interpretative Quilting. Interpretative Quilting grew out of a number of different experiences and research approaches. It is embedded in phenomenological hermeneutics, action-based research, and art as inquiry. The works by Berger and Mohr (1982), Courtney (1987), Colilli (1993), Darroch-Lozowski (1999), Darroch-Lozowski and Silvers (1982), Gadamer (1985, 1986), Heidegger (1977), Meekums (1993), McNiff (1998), Montgomery-Whicher (1996), Payne (1993), Silvers (1988), Spiegelberg (1971), and Van Manen (1990) were instrumental in a number of different ways in the development of this approach to inquiry. I would like to look at Interpretative Quilting here from its metaphorical and theoretical perspective.

The integration into a coherent whole is a central theme in the Healing-Flow Model and the practice of art and research are intrinsically linked with each other. In a sense, the research methodology described in this book is grounded in hermeneutical and phenomenological inquiry as both these approaches are strongly connected with a practice that leads to an embodied knowledge. Montgomery-Whicher (1996) presented a strong case in her paper to illustrate a parallel between the practice of drawing from life and the phenomenological approach to research.

> As a practice of inquiry – a way of questioning our experience of the world – a phenomenological approach to research shares two important characteristics with drawing from observation: one, it begins in the everyday world in which we live; and two, learning to do this kind of research, like learning to draw, is largely a matter of re-learning to see. (Montgomery-Whicher, 1996, p.3)

I would like to expand on these two notions and present my belief that drawing from lived experience not only dwells in what our senses perceive but it also engages us in a spontaneous, dialogical process which can vary in the degree of primal, meditative, reflective, and interpretative processes. Therefore, creating an image can extend into the abstract, interpretative realm of being, which makes it more hermeneutical in nature. Drawing from observations and translating them into different kinds and degrees of abstractions using lines, shapes, textures, and colors can take many forms and involve many conscious and unconscious processes that are grounded in the continuous, dialogical process between artist, art media, and the world. The final picture that is created is a composite of many experiences that draw upon visual, kinesthetic, emotional, and intellectual as well as symbolic and spiritual experiences in a playful manner (Lusebrink, 1990). These experiences can enter into and give form to the final picture from many different temporal zones from our lives. They are not limited to the lived experience of that moment but are rather filtered and interpreted through the tapestry of being and our lived experiences as a whole. The final image that is created on the page through lines, colors, shapes, and textures is a coagulation of lived experiences that synthesizes into a coherent picture of an embodied experience of this world that can be ontic in nature. The interpretation of surfaces was expanded and interwoven to give depth to the Interpretative Quilt. As Wilber (1995) noted, depth must be reached through interpretation, whereas surface structures can be measured with empirical tools. The dialogical processes of creating the Interpretative Quilt through external pictorial or sculptural figures allows for resonating with the world while creating layers of lived experiences.

Play and creativity are an essential part of the dialogical image/word approach and bring about perceptual shifts. These shifts make it more akin to a form of research. "The modern artist is less a creator than the discoverer of the as yet unseen, the inventor of the previously unimagined that only emerges into reality through him" (Gadamer, 1986, p.91). According to Gadamer (1986), play and seriousness "interact with one another, and those who have looked deeply into human nature have recognized that our capacity for play is an expression of the highest seriousness" (p.130). Play and what we would call seriousness should not become separated and dissociated from each other because play is an essential part of giving shape to creativity and what comes through creativity allows us to adopt, invent, and discover. It is an essential part of creating an Interpretative Quilt.

When looking at the work of McNiff (1998) on art-based research retrospectively, I would locate the creation of this Interpretative Quilting as a research modality within the following different approaches. As already stated earlier, it drew heavily upon elements of phenomenological and hermeneutic approaches to inquiry but it also, over time, evolved into what could be called action-based research that is grounded in a practice of art. According to McNiff (1998): "*Hermeneutic studies*...emphasize the interpretative dialogue between the researcher and the objects of inquiry while accepting the inevitable influences of personal, cultural, and historic biases" (p.113). These are also elements that are involved in creating an Interpretative Quilt. McNiff (1998) continues with: "*Action research* which uses the investigation as a way of encouraging change within a particular setting" (p.113). This is also an aspect of the Interpretative Quilt.

Interpretative Quilting, as shown above, has elements that would locate it within the following recognizable approaches. It is a synthesis that reintegrates the power of visual images and arts with the power of text and literacy. "Art-based research grows from the trust in the intelligence of the creative process and a desire for relationships with the images that emerge from it. These two focal points are the basis for a new tradition of inquiry" (McNiff, 1998, p.37). We cannot regress into the primal power of images and ignore the gains that have been made through literary efforts and scientific methods, but we do need to recognize their limits and we cannot forget that we are body, mind, and soul/spirit. Van Manen (1990) states that "a rigorous human science is prepared to be 'soft,' 'soulful,' 'subtle,' and 'sensitive' in its effort to bring the range of meaning of life's phenomena to our reflective awareness" (p.18). That is to say, in spite of all these gains made over recent years, we cannot ignore our basic human needs. We cannot ignore the power and wisdom of images and dreams. We need to integrate these images and dreams with the knowledge and methods of our days in order to maintain the part/whole relationship of all being.

Meekums (1993) draws a parallel between the creative process and doing research. He suggests that "research can be viewed as the creative process" (p.136). He describes similar aspects to what is explored in this book; namely, the aspects that are involved in creating an Interpretative Quilt. There appear to be different phases or stages, beginning with dreams or images, which he calls "striving for something," which are followed by incubation, illumination, and finally verification. In his work, he also makes a connection with the spiritual dimension that is involved in this process. Meekums (1993) writes by making reference to "many other works and suggests that it is at the interface of action and stillness that insights and inspirations occur" (p.131). According to him and others, "The individual's original nature is that of the enlightened Buddha, temporarily forgotten; in the moment of creativity, one's Buddha nature is connected" (p.131). Part of the development of the Interpretative Quilt involved finding ways of bringing to this inquiry intuitive knowledge and ways of being in this world.

The water dream that gave birth to the metaphor of the Healing-Flow Model allowed me to connect with, express, and understand creative energy and its flow from one's being in the world. It allowed me to envision that creative energy can be expressed in images and developed through a dialogical process between self and the world. Working with images allowed me to find words and gradually more refined metaphors that could adequately describe my experience.

In order to capture the complexity of the phenomena under investigation with its essential features, I needed to create a metaphor that would help in communicating my experience. Peavy (1996) in his paper on "Sociodynamic Counselling™ Beyond Twentieth Century Forms of Helping," that he presented at the Fifteenth International Human Science Research Conference, believed "that progress in human social life is constituted through the invention and adoption of increasingly useful metaphors" (Peavy, 1996, p.4) and images and the language of the arts help us to do that. By creating and recreating useful metaphors through images and a continuous dialogical process, we evolve and communicate the complexities of our lived experience through symbols and metaphors that will contribute to a regeneration of creative energy. This biologically grounded process between internal images, feelings, and thoughts connects us deeply with others and with the larger web of life. It is this process that helps to create shared meaning that is embedded in lived experience and that propels us into the future. The metaphor of the

Healing-Flow Model started with a dream image. The metaphor of the Interpretative Quilt began with putting together visual images. Both metaphors were agents of change that led to deeper understanding.

In my Masters thesis (Schnetz, 1990), I also explored the process of art toward healing. In this work, I drew upon what I would now call primal images or what Darroch-Lozowski (Darroch-Lozowski, Crawford and Ponti-Sgargi, 1997) called maternal images. These images led me to explore my personal relationship with the creative process as it related to childbirth and to the dialogical process with the growing child through the use of sculpture, painting, photography, and text. The works of Assagioli (1971), Barthes (1981), Courtney, (1982, 1987), Darroch (1984), Darroch-Lozowski (1989), Larsen (1988), Silvers (1988), Stern (1985), Storr (1988), and Winner (1982) were explored there. They were fundamental to my understanding of the process of art toward healing. Although I will not explore these writers in the same way as I did in my Masters thesis, I would like to acknowledge here that the understanding I gained from their works also influenced my later inquiry and the development of this book. I understood that the image-making process is central. I also saw the shamanistic and mythic relevance to the soul and spirit, the importance of developmental issues and the mother–infant dyad, the connection of images and their ontological nature, as well as the importance of acknowledging one's historicity, while at the same time moving beyond the personal into discovering more universal truths.

Silvers and Darroch-Lozowski's work with images has continued over the years to help me gain important insights into the role of images in inquiry. In her later works, Darroch-Lozowski (1993) writes about the function and origin of the immemorial images from her experience:

> ...immemorial images is that they are omnipresent; that they impel us steadily toward their own reason, which is an ontic one; that, ideally, we may discover one which explains everything about our lives. What alters in chronological time is where these images place themselves – in memory or matter – and how, emotionally and concretely, they become active within us, and around us. (p.25)

Interpretative Quilting, with its dialogical image/word approach to inquiry and its use of psychotherapy guided by metaphors and images of the Healing-Flow Model, was an attempt to honor my own historicity. At the same time, it was also an attempt to move beyond my historicity and to honor my more objective role as researcher, artist, and psychotherapist; thus, creating a more integrative view of the phenomena under investigation.

Darroch-Lozowski writes about women's experiences in history and time as they were propelled by what she calls maternal imagery:

> Maternal imagery gave birth to the Woman's Institute. The network was conceived, born, and nurtured by women's voices. Voices of women weave past, present, and future together. The interwoven nature of the women's voices is apparent here and now as we remember, imagine, and bring forward aspects of women's places and times in Canada and beyond. Voices are our links – they are like golden threads which endure and connect our stories to others'; our times and places to those before and after our own. (Darroch-Lozowski *et al.*, 1997, p.14)

As the creator of this Interpretative Quilt, I feel that I am just one of many voices adding, through this inquiry, to our understanding of lived experience. My own history, my present, and my future become interwoven with the voices of others. Like the women whom Darroch-Lozowski (Darroch-Lozowski *et al.* 1997) honors in her writing, I also have had a long and difficult journey of trying to attain a balance between my role in the domain of the private and personal and my role in the public sphere – the role of a woman and a mother balanced with the role of a researcher, artist, and psychotherapist. In this work, the voices of the researcher, artist, and psychotherapist are more visible; nevertheless, I speak from the embodied knowledge that emerged from both the private and personal domain and from my whole being. The Interpretative Quilting needs to be authentically grounded in lived experience in a way that moves beyond the personal through a reflective, dialogical process that can hold the many voices and experiences of the individuals who helped to shape my understanding of the process of art toward healing.

Maternal imagery, as mentioned earlier, is part of the water dream and the Interpretative Quilt. The relationship between creativity in its primal form, childbirth, and the interpersonal relationship with mother and child, and how these related to creativity and the process of art toward healing, is grounded in the work I did in my Masters thesis. My observing and engaging in the process of art toward healing further developed my understanding, as it unfolded within the dialogical dyad between my first son and me. My readings of the works by Brazelton and Cramer (1990), Mook (1996), Pearce (1992), and Stern (1995) further developed my understanding in this area. The work of

Dissanayake (2000) confirmed my sense of the function of the arts in relationship to human development and health. According to Dissanayake (2000):

> Being a baby means wanting to participate in patterned, multimodal, emotionally communicative improvisations with other people, to imitate their sounds and activities, handle things, and play with vocal sounds and physical materials... These impulses or needs are primary and pleasurable; they are among the abilities that make us cultural, able to socialize and talk, find and share meaning, and develop competencies in our lives. (p.178)

She continues stating that infants do not have to be trained to do these things, as animals do, and that babies learn quite naturally without being prompted. This means that they are ready and emotionally motivated to learn through play and through creating sounds and images in order to engage the world. I would like to acknowledge here the process of art and the dialogical process between self and the world where explored with individuals whose natural, adaptive patterns and ability to engage with the healing flow have been severely interrupted. However, in the early phase of this inquiry, I originally had explored images that connected me with my own roots and childhood experiences, as well as with emerging maternal images that allowed me to connect with my first child through images and words.

In the early part of creating the Interpretative Quilt of this book, the imagistic pauses were comprised of images of my childhood, as well as of drawings and paintings that I had created with my first son, starting with his earliest scribbles and moving on to his more refined images. From these experiences I developed the understanding that it was not actually the final image that was essential to the process of art toward healing but rather that it was the dialogical process that evolved and those connections and meanings that were shaped through engagement with the physical world and close human relationships; it was the energy flow, not the static image, that was essential. Out of this understanding I started to develop the different functions that images can have for the person who creates them and for those who see them.

It appeared that in order for me to become sensitized and receptive to the manifestations of the healing flow, I first needed to engage in a dialogical process with images that connected me with my own life and with how these images, in turn, connected me with the world, as they had affected my development as a human being. Although these early explorations were not included in the final version of this book, they, nevertheless, are important to acknowledge here. The awareness that was gained through these early explorations formed the foundation for what was later developed in this book. This awareness allowed me to see possibilities for this contemplative, ongoing, dialogical process and to see how images could play different functions within this dialogical process. It was this sensitivity and embodied awareness that I was then able to bring to my work as a psychotherapist and a researcher. It was from these early maternal images, experiences, and observations that the Healing-Flow Model was able to emerge.

Observing the process of art toward healing within the clinical setting allowed me to gain a different perspective and it appeared to amplify the underlying dynamics. Shifting the focus to a clinical setting rather than observing the process of art toward healing within normal developmental situations within the individual, family, and community further allowed me to make visible how this process could be harnessed in psychotherapy. Before moving into this clinical aspect and the role that the process of art toward healing can play in restoring inner balance and health in the subsequent chapters, I would like to look at how the process of art toward healing connects with early childhood development, interpersonal relationships, and community, as this aspect is essential to our discussion here.

This connection between early childhood development, the role of images, play, and the dialogical process that unfolds between infant and the world is vital to our understanding of the Healing-Flow Model and the dialogical image/word approach. Dissanayake (2000) explores the role of art and intimacy from an evolutionary perspective when she shows the adaptive function of art and how it has helped us to survive and evolve. She writes:

> My thesis begins with the assumption that it is in the inborn capacity and need for (1) *mutuality* between mother and infant (the prototype for intimacy or love) that four other essential human capacities and psychological imperatives are enfolded or embedded and gradually, in their time, emerge. Mother–infant mutuality contains and influences the capacity for (2) *belonging to* (and acceptance by) a social group, (3) *finding and making meaning*, (4) acquiring a sense of *confidence through handling and making*, and (5) *elaborating* these meanings and competencies as a way of expressing or acknowledging their vital importance. (Dissanayake, 2000, p.8)

The arts are not a self-absorbed, narcissistic endeavor, as they may have been seen in recent years of human evolution, but rather they have an evolutionary and necessary function. As already discussed, Dissanayake's (1988, 1995, 2000) analysis of the arts is that they have great value for the artists as well as for the audience and the community and "they are much more than self-esteem therapy. Participants are made aware of their common humanity and hence become more fully engaged – body and mind – in life" (Dissanayake, 2000, pp.189–190). In this book, the process of art toward healing was uncovered within the microcosm of psychotherapy. It is my hope that this book will inspire works that will re-examine the role of the arts so that they can play, once again, a vital part in human evolution and health, as they have in the past. "Taking the arts seriously means arts for everybody, not simply as enrichment or appreciation but – in schools and communities – as encouragement and opportunity to participate from the first year of life and throughout life, as was the human birthright" (Dissanayake, 2000, p.185). The opportunity to reintegrate and connect in a meaningful manner with an image-making process on a deeper level is not only important for artists and the privileged few, but it also needs to be part of everyday life and needs to be embedded in a receptive community and in the greater part of the whole of being. This is important for the development and health of the individual as well as for humanity as a whole.

> I make the case that the arts remain the birthright of modern individuals and that even in societies that no longer take the arts seriously, they still provide avenues for belonging, meaning, competence, and an enlargement of the sense of being. (Dissanayake, 2000, p.17)

Taking the arts seriously is one step toward a reintegration and a respect for the natural laws of part/whole relationships. Taking the arts seriously also implies that we can study them and that they can be a legitimate way of obtaining and representing knowledge. However, before exploring how art can be a form of research, I would like to look at the role of the arts and sports, as Dissanayake (2000) has addressed so well in her book.

One could argue that sports may have, in part, a similar function to that of the arts. One difference is that, at this point in time, sports seem to play a more prevalent role in our society, as is reflected by the money spent on sports-related activities and the attention sports receive in the media. However, according to Dissanayake (2000), there are important differences, functions, and needs that are not met through sports:

> In contrast to sports events, which can also be a kind of theater, a drama production is a noncompetitive, collaborative, "team effort" in which spectators, cast, and crew are interdependent and *all win*. All roles are important, including that of the audience, which helps to create the performance and then appreciates its co-creation. Ideally, something remains afterward to affect the lives of the participants. (Dissanayake, 2000, p.188)

Although one could argue that in sports there are elements of cooperation and teamwork, overall there is a competitive nature to sports. Conflict is generated rather than de-escalated and transformed, as is possible in the language of the arts. Through the arts, if they are integrated in a meaningful way with lived experience and culture, something remains afterward that affect the lives of the artist and the viewer on a deeper level. According to Rothenberg (1990):

> ...creation in any field is a healthy means of dealing with destructive feelings. Because creation has the *potential* for increasing self-knowledge, there is the possibility of creative persons freeing themselves from their psychological past and making themselves, or aspects of themselves, anew. (p.70)

Through arts and rituals, aggressive energies can be worked with in a way that can lead to a deeper understanding of what it means to be human in this world.

Dissanayake's (2000) writings make us aware of how the arts, with the importance that they play in human evolution and culture, are trivialized in our culture. One only needs to look at how the arts and sports are portrayed and handled in the media. Yet it is the healing powers of the arts that I believe will be essential for our next evolutionary development. These healing powers will be necessary to enable humanity to transcend and transform competitive, aggressive energies into more cooperative interactions on an interpersonal level, as will be seen within the context of psychotherapy groups, as well as on a social and global level.

When looking at how we, as humans, have dealt with human suffering and trauma over the years, it becomes apparent that we have moved away from dealing with it through rituals and art in a social, collectively connected manner to dealing with it by pathologizing it; thus, placing it within the context of medicine, therapy, and the sciences. Yet issues related to human suffering are not necessarily successfully dealt with through these avenues, as they, at this point, fail to address the basic human needs and issues of the soul.

Hacking (1995), in his discussion on memory, illustrates how suffering is treated in a way that avoids the real issues by relying on the sciences to provide answers that are ontological and ethical in nature: "Only with the advent of memoro-politics did memory become a surrogate for the soul. Even today there are plenty of kinds of false consciousness that have nothing to do with memory" (p.260). This inquiry described in this book is using a research approach that is able to give voice to issues related to the soul.

In order to transcend and prevent the continuation and cycle of abuse, we need to shift from a competitive approach to one that fosters cooperation, problem solving, and the development of an authentic self that is grounded in lived experience and a whole being (body, mind, and spirit); and to working together collectively for a common goal. "The arts – ours and those of others – are *ways of treating the inner life seriously,* embodiments of our affective experience" (Dissanayake, 2000, p.192). Interpretative Quilting attempts to take the arts seriously.

An engagement with the external, material world through dreams, images, metaphors, and the arts allows life's energy or creative energy to become shaped and externally expressed, where then, in turn, they become shaped by the world. The physical object of the image or the artwork has some quality that suggests permanence in the world "out there" where it can play a vital function for an individual and the community. However, it also reminds us of the ambiguity and impermanence of existence and creates a place for contemplation of that for which we do not have clear answers. "Unfortunately, today in our North American culture it is rare that serious works of contemporary art are intimately engaged by viewers as a field of discovery, or as an offering for mutual creation to the viewer" (West, 1993, p.1). It is not only in the world of modern art but also in our daily lives that there seems to be an absence of spaces for art and rituals as a means of contemplation.

Spaces where the creative process can resonate and be received into a group consciousness in a reflective, non-judgmental way of experiential practice that rekindles the flow of energy throughout our being are not readily available within this culture. Anne West (1993) reflects in her thesis on how contemporary art is viewed in our North American culture that it becomes clear that an essential aspect of the role of art and the creative process has been rendered impotent. "Generally, artworks are encountered in opaque meetings, without penetration and insight" (p.1). Artworks are encountered in sterile environments where our interactions with them and perceptions of them are guided by the view of those who we call "experts and professionals," disembodied from our own sense of being and our perceptions. Within this context, art no longer can play a role in "soul making" and yet not many other forms of expression provide the same opportunities to fulfill this function as art can (E. Levine, 1995; S.K. Levine, 1992; McNiff, 1992).

Subsequent chapters will reveal that the process of art toward healing can also be utilized in psychotherapy and can play an essential part in helping people transcend and transform traumatic experiences. It also helps them to find meaning and connection within the community through the dialogical image/word approach to psychotherapy. Within the supportive context of a group, the arts once again can play their vital, adaptive role and help with healing and transcending what cannot be understood verbally, just as they have done for many years for our ancestors. Thus, they connect us with the vital force of being: the energy flow that connects individuals with the social and collective realm. As Dissanayake (2000) points out, this energy is part of survival and human evolution. Nature seems to have assured that: "Individual success may feel good, but our evolutionary history has ensured that successful *group* efforts feels even better" (Dissanayake, 2000, p.186). Therefore, the social context and the dialogical process that connect the arts with its community prevent dissociation and fragmentation. This is essential in maintaining health and the well-being of the mind, body, and soul/spirit. How can this knowledge aid us in finding research approaches that are respectful of the phenomena under investigation while at the same time serve the larger community?

As already mentioned, the metaphor for the Interpretative Quilting evolved for me as I was putting together the images that patients had created during the art therapy sessions in order to organize them and to see them as a whole. Through manipulating the images and creating the imagistic pauses, the metaphor of the quilt presented itself. The patterns that had evolved and the way I had arranged the images visually resembled that of a quilt. The quilt quickly became an appropriate metaphor as I continued to work with the images. On the symbolic level, the making of the quilt also very much mirrored how this work evolved over the years.

The making of a quilt tends to be associated with folk arts and crafts and is closely connected with lived experience and everyday life, as it is saturated with deeply personal meaning for those who have created the quilt. Over the years that I worked on this book, I also explored my personal history and the different life events that had shaped my perceptions, choices, and understanding of the world. Although I decided not to explicitly make the personal experiences of my childhood, my relationship with my own children, and my role as a mother a visible part of this work, they nevertheless are present in the Interpretative Quilt. The Interpretative Quilt evolved over time through a continuous dialogical process alongside lived experiences of marriage, motherhood, divorce, and work as a therapist, researcher, and artist. It was marked by my dealings with everyday demands and life challenges. At times, like the many women who have worked on quilts, I had to put the quilt aside to attend to my family's needs and other demands. It is these interruptions that actually add to the depth and richness of the quilt that is created, as layers of time and lived experiences become embedded and interwoven into the work.

Although Interpretative Quilting is a metaphor, it still shares some parallels with the history and culture of quilt making. It is deeply connected with the lives of women and everyday life, it is an art form and a way of expression that is not exclusive to an elite few, it is usually done and appreciated in a social context, and it serves many functions. Quilts have been used as a way of expression and to communicate messages for many generations over hundreds of years. The graveyard quilt, the murder quilt, family-album quilts, and wedding quilts, as well as more personal types of quilts, all have been used as a medium through which to express resistance, rage, grief, and celebration. "They have contained stories and held meaning for those who knew how to read them. To many people they are just quilts. Pretty patterns and lovely color. But if you stop and look there is always a story. Quilts are the perfect social text" (Ball, 1999, p.46). In her doctoral thesis, Ball (1999) used quilts that were created by women and men who were in a treatment program for post-traumatic stress recovery in order to create a social text. This social text challenges traditional ways of representation and is cross-disciplinary in nature. Her work contributes to the creation of alternative, textual styles in the social sciences that include images as a way of representing experience. According to Ball (1999), "Mental health professionals, academics, and researchers need to acknowledge and draw attention to the kind of realities that are created and maintained through the textuality of social science scholarship" (p.5). In my work as a therapist, I facilitate image-oriented art therapy groups. As already stated, I have explored the process of art toward healing through my personal work as well as through my professional work. As a researcher, I struggled to find a voice that would authentically represent my experience, as well as allow me to draw upon the works of other researchers, artists, and therapists.

Ball (1999) makes it so clear in her thesis that we need to question how we represent experience in inquiry and how our writing style in the social sciences, as therapists and researchers, affects what can become visible:

> While we may be able to recognize practices/behaviours that deviate from the previously established norm of practice (i.e., ethics, abuse) within the discursive field, we are not able to recognize the constitutive nature of our writing styles and the worlds that they construct. (Ball, 1999, p.9)

I worked with Helen Ball for a number of years. We had many interesting discussions as we shared our research work and therapy work as friends and co-workers. However, the Interpretative Quilting differs from her work in a number of ways. She writes:

> In its self-consciousness, the poststructuralist text invites the voice of an engaged and present writer – who draws attention to the influences of the circumstances of the construction of the text, the ambiguities of [its] constructions, and leaves open the opportunity for more discussion. (Ball, 1999, p.24)

According to Ball (1999), "Poststructuralist text has the potential to reflect honest and engaged *social* processes. Just as a therapist must consider social, economic, class, racial, gender, political and historical influences affecting him/herself and the client – so too does the poststructuralist text" (Ball, 1999, pp.24–25). Dissanayake (1995) argues that "the concept of art has indisputably been dealt a mortal blow by postmodernist theory and practice… 'Fine' art has been demoted to little more than a transparent ideological banner by means of which one both displays and attempts to preserve one's elite status" (p.220). I believe that we can learn from both and that any theory or banner that is not grounded in life can go awry as the part/whole relationship becomes disrupted.

When the text or image becomes more important as an object and is no longer embedded in its contexts, its function and meaning become lost to the individual or the social group. Within the therapy context described, the risks involved in this objectification and overemphasis on the picture as object are further explored. When looking at a phenomenological approach to research, the following observations become important for the creation of an Interpretative Quilt. "Phenomenological research has, as its ultimate aim, the fulfilment of our human nature: to become more fully who we are" (Van Manen, 1990, p.10). This is also true for the process of art toward healing, as it allows the person to explore within the therapeutic context of the therapy group. "What we must do is discover what lies at the ontological core of our being. So that *in* the words, or perhaps better, *in spite of* the words, we find 'memories' that paradoxically we never thought or felt before" (Van Manen, 1990, p.13). I would argue that this is even truer for dreams, images, and metaphors because of their primal nature. That is why I believe it is so essential that we allow images to speak and inform us about what it means to be human in this world.

Interpretative Quilting is a metaphor. It did not involve the actual creation of a physical quilt. It allowed the bringing together of images and text from many different sources so that they could become interwoven in a more integrated manner through the use of imagistic pauses and a continuous dialogical process. The bringing together of different experiences in order to form a cohesive whole was, however, mediated and filtered through my interpretations and my working with the images. Therefore, I do not think that I have created a social text as Ball (1999) did in her work; even though this work does include the lived experiences of others, their voices have been changed by my actions – the transformation of the original images and the fictionalization of lived experiences to reflect more universal themes. I need to acknowledge that the way I organized, analyzed, and formed the text and images into the Interpretative Quilt added a thick layer that is grounded in my own historicity and in my working with the images. It is this layer that gives the Interpretative Quilt its depth but it also is this layer that moves toward more universal rather than personal truth.

The Interpretative Quilt, with its dialogical image/word process, is perhaps a way to make visible the many dimensions of the phenomena under investigation and to move beyond isolation and the duality of subject and object. This again is more hermeneutical in nature.

> Unlike the phenomenological text, where the reader observes a portion of the subject's consciousness (as it relates to understanding a specific phenomena), the hermeneutical text is based more on establishing a narrative between the subject and the object of knowing. This process of understanding and the resulting reduction of distance between the subject and the object of knowledge characterize the hermeneutical text. Ultimately, the hermeneutical text creates a metaphor of recovery

> (Shapiro, 1985–86). It is the re-covery of understanding by the subject within the text that is re-trieved through reciprocal dialogical process that moves the subject and object of knowledge closer together. (Ball, 1999, p.16)

Interpretative Quilting, in a way, shares elements of both phenomenological and hermeneutical approaches. When creating an Interpretative Quilt, the researcher shifts back and forth between being an active participant and a reflective observer. It is an approach that allows intuitions, knowledge, and dreams to speak in their primal form through images and metaphors and to have an equal place with the more reflective processes of creating an interpretative, analytic text.

In creating an Interpretative Quilt, it is the openness and receptivity of the artist, researcher, or therapist that gives the interpretation its depth and embodied knowledge. The time spent in an active, engaged, and honest dialogical process is what gives the Interpretative Quilt the special, embodied knowledge of phenomena. The knowledge gained through an embodied, dialogical process with lived experiences gives the Interpretative Quilt a special place within a specific context that is grounded in the artist's lived experience and limited by his or her skill and sensitivity with the media and receptivity to the complexity of the world. Dissanayake (2000) writes:

> That humans have an inborn capacity for engaging in and responding to the arts may seem even more astonishing to a contemporary reader than having a native capacity for mutuality. Evolutionary scientists, like many other members of society, often seem uncomfortable with the arts, just as they seem to be uncomfortable with emotions and what cannot be verbalized. (p.17)

Speaking from the perspective of a visual artist, therapist, and researcher, I was aware that I needed to develop a research approach and a way of representing experience that was congruent with my practice in these areas and that was authentic to the creative process. As a visual artist who has used the creation of images through drawing and painting for many years, I was well aware of how the creation of a painting, in a way, can be a form of inquiry that can be equal to the use of the written text. McNiff (1989) supports the need for innovative ways of inquiry in the area of art therapy research that "emerge from the essential dynamics of the art therapy experience" (p.121). Even if one does not express oneself through visual images, internal pictures and metaphors appear to play an essential part in creativity and in how we, as humans, think, process feelings, gain knowledge, and adapt to the world. Internal images and dreams have inspired and propelled many discoveries.

Images are an integral part of inquiry and connect us with the world; they aid us in gaining insight and understanding and allow us to deal with experiences that are beyond our control or understanding. Images and the arts need to be given equal value in our quest for knowledge and in order to obtain a more integrative view (Wilber, 1995, 1997). "The work of art serves as an optical instrument in which one comes to see the unexpressed or unrecognized depth of oneself" (West, 1993, p.5). While images get us in touch with our deeper sense of self, they also allow us to expand this personal experience into the broader realm of the community we inhabit.

Researchers in the social sciences need to go beyond words, numbers, and texts in order to include the personal dimension of lived experience, as well as to move us toward the understanding that is embedded in ontic truth. Wolf (1994) writes: "Ontological ambiguity is slippery. It doesn't quite fit into reality as we perceive it normally, and it isn't fantasy. Perhaps it is an indication of a deeper reality, one that we are evolving..." (p.265). This intuitive/felt sense can be fostered and developed so that it can help inform us as scientific endeavors have done.

> The tendency to identify research exclusively with science has created a limiting imbalance. The application of a one-sided skepticism to the creative process is an attempt to fly with only one wing and the same applies to a disregard for scientific understanding. (McNiff, 1998, p.31)

The Interpretative Quilt, like many other art forms, communicates and allows us to connect with the larger web of life in an affirming and transformative manner and is an essential part of human evolution and the development of culture. It also incorporates the more rational, analytic, linguistic, interpretative, and objective side of acquiring knowledge. The use of images, symbols, and metaphors plays an essential role in human evolution and in the development of culture. It also can play a vital role in inquiry and in our quest for knowledge, as will be illustrated through this Interpretative Quilt.

In the following section, some of the literature discussed so far will be connected with the material pertaining more directly to the development of the dialogical image/word approach, and to the conceptualization of the Interpretative Quilt. Experiential aspects have also shaped both. I will begin by giving examples from my life that illustrate the essential role that lived experience has played in the development and practice of this method. This material is included to orient the reader to the history and thought behind the practice of this approach to inquiry. Biographical reflections became important in this type of research as they shaped the qualitative data and experiences, and they were given voice to through the Interpretative Quilt. Throughout the following section, examples and verbal explorations will be used to familiarize the reader with the lens through which the researcher saw the phenomena under investigation, and with the lived experience, or Bildung[1] (education), that guided the approach to this inquiry.

Biographical Reflections as they Relate to the Dialogical Image/Word Approach

The seeds of this inquiry were planted many years before its formal conceptualization. It is deeply grounded in my informal and formal training in the visual arts and has been shaped by years of study and practice in Fine Arts, where observing, recording, and interpreting through images became an intuitive and spontaneous act. As part of this training I spent many hours observing and then translating my perceptions into visual images using different art media. In the beginning of my formal training the focus was on learning to understand and capture subject matter (i.e. the human figure, landscapes, or still lifes) in a direct and unmediated manner. The focus of this early training in Fine Arts was on learning to develop skills by experimenting with different representational styles. The main method for developing one's personal representational style of working was through studying the human figure and drawing from life models. Although I spent some time working with landscapes and still-life paintings, most of my skills were developed through working from the life model. The dialogical process that I observed from the many sessions of studying the human figure could be best described in the following manner.

In Japanese painting, the student is asked to paint the image of a bamboo over and over again until he/she no longer thinks about painting it but actually has internalized the image of the bamboo to such a degree that it has become embodied in the artist's being. Through the practice of the numerous quick sketches, the artist internalizes all the subtleties of his or her subject matter. Through this internalization, the artist is almost able to sense what it would feel like to be, in this case, bamboo blowing in the wind. In this sense, the artist's keen observations and the awareness that he or she is able to gain through the many sketches elevates the mundane into the realm of the contemplative. The skills and grounding of the daily practice allow the artist to move into this strange intersubjective fusion between "self" and "other" without getting lost.

In the process of figure drawing, one appears to be in a qualitatively different state of consciousness in which connections between the internal and external world seem softer and more plastic, spontaneous and flexible. Both the one-minute poses as well as the studies of the model that extended for up to forty hours evolved and advanced through the dialectical process. This involved experiencing the model as he or she was colored by the physical quality of the light, recognizing other contextual cues, and utilizing the more internal subjective state of the artist's internal landscape. The image creates an interesting transitional space that is a synthesis between "self" and not "self." Within this space a dialogical process is set forth that creates increasingly complex and deeper understandings of the subject matter. Over time, one's ways of understanding and being in the world are altered and enriched by this internal experience, and then are echoed externally through the emerging image. In this process, the artist may experience moments of intersubjective fusion, while staying grounded through the physical reality of the art media. In this way, the artist temporarily is able to break the sense of duality between self and world without losing the feeling of a cohesive self.

The continuous dialogical process between the art materials and my internal and external perceptions of the human figure gave rise to the emerging image. My experience of the model became translated into shapes and colors that were mediated by the art materials. Within the symbolic realm of the paper or canvas, I was able to give form to the many layers of experience associated with the subject matter. The symbolic representation of the human figure was a coagulation of the many different experiences that had collected over the time that I studied the model. The image that emerged in front of me was encoded with many layers of feelings, thoughts, and sentiment. This aspect of the painting process came to resonate for me with the terms that we use in psychotherapy to describe transference and counter-transference issues. Thus, even the most realistic representation of the model has embedded in its image many layers and interpretations by the artist.

In the early phase of my training I focused on the exploration and methods of drawing and painting that were grounded in more representational and traditional styles. I learned different iconographic/representational styles that allowed me to create images that were more realistic in their painting manner. These images closely mimicked the world as we see it through our eyes. The different representational styles were based on distinctive schools of paintings that I learned from my teachers as well as from studying the works of the great masters. My interpretations of the subject matter were influenced by the styles and methods of other artists whose works I was exposed to during my training.

The life-drawing exercises that involved making many sketches of the life model developed in me a tacit, intuitive knowledge of how to translate perceptions into lines, colors, textures, and shapes. This tacit knowledge developed into a visual style. The years I spent working from the life model, studying the human figure, and creating many different drawings using various art media deepened and sharpened my understanding of the human form. I made an effort to grasp every detail and to represent it in the drawing, but the more my attention was occupied by focusing on surface likeness, the greater was the risk of the drawings becoming over-worked, lifeless, and empty. Often, quick gestures were more likely to capture the moment in its essence. I became very much interested in finding ways to encode psychological, emotional, and spiritual perceptions, as well as those that were literal and realistic, into the paintings and drawings. I will refer to these images as *embodied iconic abstractions*.

The images that I created during my training were saturated with the techniques that I was being taught. In this way my intuitive manner of working with images became mediated by a more reflective and analytic stance that I learned from the different teachings that I had experienced over the years. The focus of my training, at that time, was to learn to execute relatively realistic renderings of the human figure in a truthful manner.

Although the greater part of my training was spent drawing and painting from life, my manner of working was also influenced by the study of other artists' work. The following artists had inspired me in many different ways: Michelangelo (Hupka, 1979), Caravaggio, Artemisia Gentileschi, Joseph Beuys (Stachelhaus, 1987), William Blake, Francisco Goya, Claud Monet, Vincent Van Gogh (Stein, 1986), Gustave Klimt, Franz Marc, Vasily Kandinsky, Max Ernst (Pritzker and Dopagne, 1975), Paul Klee, Georgia O'Keefe (Bry and Callaway, 1989), Franz Kline and many other artists (Boltin and Newton, 1978) whose work I had encountered over the years; all had something to offer me in terms of how to see and experience the world around me and how to portray it through the different art media. Many other artists, not mentioned here, that I learned about in my art history and aesthetics classes further contributed to my way of seeing and learning about many different art media and their use.

When I had encountered the original artworks in the different museums, I was able to experience them very differently from when I had learned about them in my art history classes. This had further made me aware of how much the experience of a work of art or image is influenced by the context in which it is viewed and by the knowledge that we bring to it. Because of the nature in which artists' works are presented in the different museums, I was able to notice how much each time period appeared to be connected with a predominant style of working. This way of presenting and organizing artists' work may not be a true or the best representation of the work of a particular time period but it allowed me to see their work in a certain light that touched me in a special way. However, sometimes it was difficult to integrate this experience into my own work as their worldviews and life choices were so different from my own. Thus, the artworks by these different artists provided me with a window into their unique worlds. This made it difficult for me to simply imitate their styles without modifying them to a point where it was hard to tell in which way they had actually influenced my own process and working with images.

The studies of other artists' works allowed me to realize that although I could draw upon their works to some degree, I had to live and work from my experiences of the world. The perspective that I had of the world as a woman, a mother of two sons, a therapist, and a researcher living in a small town in southern Ontario was very different from those of the artists previously mentioned. Thus, my own historicity was the ground from which all my work grew. I felt that the image-making process was a way through which I could learn and connect with the social, economical, and ecological aspects of my times. Other artists' artwork could show me how to use the different media, but I needed to work from my experience of the world.

The only thing that I could clearly note about these experiences is that the studying of works by other artists had, to some degree, sensitized me to different iconographic representational styles that had opened many possibilities for me to find my own voice. Most of the time the connection between other artists' way of working and the discovering of my own iconographic language was complex. It was predominantly grounded in the practice of the dialogical image-making process that was mediated by the experimentation with different art media. The iconographic language that gradually evolved over time was a synthesis of visceral, unconscious, and unmediated processes guided by intuitive perceptions, feelings, emotions, and intellectual reflections. Out of this practice evolved a tacit, practical knowledge of techniques and a way of seeing the world. Many other influences, such as my relationship to people and important life events, contributed to the way I expressed myself in the images that I was creating. That is to say, my iconographic style was shaped and mediated by the practice just described and by the dialogical reflective processes involved in the perceiving, describing, interpreting, reflecting, and sharing of what had been created.

The iconographic style is a synthesis of unconscious and conscious experience shaped by cultural and archetypal forces. Therefore, the images that I created were bound by my historicity. Although the images emerged through a tacit, embodied knowledge that is grounded in practice, the act of painting or drawing is filtered through the historicity and iconography of my times. That is to say, cultural, psychological, personal historical, emotional, social, archetypal, and spiritual forces shape the iconographic style. Through a dialogical process between all these elements, my understanding emerges, beginning with a felt sense and gradually moving into more verbal intellectual responses. I felt that it was important to preserve and honor the non-verbal contemplative aspect of this dialogical process and to integrate it in a balanced way with a more theoretical analytic stance to inquiry.

Over my six years of training in Fine Arts I became aware of the complexities involved in creating images through this continuous dialogical process. With this recognition my work became increasingly conceptual and abstract in nature, as this allowed me to give voice to the richness and depth of my external and internal experiences. When I created an image I was able to rely on the dialogical process between internal experience and external perceptions, my familiarity with the art materials, and an internal multi-leveled interpretative process. Although there were many unconscious as well as conscious layers of processes that influenced the emerging image, there was also a sense of direct and immediate connectedness with the subject matter. Working in an unmediated, spontaneous manner was energizing, rejuvenating, and provided a meaningful way to more fully connect and resonate in the moment with the phenomena under investigation. It provided a type of meditative, contemplative portal that allowed me to deepen my understanding of the world. I felt that the images that emerged out of this process contained or exhibited a freshness that kept me in close connection with the subject matter. The knowledge gained through this process seemed to be qualitatively different from that of more verbal, analytic contemplations.

Within the symbolic realm of the image-making process shapes, colors, thoughts, and symbols could float freely. Meaningful patterns could emerge gradually as they resonated on a somatic, emotional, psychological, and spiritual level. These experiences could be synthesized through the dialogical process between art materials, visual images, and the artist's subjective experience. This dialogical process is qualitatively different from one that is carried out on a more verbal and analytic level. The image-making process consists also of analytic components. However, they seem to engage and draw upon different aspects of one's being.

Working with art materials in a spontaneous manner allows for the integration of different and, at times, contradicting information into one image. Within the symbolic realm, conflicting ideas, shapes, colors, and lines can be brought together to form a new understanding of the phenomena studied. The image that is propelled by the dialogical process creates a representation that synthesizes the ongoing, complex relationships between the artist's perception and the subject matter.

Drawing from life has another important aspect that is more difficult to put into words. There seems to be a kind of energy flow that connects the artist with the subject. When engaging in the image-making process this energy flow appears to be mediated by the artist's perception, his or her skill with the art materials, and the subject matter. The artist's focused attention and contemplative stance allow the energy to flow from the subject through the unconscious, non-verbal part of the artist's being into consciousness, where it is then incorporated into the emerging image. This flow becomes disrupted when the artist shifts from his or her direct experiencing of the subject matter to a more analytic contemplation of what has been created in the image. The energy flow does not appear to be unidirectional, and shifts with the artist's internal stance and focus. Working directly from life is a contemplative, meditative act. It allows one to connect with the world in a deep and holistic manner.

My experience during drawing from life and the energy flow that I have described above fostered my interest in Eastern art and philosophies. For many years I became fascinated intellectually, as well as on an aesthetic level, by Japanese and Chinese ink-brush paintings (Cahill and Skira, 1977; Sirén, 1963). The quickness of the brushwork and the spontaneity and life that emerged from repeated practice, which led to the embodiment of the subject matter within each brushstroke, resonated with my own experience. On a theoretical and philosophical level the Zen paintings, with their minimalistic lines and their concept of life force or energy (Ki or Chi), which was expressed in every brushstroke, echoed my experience of the energy flow that I had become aware of during painting. This concept of energy and the embodied images that are grounded in this meditative practice described above informed the development of the metaphor of the Healing-Flow Model and the development of the dialogical image/word approach.

Within the dialogical image/word approach, painting or drawing is conceptualized as being in a continuous, dialogical process from which the image emerges with each brushstroke. There is a continuous flow of energy that connects body (matter), mind, and spirit in a continuous feedback loop. At each step, the emergent image is responded to by the artist's subjective experience of the world. The emerging image depends on how well one is attuned to the subtleties of the dialogical process between self and the world, between art media, emerging image, and one's response to the image and the subject matter. Within the symbolic realm of the emerging image, the transitional space between the internal and external forces of being can become filtered through the media. Perceptions are materialized and coagulated into the emerging images in a way that resonates on many levels, thus creating a new awareness of one's way of being in the world. There are many unconscious processes involved in making a visual image, yet when engaging in the process it is a fully conscious act in which our usual way of perceiving is expanded; the images emerge through the filter of one's being, where the source of the actions originates, beyond the realm of the ego (Schnetz, 1990).

Within the Healing-Flow Model, the final image represents the coagulations of the many moments of lived experiences synthesized into its essence. Thus, the image emerges out of a direct and immediate dialogical process between external world and being. I will refer to images created in this manner as *dialogical iconic abstractions of being.* The art materials and the emerging image that were shaped by this fluid, dynamic, dialogical process provided a link between my being and the world. Working in this manner seemed to bring me closer to understanding myself in the world and in this sense it became a way of inquiry.

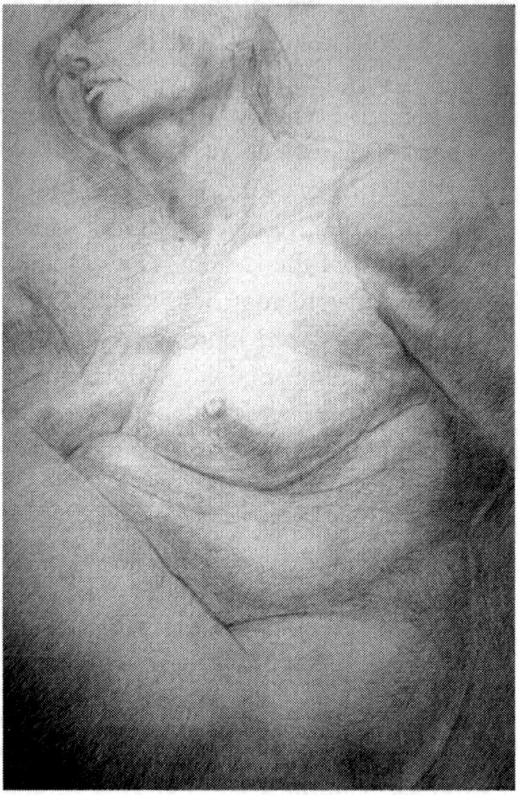

Figure 2.1: Drawing from life (completed in 1984)

The awareness gained through my training in Fine Arts and this direct manner of working contributed to my later interest and attraction to phenomenology and hermeneutics. Within the dialogical image/word approach the researcher, like the artist, plays an active part in investigating phenomena. The artist or researcher explores the phenomena through the different media and tools. As he or she shapes the emerging image and dialogues with it, different types of understanding are brought to light; each medium offers its own unique perspective. The awareness I was able to gain through my years of studies in Fine Arts combined with my respect for some of the more traditional research methods gave rise to the development of this dialogical image/word approach and the Interpretative Quilting used in this inquiry.

In my doctoral thesis (Schnetz, 2003) I have explored in more detail the different research tools that were used to create the Interpretative Quilting that is described in this book. The tools and experiential data that informed the inquiry in my doctoral thesis consisted of (1) clinical progress notes/forms; (2) patient-feedback forms; (3) photographic reproductions of images created during therapy; (4) images produced during therapy sessions; (5) the creation and use of a visual database; and (6) personal reflections. When creating an Interpretative Quilt, it becomes important to use tools that are sensitive and in tune with the phenomena under investigation. The tools should provide a wide perspective and include the domains of the natural sciences (the it-domain), the interior, subjective, moral, and cultural domains (I and we) (Wilber, 1995), as was illustrated earlier. Although the Interpretative Quilt emphasizes the use of images through the dialogical image/word approach as a practice-based research methodology and an approach to therapy, I would like to note that all dimensions are important.

My stance toward the phenomena under investigation was not one of a detached observer but rather one of being directly and experientially involved. The dialogical image/word approach was grounded in a phenomenological and hermeneutical approach to research. According to Van Manen (1990), hermeneutic phenomenology is not just a "descriptive or interpretative methodology" (p.154) but also an action-oriented approach to inquiry. Thus, with the image/word approach to inquiry, subjectivity was seen as a strength that provided the focus, which helped to create the final version of the Interpretative Quilt.

Note

1 The term "Bildung" can be understood to be somewhat similar to the word "education" but it is used here in a broader sense that is more holistic and inclusive in nature and refers to more than one's formal education.

CHAPTER 3

The Nature of Truth in Interpretative Quilting

The images that were created within the Interpretative Quilt of this book represent different aspects of the phenomenon of art toward healing. These aspects were excavated through the continuous dialogical image/word approach to inquiry. Through this approach, theory and practice have been merged through the synthesis of many different experiential data into what I have called an Interpretative Quilt. Within the Interpretative Quilt, different experiential data have been summarized into images and texts. The different images or quilt blocks were then interwoven to create a cohesive picture of the phenomenon of art toward healing as it was observed within the specific clinical context.

The nature of truthful representation is an issue that must be faced by all qualitative researchers. Each quilt block, each descriptive text, and each interpretative border portrays some aspect of the phenomena. However, how do we ensure that what is presented in this Interpretative Quilt is a truthful rendering of the phenomena under investigation? To return to the metaphor of painting, each image emerges on the surface of the paper or canvas and is shaped by my ability to observe and to translate my observations into truthful representations. My familiarity and skill level with the different media that I have chosen, combined with my intentionality, my historicity and the context within which I create my work, further affects the rendering.

Given these assumptions, the following questions become an important part of a self-reflective process that helps guide one's perceptions and methods of rendering. When I set out to paint a picture, what parts do I portray as visible and what do I decide to leave out? Is my unconscious or conscious sense of creating an aesthetically pleasing image guiding me to leave out essential aspects of the phenomena? To what degree do I abstract my perceptions and stray away from a literal likeness in order to get a deeper meaning that lies behind the surface? How far can I stray into the interpretative, abstract symbolic realm of representation before I lose the essence of the phenomena? As was discussed, intentionality is an important aspect in qualitative research as well as in art.

There are many types of images that were already introduced in Chapter 1. These different types of images, when observed in real life, are not that clearly delineated. An image may have many different functions. Thus, the reasons for creating an image or conducting an inquiry will to some degree determine the methodology and way of exploring the phenomena. Different images are created by various conscious and unconscious dynamics that change both over time and with the context in which they are viewed. Images can be created for many different reasons, which can determine whether they help us to become more grounded in the world we live in or to escape into the realm of fantasy. There is a fine line between fantasies and dreams that redirect us toward life and help us to live more creatively and images that lead us astray. Creativity is an essential aspect of evolution and allows us to move beyond what is known. However, it is not easy to predict how an image or dream will lead us along certain evolutionary trajectories. There are always risks involved when we move into the unknown and sometimes only time will tell the difference.

There are times when it is easier to determine if an image is reality-oriented. Many times this depends on the relationships within which the image is created and experienced. In the case of psychosis, an individual is unable to deal with their anxieties about the world and its unknowns; thus, the fantasies or delusions about the world become an unconscious way of dealing with the unpredictability of life. In this case the images lead the individual further and further away from living in the shared reality of his or her community and the world.

In the case of propaganda or advertising, conscious intent is behind creating images that distort one's perception of reality in order to mislead and manipulate. These types of images can have a great impact on a community because of the distortions about the world that they portray. In these manipulated images the real essence of the people or situations portrayed is lost. There is a risk that the person who is viewing the propaganda or the advertising will lose contact with others and the world in which he or she lives. In these cases the conscious or unconscious intentionality is to distort or disguise reality for political or business purposes. It is the goal of this type of inquiry to create an image of the phenomenon of art toward healing that is truthful and helps others to enter into the process in a deeper and more meaningful way.

What happens when the "truth" brought forth through an image or inquiry is incongruent with the cultural norms of society? The artist or researcher continually needs to balance social responsibility with new and creative ways of discovering the world. In qualitative research, like in the arts, the risk of misrepresenting one's subject matter is real, but it must be weighed against the opportunities of gaining knowledge that lies outside the realm of the known. Thus, non-traditional ways of representation allow the expression of experiences that cannot be captured through traditional methods of inquiry. The language or style of representation guides, but at the same time limits, what can become visible. In this sense, the nature of language always restricts possibilities for new knowledge. This explains why the Interpretative Quilt of this inquiry includes many different types of representational styles and interpretative methods; each method provides a unique way of experiencing and portraying the world.

The questions just listed have been presented for the most part in the form of dualities; however, I conceptualize them more along a continuum of possibilities, which may lead to similar but qualitatively different end points. The contemplation of the questions has been crucial to me as a therapist and researcher. The rendering of my experiences with the phenomenon of art toward healing, and the interpretations that I have made of what was gathered, were also subject to many contemplations. Questions such as these have been key: How much of the original voice of those who have informed this inquiry should be included in the text and images? How well and how sensitively do I use this material in my interpretation of the process of art toward healing? It is a careful balancing act to include the voices of others in one's interpretation without distorting the phenomena under investigation. I needed to be careful that my own voice and style of representation did not overshadow those of others. The way I allow myself to be included and become visible in the interpretation or image that I render affects what will become visible. Thus, I have had to make ongoing choices about how much to conceal my presence behind already well-accepted interpretative styles and how much to let my own voice speak.

Well-established ways of working can provide guidance, but can also silence one's voice and thus one's experiences of the world. I had to ask myself what my motives were for developing my own method of working in a new representational style. I had to ask why I wanted to be visible in the text and images of this inquiry. What purpose did it serve for others or myself? In a metaphoric sense, if I made my brushstrokes more visible to the viewer/reader, was I in danger of concealing that which I was attempting to study or was I actually clarifying something to myself and others that would have been lost otherwise? After long deliberations I have come to the conclusion that it is an ongoing process of questioning, reflecting, and re-evaluating my method of working that helps me to stay true to the nature of the phenomena I am trying to study.

When I speak with the voice of the artist, the voice of the therapist, or the researcher I am able to see and to communicate different aspects of my experience. Through the Interpretative Quilt I am able to create a congruent whole through different media that consists of images and words. In this way I am able to honor the part/whole relationships of the many elements that were in the study of the phenomena under investigation. When I give a rendering of what I see, many internal and external forces that influenced me need to be accounted for. The historicity of my times and my cultural and personal biases all influence what I am able to see and communicate. I communicate through the subjectivity of my being and it is this subjectivity that gives shape and focus to the way I represent my subject matter.

Some of the questions I asked have made me more aware of the complexities involved in the phenomenon of art toward healing. The dialogical image/word approach to inquiry is in part a response to the issues of studying these complex and multidimensional aspects of the process of art toward healing. The methodological procedure described here has allowed me to work with my subjectivity in a way that has strengthened rather than weakened the rendering. I would like here to explore the issue of subjectivity and intentionality within the context of painting. The following example is included to illustrate some of the ways in which subjectivity and intentionality can affect the image-making process and to explicate it from an experiential perspective.

I come upon this beautiful spot in a scenic landscape to which I feel drawn. As I contemplate the view I become aware of a telephone pole that disrupts this landscape. I find myself frustrated with how this telephone pole disrupts the beauty of this landscape. My first reaction is to find another place to paint; yet I pause to reflect on what had initially attracted me to this view. On the one hand, something propelled me to look at this landscape again with a deeper concern. There was a wish to capture what attracted me to this scene, which was in some conflict with the presence of the telephone pole that I perceived as a disruption. This disruption caused an opening.

After looking at the scene for some time I came to question my own stance in relation to the subject matter. If, after contemplation, I was to proceed with the painting of the landscape, my rendering may then focus to accentuate certain aspects of the landscape, such as the presence of the pole as an important symbol of modern technology that is in stark contrast with the rugged nature of the landscape. In my rendering, I could also change my perspective to deaccentuate the presence of the telephone pole because I do not see it as an important or essential part of the essence of what I am attempting to capture.

When the layers of discovered experience are in conflict with the overall harmony of the emerging picture, something becomes an interruption. This rupture causes one to step back, to be outside the prereflective flow of the dialectical process between self, world, and image. An opening is created that allows one to access and draw upon a different, perhaps more analytic, perspective than one has been using. This interruption of the flow may lead to further contemplations and perhaps a new engagement or abandonment of the image in order to start anew. In both cases, an understanding of one's way of being in the world can be furthered.

The choices I make in my rendering of the landscape will create very different views of the subject matter. Each of these different views communicates, through my iconographic style, a different reality to a viewer. My stance as an artist and the reasons for my painting this picture will affect every nuance of the image. There is an intentionality in each brushstroke that creates a specific sense of reality. Do I want to make a political statement about the nature of our environment or do I want to celebrate the beauty of the flowers, sky, and trees? How much do I keep the rendering on the level of my perceptions and how much do I let my inner landscape and vision guide me? What is the difference between a functional image such as a "map" and a painter's rendering of a landscape? Both create visions of the world. Each provides a view into slightly different territories. This brings me to the subject of distinguishing between "imagination" and "fantasy." I note here that many different unconscious and conscious forces propel the choices that I make. Depending on the dynamics of these forces in relationship to my external world, these forces will determine if painting the image is an act of bringing me closer to the world or pushing me away from it. It will determine whether it is an act of discovery of a new vision, or an act of escape from the world.

Although the focus of my training was realism and the creation of representational images, I became more and more aware of and interested in the dialogical/interpretative aspect of this process. I learned about the use of different art media and discovered how each medium had its own dynamics. For example, I noticed that oil paints brought out very different ways of seeing and interpreting my subject matter than watercolors or pencils. I found that each medium set off very different resonances and dialogical processes. These resonances were qualitatively different and not directly related to the technical skills needed for the use of the different media, but seemed more connected with a mood or a felt-energy flow. Some media seemed more fluid and free while others were heavy and slow, thus allowing the energy and dialogical processes to move at different paces. Some media, like watercolors, were more transparent and others, like pencils or oil paints, almost invited a constant reworking and reinterpreting, thus creating thicker interpretative layers (in a metaphorical as well as in a literal sense). I found this also somewhat true in the writing process and in the creation of different types of texts. Some texts tend to be more prereflective, lighter, and fluid while others tend to be heavier, and denser with many interpretative layers. Whether it is the medium and nature of an image or the quality of a text, each opens different possibilities in the dialogical process, and alters the awareness that could be gained from it.

Photography and computer art are media that I also explored, each with its own qualities, and later incorporated into what became the multi-modal approach to research of interpretative quilting. When comparing the nature of taking a photograph to making a painting some very important distinctions can be made. As Berger and Mohr (1982) remark: "Photographs do not translate from appearance. They quote from them" (p.96). The person making a painting creates it through the lens of his or her being and coagulates his or her observations over an extended period of time while the camera (although guided by the interpretative function of the person taking the picture) is interpreting the phenomena through the optical mechanics of its inner working over a relatively short period of time. "Photography, unlike drawing, does not process a language. The photographic image is produced instantaneously by the reflection of light; its figuration is *not* impregnated by the experience or consciousness" (Berger and Mohr, 1982, p.95). The function of time and the dialogical process between the inner landscape of the person or artist and her or his subject matter allows for a different process of discovery. The image does not simply mimic visual "reality" but interprets it through a complex experiential process that takes place between the inner landscape of the artist and the physical outer landscape of the subject matter, the art media, and the emerging shapes of the images. The contemplation of the extended pose and the melting of internal intuitive perceptions with the optical reference create the emerging image. In painting, the model, who may never speak and reveal information about herself, will still communicate, through her non-verbal stance, qualities about her way of being in this world. The artist will respond to these non-verbal signs and they will be represented in some form in the rendering of the model. The final emergent image, then, is a synthesis of self and the other. In painting, there is an energy that underlies and carries the process forward that is qualitatively different from the interpretative process involved in rendering lived experience through photography.

Photography shares some similarities with the painting process just described, but it also has very distinct features that set off slightly different dynamics. The main difference appears to be not so much a function of the level of interpretative abstraction, but more a relation to the passage of time and the opportunity to engage with an emerging image in a dialectical process that allows subjective engagement and intentionality to come into play. The painter/drawer has more choices in gradually shaping the image, whereas in photography, once the picture is taken, the image is captured on the film. It is my own history as well as the motivation that I bring to the image-making process that determines the different possibilities of what becomes visible. This experience may change over time. There is also a difference in how I see and experience the subject matter that I try to understand through my painting or photography. With the camera, my engagement is through its lens and, unless I develop my own film and make my own photographic prints, the dialogical process between myself, subject matter and image evolves along different processes, mediated by the technology involved, than when I paint or draw.

Many works by artists and thinkers have influenced the dialogical image/word approach to inquiry and the methodology of interpretative quilting. However, no particular predominant school of thought guided either. The autobiographical text has been included to give voice to my own experience of the process of art toward healing. I have explored the dialectical process between emergent images and the exploratory/interpretative process as it unfolded within different contexts; thus, illustrating the methodological approach that was developed in order to gain a deeper understanding of the process of art toward healing. I have also endeavored to convey how the researcher's "lived" experience has played an integral part in the methodological approach. From the exploration above it should be evident that the qualitative multi-modal approach to inquiry is grounded in the practice of observing *and* in the translation of perceptions into interpretative forms of drawings, paintings, and writing in order to gain awareness or sensitivity toward the subject matter and the process of art toward healing. This approach is grounded in lived experience and in the dialogical process between lived experience, theory, and practice.

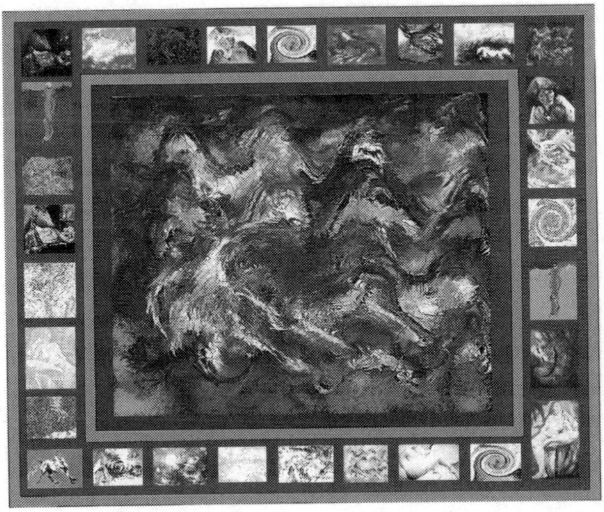

Figure 3.1: Interpretative Quilt of dialogical iconic abstractions of the author's work (completed in 2001)

Part 2

An Interpretative Quilt: A Qualitative Study of the Healing Flow within a Clinical Setting

CHAPTER 4

The Role of Contextual Factors in Interpretative Quilting

The focus of this chapter is to make visible the context in which the phenomenon of art toward healing was examined. It is to give voice to and acknowledge some of the contextual forces, which shaped this work as a whole. Furthermore, it is to provide a brief historical account of the process by which art therapy became gradually more accepted and utilized as a treatment modality within the clinical context described. Therefore, the information provided here is essential to the understanding of the interpretative stitching that weaves the symbolic quilt blocks into a cohesive whole.

As mentioned earlier, this work is grounded in the supposition that everything is embedded in an endless chain of part/whole relationships. It draws upon "an integral or holonic theory of art interpretation" (Wilber, 1997, p.119) that is complex, context bound, and universal in its essence. The description of the Program for Post Traumatic Stress Recovery is essential to this work because meaning and understanding are dependent upon the information provided about the context from which it emerged.

In the following section I will acknowledge some of the background noise that is part of lived experience and daily clinical practice, which is not made visible in the Interpretative Quilt. The descriptive border will provide some practical and clinical information to clarify the process of art toward healing in a way that includes some of the challenges of practice-based research. A conceptual map of the group structure and its functioning will also be given, thus providing the relevant information by which the Interpretative Quilt and the fictionalized art therapy sessions can be understood.

Contextual Features of the Dialogical Image/Word Process in Therapy and the Interpretative Quilt

The Program for Post Traumatic Stress Recovery is a six-week inpatient comprehensive treatment program that is based upon the therapeutic community milieu approach and trauma theory. The program includes a combination of biological and different psychotherapy treatments that are adapted to suit individuals' needs and treatment goals. Treatment options consist of educational sessions, skill development, group therapy, spirituality, and creative arts therapy, as well as horticultural and recreational therapy. The program shaped to various degrees what could unfold within the art therapy group. The program schedule, the patient population within the therapeutic milieu, and the different clinical and non-clinical staff all helped shape the therapeutic container of the process of art toward healing. Factors such as: the support and understanding of the art therapy group by other team members; the number of referrals to the group; the time the group was scheduled; the pre-group information provided to the patients; and the co-leadership also influenced its overall functioning. These factors as well as many other more subtle and personal ones fluctuated over the years.

The support and understanding of the art therapy component varied between team members and changed over time. The strong theoretical support and focus that the Sanctuary Model had provided helped with the integration of the art therapy component. This theoretical model (Bloom, 1997) will be explored further in this section. However, the many practical challenges that presented themselves over the years brought forth various issues and confounding factors that were associated with clinical practice. Trust in this treatment modality slowly grew as the program evolved and as staff encountered patients responding to art therapy. This was particularly true for those who had seen the process of art toward healing in practice. The support of co-therapists helped to build trust within the team and to integrate the art therapy component into the program. However, at times of constraints and pressure caused by limited financial or human resources, overall program deliveries, including the art therapy component, were affected.

During stressful times it was easy to go back to what each of us was most familiar with and to become somewhat defensive about our own specialty areas. This tended to create an atmosphere that made it more difficult to be receptive and open toward each other's perspectives. Although this affected everyone equally it seemed that perhaps this dynamic was amplified for team members who were practicing in more non-traditional therapies. This, to some degree, parallels the role that the arts play in our culture.

In Part One of this book I explored some of the issues related to the cultural container in which the arts and art therapy are embedded. This cultural container or border speaks to the part/whole relationship of the process of art toward healing. The fragmentation and dissociation of knowledge as it has been discussed so far echoes observations made in this particular clinical context. The theme of fragmentation of knowledge and different approaches to understanding one's way of being in the world, as discussed by Wilber (1995, 1996, 1997), echo the continuous struggle that was associated with establishing and maintaining an integrative and holistic manner of working in this Program. On a micro level, the integration of the art therapy component within the Program of Post Traumatic Stress Recovery provides an opportunity to explore some of these issues in a more direct and concrete manner.

Within this microcosm, I would also like to note that there is a parallel between the process within the clinical team that unfolded during stressful times and the process that patients were moving through during their treatment. In the program, patients were exposed to many different and intense therapeutic interventions. During times of distress patients, similar to staff, found it more difficult to trust their own creative powers and to be open to new possibilities. Thus, this struggle was reflected to some degree in the challenges that we faced as a team.

Trust and security appear to be at the core of the patient's ability to step into the unknown and to enter into the creative process. During times of difficulties related to financial and staffing resources and general program planning, great care had to be taken so that the art therapy component would not become trivialized and rendered impotent or pushed toward the periphery of the program. As already mentioned, this tendency to trivialize was probably not unique to the art therapy component but it seemed to be amplified by the cultural role the arts play in our times. In her work Bloom (1997) has also drawn a parallel between the arts within the current cultural milieu and the struggles of the creative arts therapies to become recognized within the mainstream therapies.

During times of difficulty it was important to identify the issues that were arising from the situation and to acknowledge the problem so that we could work together in order to re-establish trust in each other's abilities and methods of working. This was particularly important because the art therapy process seemed to unfold along different parameters than some of the other treatment modalities. In some ways, the process that is explored in this book makes visible the difficulty of measuring the phenomena of art therapy. It appears that the process of art toward healing generally unfolded in a less than predictable manner. When I speak of predictable I mean the pattern of the process and how it unfolded, not its actual effect.

It seems that this aspect led at different times to the perception that the art therapy component could perhaps unravel and regress patients more quickly than other treatment modalities. This difficulty was related to the fact that each member of the multidisciplinary team had slightly different training and ways of conceptualizing how treatment should unfold. This led at times to misunderstandings, skepticism, unrealistic expectations, and other challenges that presented roadblocks to integrating the art therapy component as a vital and dynamic part of the program. It was a continuous process of education, clarification, and patience that slowly transformed skepticism into trust and understanding.

The common language that the Sanctuary Model provided aided this transformation. The theoretical framework and language of the Sanctuary Model that Sandra Bloom and her colleagues developed allowed us to communicate with each other and to integrate the many different aspects of the program. In this model, the creative arts therapies are seen as providing essential aspects of the treatment for trauma survivors that cannot be fulfilled through other types of therapies. Bloom (1997) identifies that traumatic experiences, particularly those from early childhood, are at times difficult to access and process through verbal therapies. The experiential and creative arts therapies are a potential channel through which patients can express their feelings on a non-verbal level so that they can be transformed and reintegrated (Bloom, 1997). Following this model, these observations can be made about the role of art therapy within the Program for Post Traumatic Stress Recovery. According to Bloom, the art therapy component can work in conjunction with and complement the verbal therapies offered within a program.

This potential was further supported by some of the literature in the area of Post Traumatic Stress Recovery and art therapy in which other research on memories indicate that traumatic events may be encoded differently from ordinary lived experience (Cohen, 1996; Van der Kolk, 1989). Cohen (1996) argues that therapists who can capitalize on visual-oriented therapies will be able to provide more effective treatment than those who use verbal therapy alone: "When experiences are found to be overwhelming, unexpected, or undesirable, they cannot be adequately processed" (p.528). Cohen continues by explaining Horowitz's work on congruent and incongruent schemas and memory, which states that incongruent schemas or patterns cannot be translated into verbal language patterns. According to his thinking, these "disrupted schemas are stored in short-term memory, primarily on an iconic (visual) and sensorimotor (body) level" (p.528), where they make up the basis of traumatic memories. He describes these memories as being wordless, de-contextualized, meaningless patterns that affect the individual on many levels without them being able to consciously work with them on a cognitive and verbal level.

According to Cohen's thinking, there are many parallels between the dissociative reality and the art reality. He draws the parallel between the two realms and in support of his argument he identifies four aspects that apply to both the dissociative realm and the world of the arts. The concepts are bisociation, plastic, absorptive, and multi-leveled in nature. Some of these concepts bear kinship to other thinkers in this area. Cohen (1996) draws the term "bisociation" from Koestler's work. It refers to "the combining of habitual, incompatible parts during the creative process." Rothenberg (1990) had a similar concept, which he named "janusian and homospatial processes." "Unlike psychopathological processes, which involve rigidity, irrationality, and extreme self-absorption and self-focus, janusian and homospatial processes are flexible and rationally based as well as directed toward other human beings and the environment" (Rothenberg, 1990, p.161).

According to Cohen (1996), the incongruent images of traumatic memories can be worked with more easily by drawing upon the creative process and the visual arts. He states: "Because visual and sensorimotor functions are critical in the storage, coding, and recall of traumatic events, one must be willing to learn about the impact of trauma on imagery and how they manifest through art making" (Cohen, 1996, p.527). He draws a parallel between creativity and the utilization of the arts with the dissociated, fragmented world of traumatic memories. As already discussed in different parts of this book, in spite of the similarities there are also many important differences between the creative process and the dissociated realm of traumatic memories. However, within this specific clinical context an important part of the art therapy component is that art therapy with the image-making process can help break down fragmentation and provide a vehicle for working with and integrating traumatic memories.

The literature on childhood trauma generally supports the notion that traumatic experiences, particularly those from early childhood, are at times difficult to access and process through verbal therapies and that the creative arts therapies including art therapy seem to offer an approach that can complement the verbal therapies. Bloom (1997) writes that "[t]he arts give form, shape, and sound to the numinous, the traumatic, and the nonverbal, which can therefore be brought into full awareness and integrated into overall functioning" (pp.234–235). Therefore, there is much evidence that the art therapy can be seen as a channel through which patients could express their feelings on a non-verbal level.

Within the symbolic realm of the art therapy group, patients could work on many levels with materials that emerged during therapy. This aspect is well described by Bloom (1997) and relates to the non-verbal and encapsulated aspects of traumatic memories. The verbal self had to experience, for the first time, the traumatic event with the accompanying overwhelming emotions. Only then could the patient put the event into a narrative form so that the traumatic experience could become a true memory, safely stored in the past, no longer able to non-verbally direct and control behavior (p.161).

Although this aspect of working with traumatic memories is a strong feature of the art therapy component, I would not want to limit the process of art toward healing to it alone. In this book I have looked at some of the broader curative factors that an art can provide. Within the Program of Post Traumatic Stress Recovery, patients were referred for a number of different reasons that included, but were not limited to, working with traumatic memories.

General Objectives and General Goals of the Art Therapy Group

These objectives and goals were as follows:

- to encourage communication through the use of art media and to increase awareness of self (emotions, feelings, images, thoughts) in relation to others
- to facilitate exploration of communications with the unconscious
- to allow individuals to discover their unconscious in a non-threatening way and to learn from it in a constructive manner

- to learn how to work with and understand frightening/intrusive internal images through the use of art materials
- to provide opportunities to discover and utilize one's creativity and to become one's own tutor
- to encourage group interaction through sharing the images on an implicit or explicit level as well as through group discussions
- to provide a situation where the reflecting on images within a group setting can bring about a shared understanding of how trauma can be metabolized and transcended.

As illustrated by the goals just listed, the art therapy group could facilitate many more processes that reached beyond simply working with traumatic memories. Independent of the theoretical and interpersonal factors discussed so far were the many practical issues that presented obstacles to the integration of the art therapy component. Even with the support of other team members and of the program co-ordinators, many practical issues, such as time schedules, studio space, and co-leadership, provided obstacles for integrating the art therapy group in a way that could fulfill its full potential. A number of structural changes to the art therapy group were employed to improve its functioning and integration. A good introduction to the art therapy group that described the potential benefits and risks of this therapeutic modality helped patients to get oriented to the process. It also helped them to evaluate if they felt ready for this kind of therapeutic work. Because the short-term nature of the group involved only four to eight sessions, a staggered entrance of weekly intake into the group seemed to further help patients to acclimatize, and helped to introduce new members into the unfamiliar process of art therapy.

The number of sessions that patients were able to attend further contributed to the kind of therapeutic experience that patients were able to have. The patients who attended more than four sessions had a greater chance to become comfortable with the process of art toward healing. They were more likely to learn to trust the unfolding of this unique treatment modality. This was in part due to the fact that the first few sessions were needed for individuals to get comfortable with using the art materials and the dialogical image/word process. The number of group members within the group and their commitment to the group further contributed to the quality of the therapeutic experience. The time of day the group was held and the groups that patients had attended prior to coming into the group further affected how the patient would be able to use the group. In some circumstances, the scheduling in the morning may have been very intense, thus leaving little energy left for the individual to engage meaningfully in the afternoon art therapy group. Thus, the overall programming of therapeutic experiences affected how patients were able to participate in the group.

Within the Healing-Flow Model the therapeutic container plays a central role in the way the process of art toward healing is able to unfold. For me, one of the greatest struggles in integrating the art therapy component as a vital part of the program was related to maintaining a suitable therapeutic container as well as maintaining a good group mix. From my observations, it seemed that the group structure and the group mix had a great effect on patients' ability to benefit from the group and to get familiar with this different treatment modality. As I will show in the Interpretative Quilt, with its fictional art therapy sessions that are described in the following chapter, the number of group members and the interpersonal issues affected the therapy process and the unfolding of the dialogical image/word approach.

Practice-Based Theory of the Art Therapy Group within the Program for Post Traumatic Stress Recovery

The art therapy group that was part of the Program for Post Traumatic Stress Recovery was basically an insight-oriented psychotherapy group where the image-making process played a central role. As already discussed, this image-oriented art therapy shared many qualities with other forms of verbal therapies (i.e., theoretical foundations of counselling psychology and group dynamics). However, when using an image-making process and the dialogical image/word approach within the context of group psychotherapy, many more experiential dimensions became engaged. Within this therapy process, different types of verbal and non-verbal dimensions became integrated into awareness. That is to say, an image-oriented therapy has the additional modality of the image-making process and its dialogical aspect that is set in motion through the use of the different art materials, where each material has its own unique possibilities.

The phrase "image making" as it is used here refers to any visual expression, ranging from one line on a piece of paper to abstract shapes, to blending of colors, to shapes made from clay and found objects. An image does not have to take any recognizable shape, although it may if the person so chooses.

Images can also include words that create patterns forming connections with lines, colors, and shapes.

Images themselves can reflect a state of mind and give important information to the patient and the therapist. One can return to the image at different times during treatment. An image may express aspects of the self that are not yet fully understood on a conscious level but that may evoke strong emotions or feelings in the person. In some ways the image-making process can be compared to dreams, where the unconscious is emerging into consciousness using its own symbolic language that is not easily understood by the conscious, rational mind.

Unconscious feelings can also be processed on a symbolic level without the person necessarily being aware of the content or meaning that lies behind the symbols of the colors, shapes, and images. For example, a person could work on images for a long time without being aware of the type of material/issues that he or she may be processing on an unconscious level. It is important to recognize that the actual working with the art materials may be a preparation for the person to face complex and difficult feelings, memories, and experiences. Working with the materials can engage a person in a process on a non-verbal level that needs to unfold in its own time. Premature interpretations that push for meaning before the conscious mind is able to understand the message may not lead to insight and could cause frustration, tensions, and the rejection of what the image may have to offer. The image-making process unfolds best in a safe, non-intrusive environment, where therapeutic interventions guided by the therapist's receptivity and awareness allow materials to come into an area of consciousness where they can be further processed and integrated.

This process can at first be an unusually intense experience and therefore the therapeutic atmosphere of safety is an essential part of the treatment. When an image emerges that the person who has created it is not able to fully embrace at the time of creation, he or she will have many choices about how to regain power over what the image evoked and not to become trapped in a traumatic re-enactment. For example, the patient is not in isolation and can draw on the group as well as on the group therapist for support. This can facilitate affect modulation and the learning of how to stay with feelings, how to honor them, and how to use them as a resource. If feelings evoked by the images become too strong for the individual to tolerate, the picture can be put in a safe place until a later time when the patient has become grounded again.

The image can also be explored by creating other images and/or by verbally exploring it with the therapist and the group. In some special circumstances it may be therapeutic for the patient to change the picture by painting over it, or to destroy and dispose of the object. However, the therapeutic intervention will depend on the individual's personality style, stage in healing, and the context of the group. The exploration of images with the therapist and the group allows for the discovery of patterns, the examination of symbols, and the integration of split parts (emotions, thoughts, and feelings) through insight and a layered multi-modal process.

The making of images can also help a person to get in touch with their own creativity, affect their self-esteem, and foster new ways of seeing. This process works to build an internal resilience and strength. The different phases of the creative process may include the initial gathering phase, the incubation period, the discovery phase, the evaluation phase, and the resolution phase (LeBoeuf, 1980). The initial gathering phase is best facilitated by free, spontaneous exploration and free play where judgment of what is created/generated is suspended until a later time. A sense of confusion, uncertainty, and chaos may be experienced at this stage until the patient learns that free play can bring its rewards. Depending on their personality style, personal history, and degree of internal strength, some patients may need more reassurance, support, and direction during this phase in order to stay grounded and to tolerate these feelings with the help of the external structure of the group.

During the incubation period, one may experience a sense of quietness or a feeling that nothing is happening. However, processing is taking place on some unconscious level forming connections and preparing the consciousness for what is emerging. Inherent in the image-making process is a degree of solitude and reflection that needs to be respected. Therefore, pushing for movement and understanding during this phase may interrupt the incubation period. At this point, it may be better to do something completely differently or to return to free play, allowing shapes and colors to emerge without seeking meaning or following a specific goal. It is important to note that this phase could easily be confused with the absence of movement due to what has been called avoidance or resistance in therapy. However, the incubation period is very different from resistance. Each situation needs to be assessed carefully within the context of the patient's situation. If the patient is stuck, it is important to understand and identify this in order to block a maladaptive pattern of traumatic re-enactments, and to help the patient to change.

The discovery phase is the most exciting and rewarding part of the creative process and can be compared to some extent with peak experiences. During this phase all the pieces seem to almost magically fall together in order to form a picture that is grounded in deep personal meaning. This is the period where most conscious insights are gained. However, this period, if not integrated into other experiences, can for some patients present a great risk. It may foster a sense of specialness that could reinforce old patterns of isolation. It may also, in some rare cases, increase the gap between the person's internal world as embodied in the image and the external world. This seems to connect to some personality styles and to the patient's lived experience. If the images created are treated as an object through which the person was able to get unfulfilled needs met there is a risk of the patient becoming lost in the process. The "art object" then can become more important than the individual who has created it and this may stifle the therapeutic aspect of the process of art toward healing. This could further contribute to the individual's suffering through the objectification of the image that disguises or distracts from the true suffering of the person (Rothenberg, 1990). Patients may be more prone to use art as a way to avoid their external world that seems to be full of problems that they do not feel able to deal with. This could provide a stumbling block toward using the creative energy and the image created in a reality-oriented manner that would allow the individual to direct this energy toward life.

A person may very easily enter the two or three phases of the creative process but he or she may become lost or entrapped in these early phases. It may be more comforting to stay in the symbolic and free flowing realm rather than to move to the next phase where internal images can be processed through the image/word dialogue. Thus, the patient again may become trapped in their internal world without being able to connect to the external world. The first three phases of the creative process can prepare patients for possible insights about themselves and help them to communicate through their images material that they were not consciously aware of before, or that they were not able to put into words. Depending on the individual patient's situation and personality style, this phase can present a great risk as well as providing many opportunities. The outcome will in part depend on the therapist's understanding. The appropriate intervention during this phase, which can facilitate the therapeutic process, is essential. Insights gained in this phase may occur on many levels. However, how they are integrated and carried forward will depend on many personal and circumstantial factors. Depending on the quality of the therapeutic container, most individuals are able to use this phase in a constructive manner.

During the first three phases, patients are able to gain strength and confidence in themselves through the continuous dialogue with the different art media. When patients are able to see pictures spontaneously form in front of them, they are able to engage in a qualitatively different type of dialogue than if communication was to take place only on a verbal level. The dialogical image/word approach combined with the therapist's interventions encourage patients to move through all phases of the creative process. During the initial gathering phase, the incubation period, and the discovery phase, patients are able to see and experience their and other group members' internal worlds on a non-verbal level. Through the images created during the art therapy group, many internal and external resonances can be set off. The processing of these resonances within the therapy group can help propel patients forward and encourage them to use all phases of the creative process. The dialogical image/word process as it is used in the therapy context is an important part of the Healing-Flow Model as it relates to the different phases of the creative process.

Through the first three phases of the creative process guided by the dialogical image/word approach to art therapy, patients are able to dialogue with their internal world in a more positive manner. Through this dialogue individuals can gain different types of insights. However, the way patients will use the awareness and insights generated through this process will depend on many internal and external factors. It may also affect how the individual will enter the last two phases of the creative process. A patient may stay in the first three levels of the creative process where he or she is able to experience the continuous flow of images from their unconscious without processing the material generated on a non-verbal or verbal level. Depending on the situation, this may be what the individual needs to do before being able to move to the next phase. However, it could also be a way of avoiding dealing with more existential issues.

Staying in the symbolic realm without integrating and harnessing the material generated by the images may be a sign that a patient is caught in a traumatic re-enactment that he or she is not able to move out of on their own. It may take time to distinguish the one process from the other and it is the therapist's role to help the individual, by using the different therapeutic interventions, to move through all the phases of the creative process in a therapeutic manner. This aspect is what distinguishes the process of art toward healing within the context of art therapy from the process as it unfolds outside the therapeutic container. As Rothenberg (1990) remarked, artists choose the conflicts that they like to explore in their artwork and therefore may only gain partial insights about them in relationship to the world.

The evaluation phase is part of the creative process that allows the individual to learn about themselves, their strengths and weakness, and to use this information in their daily life. This phase may be experienced as more laborious because it is more a deconstruction[1] and analysis of what the discovery phase has brought. During this phase the images, thoughts, and/or insights can be explored and assessed for their personal meaning in order to put them into a larger context.

The resolution phase is marked by a sense of having successfully worked through something. There is a sense of completion, or resolution, that has led to some greater understanding. In art therapy, this could be reflected in a picture that embodies and holds many elements of earlier images and themes from the dialogical image/word explorations. However, it is not necessary that the images created will embody all the phases described above. At times the images themselves are not important and are simply a vehicle for an individual to get in touch with their creativity. The integration of the evaluation phase and resolution phase may take place on a verbal level, or it may become visible in the way an individual incorporates the experience into their daily life. The art object itself may continue to inform in a way that goes beyond the therapeutic context (Schaverien, 1992). However, many aspects of the image may be limited to the therapeutic context and the relationships in which it was created.

All elements/phases of the creative process interplay quite freely and are not as clearly delineated or identified as may appear from the writing above. Each individual, depending on their personality style and present life situation, will experience them differently. The different phases of the creative process will also be influenced by the therapeutic atmosphere and by the group dynamics. I have found that the therapist's verbal and non-verbal communications as well as the physical space (i.e., room, studio space) and the group composition/dynamics can play an important part in this process. The kind of art materials provided, the way they are presented, and the safe storage of the images created during therapy are other important elements that can affect the different aspects of the creative process and the process of art toward healing.

The general objectives of the art therapy group, as they were listed above, are to encourage communication through the use of art media and to increase self-awareness by accessing and expressing emotions, feelings, images, and thoughts. It is also intended to facilitate exploration and communication with the unconscious. Thus, the therapeutic container of the art therapy group provides an opportunity for individuals to discover their unconscious in a non-threatening way and to learn to draw from it in order to deal with their lives more successfully. It helps patients to utilize their creativity and to become their own tutor. The group environment provides an opportunity to break through isolation. The group interaction can then lead to collaboration. This process is greatly facilitated by the sharing of the images on an implicit or explicit level as well as through group discussions.

There are many different ways the different group members can use their images. The images in the imagistic pauses speak of how some patients use the image-making process. Painting can be a means to share one's internal world with oneself and others. Through a symbolic representation in the paintings, even the most intense feelings of rage, terror, and deep depression can be shared in a way that others can receive them and reflect on them empathically. The images provide a symbolic realm through which we can share, experience, and transform feelings that would be too terrifying if they were directly expressed toward another human being. Within this symbolic realm, one is less likely to become trapped in transference and traumatic re-enactments. This is possible because at times it can be easier to understand and accept the material presented as it was offered through the images. Yet, in their own way the images are powerful in how they affect our being in this world. This power can help to facilitate clarity and understanding that are grounded in the visceral non-verbal and the intellectual symbolic level within the social context of the therapy and therapeutic milieu.

The art therapy group, as it will be brought to life in the following Interpretative Quilt patches, will illustrate how the patients have many opportunities to gain mastery over and control of their feelings, internal images, dreams, and thoughts. Through the many different kinds of images, patients can find new creative ways of expressing and giving voice to the non-verbal or pre-verbal aspects of the self in an integrated manner. The symbolic realm of the images can facilitate the exploration/communication with unconscious feelings, images, dreams, and thoughts through art materials. The examples that are brought to light through the dialogical image/word approach to inquiry further show how patients can get in touch with their own creativity in order to metabolize and move beyond traumatic experiences. Within the therapeutic container of the art therapy group, patients are able to break patterns of traumatic re-enactment and utilize their creativity and to become their own tutor.

The pictures that were created during group can act as transitional objects that allow the patient to carry forward and connect whatever they learned during the art therapy sessions with their life outside of this context. The images in the imagistic pauses of the following chapters are their own record of the process of art toward healing and the possibilities that they offer to the patient/artist and the viewer/therapist/reader. Because these images have been taken outside of the context and the relationships in which they were created, the experience of them and the dialogical process that is generated will be different from the way the images had functioned for the individual who created them.

Note

1 The word "deconstruction" as it is used here is slightly different in meaning from the theory of textual analysis, which poses that a text has no stable reference and is questioning the assumptions about the ability of language to represent reality. In this book, as already explored in the previous chapters, the reality created by the text and images is understood in terms of having been constructed from perceptions and knowledge gained from various sources that have become part of our being. The text and images are reconstructed and synthesized from these experiences and how they have interacted with our being in this world. Thus, the created reality is saturated and bound up in personal and cultural bias/historicity as well as our personalities, but it also is a reality that to some degree can be shared and validated through external references.

CHAPTER 5

A Window: Entering the Art Therapy Room

The physical components of the art therapy room or studio, the art materials, and the safe storage of the images created during therapy are all important aspects of the therapeutic container. Each part contributes to the unfolding of the healing flow. The images and artwork that patients created during therapy were important transitional objects and therefore needed to be treated with respect. They were not considered as part of the patients' clinical records. All of the images that the patients created during the sessions belonged to them. The images were a visible record of each patient's journey, and they were encouraged to take their work with them after they had completed the therapy group. Depending on the individual's journey and the nature of its images, their artwork could become useful for them in the future. Therefore, when patients completed the group, they were encouraged to reflect upon their work and to decide what they would like to do with it.

While patients were in the art therapy group their work was stored safely in a storage room and they could have the images brought into the therapy sessions when they wanted to see them. This helped to set boundaries and communicated respect toward what they had created. For reasons related to confidentiality, affect modulation, and traumatic re-enactments, patients were asked to keep the images that they had created during therapy in the storage room. Leaving the images or transitional objects in a safe place helped patients learn to engage in the healing flow and the dialogical image/word process within a safe container where some symbolic closure was created after each session. However, there were some situations in which it was therapeutically

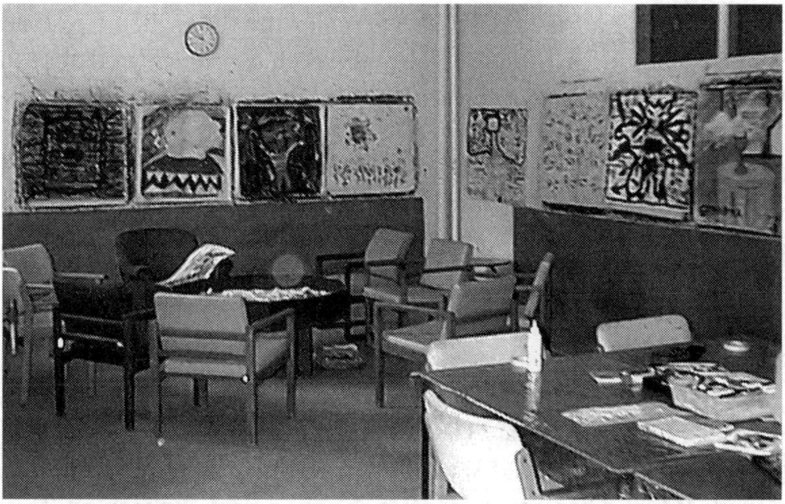

Figure 5.1: A room becomes transformed and claimed by the images that are created

beneficial for an individual to take their picture with them after they had completed it. Clinical judgment rather than rules had to be used to help the patients to understand the role of this transitional object and the healing flow.

Patients had a number of choices about how they could treat these transitional objects. They could abandon them, dispose of them, give them away as gifts, take them with them or leave them with the group therapist for safe storage. If patients left their work behind without specifying that they would like to have it kept for the future, we usually kept their work for up to one year. This symbolized that we, the therapists and the institution, valued the patients and what they had created. Therefore, a great commitment was made toward keeping works that were left behind for as long as possible so that a person could perhaps reclaim them in the future. Even when patients in later admissions did not use the pictures or look at them, for many of them it was important simply to know that they were kept in a safe place.

Group Structure and Implementation of the Group

The art therapy group usually began with an orientation phase that we called "a verbal check-in phase" or "orientation phase." As part of this check-in, patients would typically talk about how they felt about being in the group and the kind of issues they would like to explore through group discussions or the use of the different art materials. This was also the time when new members were introduced and issues could be raised that were related to patients' abilities to use the group in a constructive and therapeutic manner. The length of this group discussion depended on how many new members had joined the group and how much material remained to be explored from the previous sessions. The duration and quality of the check-in period was also affected by the overall developmental stage of the group and the group dynamics. We often started the sessions by reflecting upon pictures that had been created in the previous sessions. We hung them up so that they could be included in the dialogical process of this check-in phase.

The orientation phase was frequently followed by a time when patients could use the different art materials in a free and relatively unmediated manner. There were no group themes set by the therapists and each group member could work at his or her own pace after choosing from the many different art media. The room was usually quiet during this time while group members worked on their individual pieces. In order to allow individuals to work on what they wanted or needed to and because music can have a strong influence on the unfolding of the dialogical process and the healing flow, music was not used during this experiential part of the group. The group sessions usually closed with a reflection and processing phase that was focused upon the material that had been brought forward through the dialogical image-making process. This reflection and discussion phase was an important part of the dialogical image/word approach to psychotherapy. It included both the verbal and non-verbal processing and contemplation of the process, the images themselves, and the associated thoughts and feelings that were brought forward through the experiential aspects of the group.

The Therapist's Role

The way the therapist can facilitate and guide the process of art toward healing within a group context will be qualitatively explored through the various quilt patches. This first patch is to introduce the structure and outline which will then be brought alive and flushed out through the other quilt patches. The following list will introduce some of the main points to the reader in a manner that is similar to how patients are introduced to the role of the therapist:

1. To know, respect, and trust the process of art within the therapeutic context

2. To work with unconscious themes that arise from the group, using various clinical and creative arts interventions
3. To identify and work with issues related to affect modulation and traumatic re-enactment as they were used with the Program for Post Traumatic Stress Recovery
4. To provide suggestions and guidance on how to use the different media in a way that facilitates the therapeutic process and goals without focusing on teaching specific painting/drawing skills or techniques
5. To facilitate the dialogical image/word approach to therapy through posing questions and clarifying visual or verbal expressions in a therapeutic and integrated manner using clinical interventions.

As can be seen from the points listed above, the role of the therapist within this group was to guide the healing flow and the dialogical process through the use of different therapeutic and creative arts interventions. These interventions were grounded in the therapist's intuitive clinical judgment and were aimed at creating an effective therapeutic environment or container. Both the physical layout of the art therapy room and the therapist's attitude shape the therapeutic container, with all its verbal and non-verbal aspects. The dialogical image/word approach described in earlier chapters was augmented with clinical interventions that were specific to this clinical setting and program and that were to propel the healing flow.

The use of various interventions such as education, supportive encouragement, interpretation, reframing, confrontation, supportive witnessing, and blocking of maladaptive behaviors will be brought to life within the quilt patches of this chapter. In these quilt patches the creation of a therapeutic environment will be described and will illustrate to some degree how these interventions were used to guide the unfolding of the therapeutic process. The creative arts interventions that were described earlier were blended together with these clinical interventions and both were guided by the same intentionality of facilitating the healing flow. The therapist's tacit and intuitive knowledge, mediated by the use of self as a reflective tool, helped guide the therapeutic interactions and clinical decisions. Thus, the creation of the therapeutic container and the many subtleties of the therapeutic interventions with their conscious and unconscious forces will be made visible in the following descriptive quilt patches. However, I would like to remind the reader again that these clinical dimensions are not the focus of this book and that they will only be explicated to a degree in order to illustrate the context in which the process of art toward healing was observed.

Generally, therapeutic interventions took place at a group level with little time given for individual attention. While group members were working with the art materials, it was possible for patients to have some individual time with the therapist. These therapeutic moments were aimed at helping the patient to enter the healing flow through the different art media and to guide them back toward the group process. If needed, these therapeutic moments could also be used to help a patient with affect modulation and traumatic re-enactments so that they could find their way back to the group. However, ongoing interventions with the therapist were not encouraged and patients were expected, after a few of these interventions, to be able to use the group as a whole for their therapeutic needs.

The main mode of working was with the group as a whole by utilizing group discussions and creating images through the different art media. The group discussions that followed the experiential part of the group were aimed at exploring what was brought to consciousness through the pictures that were created using the dialogical image/word process. This exploration was done in such a way that the individuals could find their own trajectory and way of being in the world. The therapist's role was to know, recognize, and facilitate this process by drawing upon the numerous ways of using and exploring the art materials and the images created. During the group discussions, each group member had the opportunity to become a sounding board for her/himself and others. The images shared in the group allowed each member to discover something about his or her own perceptions and to learn to what extent others shared them.

Group dynamics played an important part in the way the dialogical image/word process facilitated the healing flow. As already mentioned, depending on the group's needs and its developmental stage, different amounts of time were spent using the art media and the verbal processing. The nature of the dialogical process and the healing flow were also affected by the quality of the therapeutic container, which was in turn greatly influenced by how the different group members felt and interacted within the group. Thus, the overall group dynamics, the group leadership, and the physical space had an impact on how much individuals would bring of themselves to the therapy session through their verbal and non-verbal expressions.

The therapist's ability to create a therapeutic container depended on many variables. For myself it was important to take some time prior to the group to prepare the art therapy studio and myself for the upcoming sessions. I usually would familiarize myself with the clinical information gathered since the last meeting. I also liked to go over the pictures that had been created in previous sessions and to prepare the physical aspects of the room. This preparation helped me to orientate myself for the many possibilities that could unfold during the session.

Some of the aspects of this preparation phase were influenced by the expectations and milieu of the treatment program. These preparations largely followed and related to clinical and ethical guidelines. However, some were more personal in nature and had evolved over time. I kept note of the changes within the group by checking the referral lists and attending team meetings. If possible I also tried to connect with other clinical staff between our therapy sessions in order to obtain relevant information related to the process and issues that pertained to the different group members. When a patient was struggling in the program, or in other groups, this was usually brought to my attention through clinical notes or discussions with other staff. The patient's prime nurse therapist played a central role in this preparation phase. Through this preparation I felt more connected with the work that patients were doing in the overall program, and it allowed me to work together with the Program for Post Traumatic Stress Recovery as a whole and to build on the other components in a more integrated manner.

The more personal aspects of the preparation period involved working with resonances or counter-transference issues in myself that had developed through the process of therapy. Working with these issues through discussions with the co-therapist, going over the images that were created during the groups, and reflecting upon process notes and other clinical material helped me to sort out different aspects of these resonances. They were important ways that helped to build my internal readiness for the upcoming group. From this base I was more able to be attuned and alert to different possibilities and to guide the healing flow through the various clinical interventions.

As group therapists we are endowed with a certain responsibility to help the group evolve along therapeutic goals. Thus our roles as therapists, by their very nature, created certain dynamics that contributed to the therapeutic container and to the unfolding of the healing flow. Within this therapeutic container, a dynamic interchange between the group members, the therapists, the art media, and the images was able to unfold. The different energies that developed within the verbal and non-verbal dimensions of the therapeutic container shaped the healing flow and the dialogical process. The relevant clinical information gathered before the individual art therapy sessions was filtered through and synthesized into the intuitive clinical judgment. However, all of this preparation only provides an entry point into the group process; once the group began, it developed along its own trajectory. Thus, before starting the group I tried to let all of this information fade away from my consciousness. In this way, the information would be available to inform me, if needed, without interfering with my ability to experience the individual group members in all of their complexity and humanness.

Individual Choices for Participation

Individuals have many ways in which they can enter and participate in the process of art toward healing. The following points are introduced to patients before they start the group in order for them to have some sense of what may be expected:

1. Individuals are invited to take personal responsibility within the group and to get their needs met within the framework of the group.
2. Individuals are expected to respect confidentiality of the group and its members.
3. Individuals are encouraged to use the session to deal with issues and topics related to treatment goals.
4. Individuals are encouraged to make an effort to participate on a verbal (sharing perceptions, asking questions) and non-verbal level in order to get their treatment goals met.
5. Individuals are encouraged to be respectful of other group members and to give constructive and honest feedback.
6. Individuals are encouraged to make choices about what type of art materials to use and how to use them.

7. Individuals are encouraged to make choices and take responsibility for what emerges on the paper or in the artwork (i.e. use of lines, shapes, textures, and colors).
8. Individuals are encouraged to make choices about how much to allow the image to emerge from the unconscious through free exploration and by playing with materials or to what extent to plan the image on a cognitive, conscious level.
9. Individuals are encouraged to choose how much time to spend on the exploration of the image-making process.
10. Individuals are encouraged to choose how much to verbally explore the image with the therapist or the group.
11. Individuals are encouraged to choose how much to allow themselves to experience the images on many different levels of being (i.e. the somatic and visceral, the perceptual and aesthetic, the psychological and emotional, the intellectual and symbolic, as well as the interpersonal and spiritual levels). Independent of one's choice, each group member will to some extent experience his/her own images as well as those made by other group members on an implicit and explicit level. That is to say, images created in the group are experienced on many levels even when they are not attended to explicitly through verbal explorations. They always will be experienced on a non-verbal and unconscious dimension that will propel the dialogical image/word process along certain trajectories.
12. Individuals are encouraged to respect images and to explore them for their personal meanings and the effects they evoke.
13. Individuals are encouraged to express opinions in a non-aggressive way.

The level of comfort and trust that individuals experienced within the group would influence their participation. Group themes that evolved unfolded within the different spheres of the physical, psychological, emotional, and spiritual realm of being and were shaped by the many internal and external forces of the individuals and the group as a whole. The studio space, the art materials, the images, and the verbal explorations all contributed to the healing flow. Each group member was encouraged to take responsibility for and ownership of his or her own feelings and actions in a way that was contained within the group's parameters. Members were also supported in identifying issues that they felt were hampering their participation in the group, and in working with those issues using the different choices listed previously.

The nature of the externalization and symbolic representations of the healing flow was different for each individual; therefore, each patient was reminded to respect his or her unique iconographic style and to move at his or her own pace. The social aspect of the group allowed individuals to experience and celebrate their uniqueness as well as to feel that they were a constructive part of the group as a whole. The sharing of images therefore affected many aspects of the self and the dialogical process between the internal and external world. This complex process will be communicated in the images and various types of text that make up the different quilt patches contained in the Interpretative Quilt.

The Life of Images and the Healing Flow in the Clinical Context

This quilt patch will take a perspective on the healing flow by exploring three different imagistic pauses and fictionalized text. The descriptive patches within this section were juxtaposed with each imagistic pause and are based on the artwork that different patients created within the art therapy sessions. The patches reflect the themes that emerged over time. In these patches I would like to take a reflective view of the process of art toward healing as I remember it unfolding within the symbolic realm of the dialogical image/word process and the work of different patients and their images. These quilt patches will speak to the dynamic multi-leveled interplay between art media, images, individuals, and the group as a whole that can take place within an art therapy group and which are part of the healing flow. Thus, the various quilt patches will provide different windows into the healing flow as it unfolded within a context by focusing on individual patients' images and their therapeutic work within the group as a whole.

During an actual art therapy group, as will be made visible in the following quilt patches, any reflections or interpretations of the images were aimed toward reshaping and propelling the healing flow along certain therapeutic trajectories. Thus, feedback or interpretations were not to explain a picture and its meaning but to help keep it alive through a continuous, dialogical process that moved individuals toward finding their way back into the world in a more integrated manner. Each intervention or interpretation by the therapist was to help individuals to learn to modulate their affect and to be able to move more freely between the kinesthetic and the sensory, the perceptual and the affective, the cognitive and the symbolic, the social as well as the creative and spiritual dimensions in an integrated manner.

Each individual component that makes up this quilt patch provides a unique view of the phenomena under investigation. Through the interpretative stitching and juxtaposition of images and different types of texts each part becomes shaped and at the same time shapes the greater whole. Each element summarizes themes and different aspects of the process under investigation and contributes to communicating the main discoveries of this work. However, none of the different components of the text and imagistic pauses in this quilt patch will explain the other but together they create a more integrated view of the process of art toward healing as it was observed within the specific context of psychotherapy.

The whole is greater than the sum of its parts as it relates to the creative process and evolution has been a continuous theme throughout this book. Before starting the descriptive and interpretative text of this quilt patch, I would like to note again that in the creation of each Interpretative Quilt all components or elements are unique in the way that they contribute to the greater whole. However, the greater whole, when completed, will still be qualitatively different from the sum of its parts. Therefore, neither the text nor the visual images explain each other but instead they provide different windows into the phenomena with each part playing a unique role. The following two journeys that will be described are to embody and bring to life some of the unique aspects of the healing flow as it unfolded within the clinical context described earlier. In the following components of this quilt patch, images and text will provide vital information and a window into the unique and complex phenomena related to the healing flow.

CHAPTER 6

Sam's Journey with the Healing Flow

Sam was a very intelligent young man who had been in the art therapy group for the Core Program (a comprehensive six- to eight-week program offering a full range of biological and psychotherapy treatments for depressed and anxious patients) during his first admission with a treatment focus on symptoms of depression. About a year later he was referred to the Program for Post Traumatic Stress Recovery for treatment of PTSD symptomatology and issues related to childhood abuse. During his admission in the Core Program his affect had been very flat, with little or no external expressions of feelings, and he had been more comfortable with his intellectual side. At that time emotional expression was almost completely eliminated from his repertoire.

When Sam was in the art therapy group for the Core Program he used to paint very detailed illustrations of nightmare-like images that he would work on over a number of different sessions. Because of his slow and deliberate painting style much time and effort was spent on the making of the actual images with less focus on the verbal explorations of the meaning of these elaborate paintings. Any of his explorations of these images had seemed to be carefully, intellectually crafted, with very little affect attached to them. However, the pictures that Sam did about a year later, during his admission in the Program for Post Traumatic Stress Recovery, were very different from the works he had done in his previous admission. Since his last admission, Sam's manner of working had become more fluid and open to different possibilities that were inspired more by the moment and the dialogical process between art media, images, reflection, and the interactions within the group. Overall, he seemed to be able to reflect on his work in a more integrated manner and he appeared to be able to move more freely between the psychological, emotional, and intellectual realms of being. This more spontaneous and free manner of working with the image-making process was also echoed in his being less defended and predetermined within the art therapy group.

Sam's choice of his art media now also utilized a broader spectrum of materials. He had started all his paintings by carefully sculpting shapes out of Plasticine and then pasting them onto the surface of the paper. His use of Plasticine and poster paints had come to embody for him themes that echoed his emotional discoveries and his more integrated sense of self. I noticed that he appeared to work in a much more direct and expressive manner than in his previous admission. Thus, the paintings that he was creating during this second admission appeared to echo the changes in his overall being and stance within the group and within the program as a whole.

In his first painting, Sam had started to show vulnerabilities that were grounded in deep existential and ontological uncertainties. These he portrayed through a powerful symbology of a gray, decaying head or mask that was being eaten away by a large blackbird. The way he had applied the different media appeared to propel as well as to embody the powerful symbolic messages that were emerging from the image. There was a dark and nightmarish quality about this painting that raised many questions. Some of these questions were explored during group discussions but for the greater part they were contemplated and moved forward in a more integrated manner through the dialogical image/word process and the continuous flow of images. Thus, these ontological and existential questions were explored on a deeper level through the experiential, meditative, dialogical process of producing the subsequent images.

He had begun this first image by painting a solid, deep-red background. Onto this red background Sam had constructed, out of Plasticine, a half-mask or face, which he had placed in the center of the page. The incomplete, gray face had a lifeless, cold quality to it that echoed his intellectual dimension. Although the gray mask was pasted directly onto the red background, it appeared to be floating disconnectedly on top of the surface. The disconnection between the gray mask and the vibrant red background seemed to echo the split between his intellect and his feelings. The missing parts of the gray and lifeless face reminded us of the importance of the connections between the many dimensions that make up our whole being.

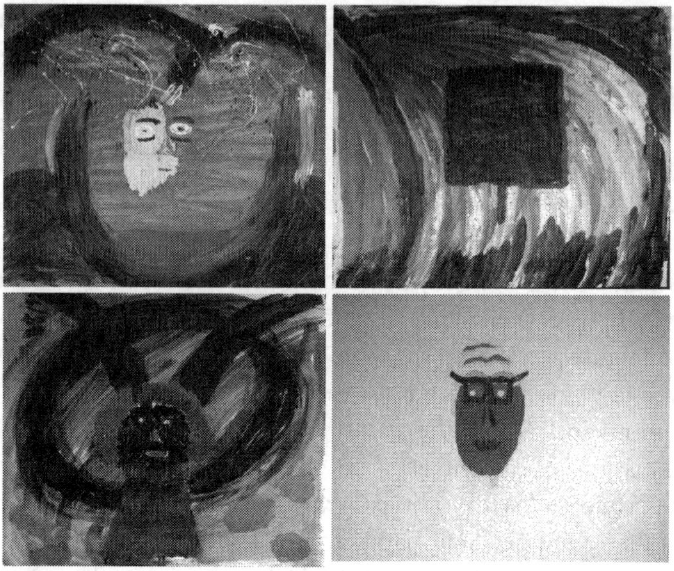

Figure 6.1: Sam's Interpretative Quilt

In an earlier chapter, the notion was brought forward that our whole being is continuously held together and revitalized through the ongoing, dialogical process between ourselves and the world and that it is propelled by our creative forces as they shape the trajectory that we are traveling along. Along this journey there are many opportunities for altering this trajectory. There are also opportunities for us to give expression to our subjective freedom through our selective use of the creative forces found within ourselves and within the world. The painting that Sam had shaped echoed some of these themes. The three-dimensional fragment of a face that Sam had created was mysteriously floating inside a larger horseshoe-like shape, which resonated with and in part completed an outline of a head. Sam had painted the black bird swooping down onto this gray fragment of a face in such a way that it completed the outline of the head while at the same time it was picking away the gray surface of the mask. The left eye was floating in space over the deep-red background, almost unaffected by the missing gray shape. However, besides chipping away at the gray mask, in a strange way the shape of this bird also completed the Gestalt of the outline of the larger head in which the gray mask was floating. Together they formed a greater whole that spoke of fragmentation and at the same time hinted at completion.

There was a brownish-yellow substance that appeared to be filling up the empty container of the space within the outline of the head. The container itself was purplish-blue and was sunken deep into the dark and thick coagulated ground. Some black and white paint had been splashed on with a large brush. The force and energy that was used to apply this paint gave the otherwise static painting a tremendous sense of movement. It was this movement that appeared to hold all the shapes together and gave life to the duality of the image.

Paradoxically, it was the juxtaposition of the textures, shapes, and colors that set off an atmosphere of ambiguity that raised many questions and invited a continuous, dialogical process. The dialogical process that arose from the ambiguity of the image, if contemplated, gave rise to awarenesses, which were frightening but also regenerating. This process seemed similar to the paradox that Thomas Moore reflected on in his conversations with Gablik (1995) where he writes that "[t]he deeper you get into the hopelessness, the more genuine your optimism is. These are paradoxes again, and we need to get beyond the opposites here – of hope and despair" (p.402). Thus, through the dialogical image/word process an opening was created in which new, iconographic representations could emerge and awarenesses could be gained that reached beyond the analytic and verbal realms. It was this paradox that was created by the broken, gray half-mask that was floating within the center of the larger head that was outlined with shapes, colors, and textures. The overall composition gave the image an eerie, nihilistic quality yet at the same time it instilled hope for a new beginning and a deeper sense of identity or being in the world.

Sam continued the theme of the first painting, including his use of materials and manner of working, in his second painting. In the first picture the broken half-mask was the central focus. In this second painting it was replaced by a red handprint on a mirror-shaped object. A red Plasticine border framed the object. The ambiguity of this object also created another paradox. If one viewed the object as a mirror, then it was puzzling that instead of it having reflective qualities it had a dark bluish-green surface, which seemed to absorb rather than to reflect light. The object, instead of providing an opportunity to examine one's reflection, displayed the red handprint, which acted like a stop sign. At that point, the mirror-like object began to take on a different meaning. The handprint, a symbol of one's unique identity, acted as a type of stop sign that prevented the viewer from looking at themselves or seeing beyond the boundaries of this red-framed object.

The paints in this second painting were applied in a much more direct and fluid manner that made the brush strokes more visible and part of the overall design. The red frame of the mirror-like object was repeated in the red pattern in the background that resembled red, flowing lava. Again, this dynamic, red texture was framed and contained by dark green and black shapes. The solid red background of the first picture here had a different characteristic. The red handprint and the red frame of the mirror-like object were accented by the color of the red, flowing lava-like background. There was darkness all around the flowing lava, which echoed the dark surface of the mirror. This reinforced the reading of the floating mirror-like object as a sign or symbol. This sign appeared to be holding something that the viewer needed to see and understand before he or she could move past the mirror-like shape into the symbolic realm of the fiery stream of lava.

To Sam, the symbol of the red handprint seemed to tell him to stop and take some time to look at himself closely before moving into the turbulent and potentially dangerous zone of the flowing lava. He thought that perhaps the lava represented his own feelings. When he looked at the picture within the group he acknowledged that there was some fear attached to moving beyond the boundaries of the known and visible into the unknown. It was not clear to him what this fear was about, though he thought that perhaps it was related to his childhood, of which he had little memory. However, one insight did not need to exclude the other and if Sam could see the symbol within the stop sign he had already begun a transformative process. Thus, the handprint within the mirror-like object that had reminded Sam of a stop sign could gradually take on more meanings.

The question arose in the group as to whether the handprint that he had placed in the center of this painting was a signal to himself to stop or whether it was an invitation to examine his own uniqueness more closely within the context of his lived experience. Could the symbology of the sign be similar to the impact of traumatic experiences that rupture one's sense of continued flow of lived experience and sense of identity? The experiences that we encounter throughout our life shape our being in the world. Perhaps some of the effects of childhood trauma are like this sign in the painting, taking one away or bringing one closer to the essence of one's existential and ontological reality; and thus propelling one along at a different trajectory. Through the dialogical image/word process one is perhaps able to re-examine one's trajectory and to integrate and reconcile different strands or possibilities within one's being.

The red handprint in the mirror-like object prevented one from seeing one's own reflection, yet at the same time it was a powerful symbol of one's identity. A handprint is unique to one's physical being. Hands allow us to do many things. They allow us to shape and manipulate the world around us. They allow us to communicate through writing, music, movement, and painting. Hands allow us to connect with and to hold each other. They also allow us to push or fight with each other. There are healing hands and punishing hands. There are giving hands and withholding hands. The same hand is capable of many different expressions and ways of being in the world. The theme of the half-mask was also echoed in the painting of the handprint and we can feel its presence through its absence. Both were strong symbols of identity. During the group, endless associations sprang forth as we looked at the image of the red handprint. They were almost as plentiful as the red, flowing lava that was gushing forth from the darkness of consciousness.

In his third painting, the theme of the mask-like face was continued. Sam again used yellow Plasticine to construct a face with wide-open eyes and mouth. He again placed it in the center of the page. Sam then painted a large red and yellow circle around the face. He then painted two even larger half circles that intercepted in the center of the page, covering the yellow mask with red paint and completely changing its appearance. At first, the half circles made the mask look as if it had two large, red horns extending from it that reached beyond the page into the universe. The two circles, as they emerged again at the bottom of the page, looked like a long red beard that gave the face an almost devilish appearance.

The continuation of the two wide, red, circular lines as they reached from the corners of the top of the page, and then went through the face toward the bottom edges of the page, echoed the red, flowing lava of the second painting. The whole Gestalt started to appear as if the two streams were flowing from somewhere beyond the page to funnel through this mysterious mask or face and then to return again back into space. The larger circle that completely encircled the mask reminded one of the first two paintings, where the gray mask was almost encircled by the shape of the blackbird and a half circle. The red Plasticine frame also encircled the handprint of the second painting and the green and black shapes framed the flowing lava. The painting once again started to take on a completely different sentiment or meaning when Sam began to cover up the whole picture with a blue-paint wash; thus again completely altering its appearance.

The yellow face and the two circles turned to dull green and the red turned to a muddy purple. There was no white left to show through and every spot was covered. Now the two purple lines that flowed through from above and funneled into one as they passed through the head had very different qualities. They had lost some of their vibrancy and were cloaked behind obscure layers of darkness, which were now encircled by a thick, purple and green rim. There were grayish-pink floating, circular shapes at the bottom of the picture, which echoed the shape of the wide-open eyes, the round face, the gray hairline that surrounded the head, and the outer rim that encircled them. This circular shape was further accentuated by the two thick lines that appeared to originate from beyond the page and then became visible through the two partial circles that met and funneled through the head and then extended beyond the page into space again. All three paintings that Sam did tended to add something beyond what is visible. They all stimulated an active and fruitful dialogical process for Sam and for the other group members.

In his fourth picture, Sam again created a face-like mask out of Plasticine, which he had placed in the center of the page. However, this time he did not use paints and he left most of the paper white. He created this mask-like face out of different-colored Plasticine, which gave the face a playful quality. Its skin was pinkish red, its nose was green, and its lips, eyes, and eyeglasses were blue. There was a playful innocence about the face with its yellow eyebrows and sparkling blue eyes that peeked out from behind the square, thick-rimmed glasses. The top of the head was left open and two orange shapes that reminded one of eyebrows were floating in the open space above. Their shape echoed the image of the blackbird in the first painting. But this mask was very different from the incomplete gray mask of the previous painting. It did not have the same nightmarish overtone. There was an open and playful quality in this image that had not been present in any of the earlier works. Sam had become aware of this new and more playful side of himself and was beginning to recognize it in many other aspects of his life.

Through the image-making process, Sam was able to gradually let go of the rigid associations that had entrapped much of his mental, psychological, emotional, and spiritual energy. This entrapment appeared to him to be related to the traumatic experiences of his past. The dialogical image/word process had provided an avenue for him to embrace more open, flexible ways of being in the world and to rediscover the creative energies within himself. The theme, which had been so central to Sam's works, was one of finding a way to return to and rediscover his authentic self; a way of being in the world where he once again was able to trust and relate to others and himself more freely and spontaneously. During group discussion, Sam expressed that when he had started the group he had hoped to find the identity or the face of the person who abused him but as he had been working on this picture he had come to realize that this was no longer important to him. Through working with the faces he had actually begun to discover himself in a way that was becoming gradually more independent from the trauma of his childhood experiences. His fourth picture had symbolically marked an opening and turning point of self-discovery and self-creation that took place on a more conscious level and in a more integrated manner. The white space surrounding the colorful face spoke of many possibilities that remained yet to be discovered. Sam continued on with this theme in his later works and carried some of his more personal discoveries into the larger social realm of his community.

There was so much that I was able to learn through the symbology of Sam's images, which was colored by my experience of him within the group. Only a small part of this experience was captured in this part of this quilt patch. Within the description of his journey, other more universal themes were integrated that represented many other voices of patients with similar experiences. His images and my reading of them were also influenced and altered by my therapeutic relationship that was specific to the therapeutic context in which the images were originally created. However, the way the images were used in the imagistic pause is to speak beyond this specific context and to illustrate some of the more universal themes that emerged through this work. They are to include the voice of the individual who created them and to make it part of the overall Interpretative Quilt.

I believe that contemplating these images in a way that allows a reflective pause for the reader and viewer could provide new and different types of understandings; thus continuing the dialogical process in an open and self-affirming manner. The reader can decide how and on what level he or she would like to explore the following images. The length of the reflective pause and the stance that one will take in part determine the experience of the images in the imagistic pause. The possible readings of the images go beyond the context in which they were created and which has been explored in this quilt patch. Some of these themes brought forward here will be picked up again and integrated in a more thematic and universal manner in the final stitchings of this Interpretative Quilt.

CHAPTER 7

Mary's Journey with the Healing Flow

The following journey will speak of issues of identity, relationships, and how trauma can affect one's way of being in the world. It will also speak of the transformative process that leads to living in the present by reflecting upon the past and opening portals to the future. Mary was a young woman in her early twenties who had been referred to the trauma program to work on issues related to childhood trauma. During her first session, Mary had identified that one of the goals that she had for her time in the group was to work on relationship issues. Mary felt that it had been very difficult for her in the past to set healthy boundaries with other people and that this had deeply affected her ability to enjoy herself and to function in a way that she would like to. For her first two pictures, Mary had chosen two small pieces of paper and oil pastels in order to explore some of her current relationship issues that she was experiencing with her friends at university. She had talked about some of these issues during her check-in phase at the beginning of the session and she was now working with them within the non-verbal, symbolic realm of the image-making process.

First Session

In the first session, Mary had made two small pictures using pastels. These images related to her struggle of setting boundaries with friends. In the first picture, she had drawn herself squished at the bottom of the page with three happy, smiling figures standing behind and above her. These three figures rep-

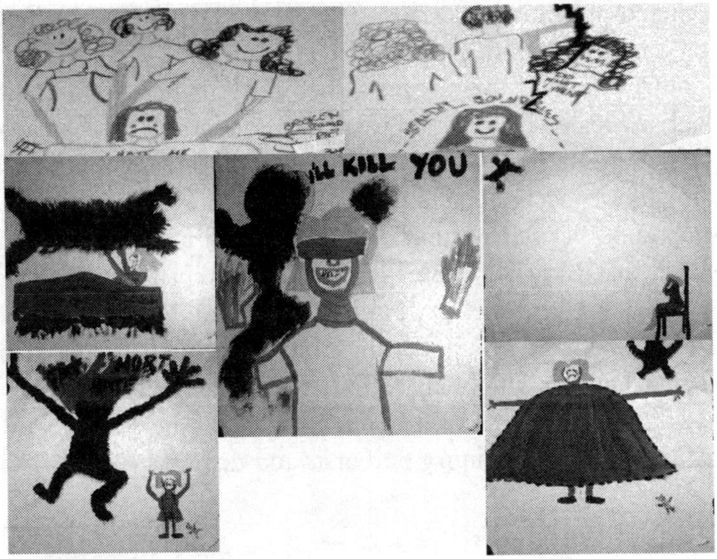

Figure 7.1: Mary's first Interpretative Quilt

resented to Mary her girlfriends at university. In the picture, they were almost taking up the whole page. Mary placed a self-portrait at the bottom of the page. The central focus of the image was the three female figures. The quality with which Mary had rendered these three figures made them look as if they were standing on top of her shoulders and that she was carrying all their weight. It looked as if their weight was pushing and squishing her toward the bottom and off the page. On the bottom right-hand side, Mary had written in blue "broken boundaries." Mary had drawn tears in her eyes and the expression on her face looked desperate and unhappy. All that was visible of her body was her head and her stretched-out arms and shoulders, the rest of the body was invisible to the viewer. Mary had written on her chest in blue marker "I HATE ME." The outline of her shirt was green and it had a balloon-like quality that hovered over these words.

In the second picture of this session, Mary had still placed herself at the bottom of the page and she had drawn herself even smaller. However, the shirt and the hair were carefully filled in with colors. Mary had depicted herself with a big smile on her face and had written on her shirt "I am me." Mary also had drawn a blue line around herself and had written "HEALTHY BOUNDARIES" around that line. The figure that was hovering above her left shoulder had an angry expression on her face. The words "DO WHAT I WANT" were written on this figure's shirt. The two other figures that were hovering over her right shoulder now had their backs turned towards her. Again, none of the figures had any legs. There was a big, black thunderbolt that separated these two figures from the one who was facing her. This black thunderbolt went through the figure facing her and penetrated the blue line that marked Mary's boundary around her self-portrait. However, it did not touch her body. The drawing style that Mary had chosen for her first two small drawings was representational in nature and she very directly illustrated the conflict that she had described earlier in the group. Setting boundaries with friends had always been associated for her with being suffocated by others' needs and wishes. She had always feared that if she set boundaries with others they would either abandon her or react with angry outbursts and disrespect.

Second Session

In the following session, Mary did not feel that she wanted to continue to work with the material from the previous session. Instead she wanted to make paintings of a recurring nightmare that she had had over the past few years. This nightmare, for some strange reason, seemed to be very important to her at this point. In the art therapy program it is essential that individuals have the freedom to work on what is significant to them, even if they are not sure why it is important at this time. Unless there are specific clinical reasons we, the therapists, support individuals in following their intuition. Usually group discussions and the creation of images help to guide, modulate, and shape the healing flow. Before painting, Mary briefly shared with the group what she knew about the nightmare and the meaning that she had attributed to it so far. Somehow she had made a connection between the nightmare and what she had remembered her relationship with her brother being like during the time when her parents went through their divorce. During this time period, she remembered him tormenting her in many different ways.

It was important for Mary's process for her to feel connected with the group on a verbal level before she could paint her images. Feeling connected and understood provided a safe atmosphere where she could explore these frightening internal images. Talking about them also helped Mary to see how the group would potentially react to them and to her as a person. When we were ready to start painting, Mary went directly to the paints and started to use them on one of the large pieces of paper up on the walls. She painted very quickly, with only a few pauses or times when she would think or contemplate what she was going to paint. It appeared as if the images were just pouring out of her. In a short time she finished three paintings that reflected different aspects of the nightmare. I noticed that while Mary was painting she appeared very grounded in the process while still being connected to the present and to the group as a whole.

In the first image, Mary drew herself lying on a blue, bed-like shape. It was resting on what appeared to be a black base that was floating in space. There was no visible ground. A big, black monster-like shape floated above her bed. It bore some similarities to the black figure in the second painting but its body was longer, with fur all over it. It looked more like an animal. Its arms and legs were stretched out and it appeared to the viewer as if the monster was going to be pouncing on the figure on the bed. This figure was reaching up and was trying to push the monster away with her arms. There were red tears dripping from her eyes. These echoed the monster's red ray-like eyes. In her renderings of the dream, the figure that represented her was always wearing a green shirt or dress. This was the same color that she had used in all her other pictures for the clothes that she wore. The green color later became her symbol for her identity.

Although Mary had identified that she wanted to work on a different issue from the previous session, I noticed that there were many similarities between the pictures done during her first session and the three pictures she had created during this session. In this first picture, again only her upper body was visible and the lower body was covered with the solid blue cover of the bed. The blue cover echoed the blue boundary that she had drawn in the picture of the previous session to identify her "healthy boundaries." Mary had also used the color blue for the words "DO WHAT I WANT" that were written on the figure in blue in her earlier picture. Here, in this picture, the blue sheet seemed to provide a protective layer between her and the monster and it appeared to be present when Mary needed to set boundaries to protect herself from others.

In many ways, the three images that Mary painted during her second session shared many subtle similarities with the images of the previous session but that only became apparent when Mary looked at all her work in her last session. Most of the time, these themes had emerged unconsciously and that gave them even greater power than if they had been in her conscious mind. Thus, in spite of Mary's conscious intent of not continuing with the themes from the previous session, she did so, but on a much deeper level. That is to say that although the subject matter was very different, the theme, the placement of the figures, and the colors were very similar. The main difference was their physical size (i.e. size of paper) and the intensity of the colors and shapes. These differences in magnitude were echoed by the greater affective intensity that was embodied and evoked by the images from this session.

In her second picture, Mary once again painted only the upper half of her body. This rendering was showing more of her upper body and she had placed herself almost in the center of the page. Her hands were raised up in the air but they were cut off from her arms and were floating strangely above the rest of the body. Mary had again painted the outline of the green shirt around her figure. She was blindfolded with a red cloth. Her mouth was open wide and the word "HELP" was written in black paint in the open mouth. Again a figure was floating behind and above her. This time it was a solid black figure with hands raised up in a threatening manner. Beside its head, the words "I'LL KILL YOU" were written in black paint. The themes of the pictures from the previous session were echoed in a more intense manner here. The theme of the pain and distress that can occur in interpersonal relationship echoed the earlier themes. The "self" and "other" were represented in an inconsolable conflict. Distress, torment, and abandonment echoed through both the images that Mary had created. The overall feelings that were evoked were that of sheer terror and extreme distress. The black monster and the broken and fragmented body symbolically conveyed this distress in a very graphic manner.

In her third painting, Mary drew herself in a green dress, sitting on a large black chair in the lower right-hand corner of the page. The black monster was now much smaller and was floating like a shadow in the upper left hand corner directly diagonal from her. The way that the figure's head was resting in her hands, which were also covering her eyes, gave the impression to the viewer that the figure was very sad and alone. This figure looked like a small child crying all alone on a large chair. Her feet were too short to touch the ground. Even if they were longer it would not have mattered, as the chair was not sitting on any visible ground. Actually, none of the images that Mary had done so far had any visible ground and everything was always floating in space. In spite of the nature of the subject matter, the figures and objects in these three images were becoming bolder and stronger. All the shapes in the last three paintings were painted in bold solid colors with strong and direct brush strokes, which echoed the intensity of the affect and content of this rendering of the nightmare.

The healing flow had begun to become visible in the pictures that Mary had done so far. Although the subject matter of these three paintings was very different from those in the previous session, there were many similarities and themes that were beginning to emerge. The style Mary had used to express herself at this point seemed to be more representational and real in nature. There was a graphic literalness to her images that appeared to reflect her nature and her way of being in the world. I noticed that the way Mary interacted with other group members was in stark contrast to what these images were conveying about human relationships. Through these images we got a sense of how painful close relationships had been for her in the past and how they had contributed to a sense of loss of identity and a feeling of abandonment instead of connectedness.

Third Session

In her third session, Mary worked on two paintings that continued along themes similar to the one in the previous session. In these two paintings, Mary was further exploring this recurring nightmare. However, some of the elements had already been altered by the dialogical image/word process and by the group discussions from the previous sessions that had led to a conscious reprocessing. Through the dialogical image/word process, Mary was able to share her experiences in a way that allowed her fear and pain from the past to be contemplated and honored. In the two paintings that Mary did in this session, she used the same green color for her dress, the same red color for the skin tones, and the same bright yellow for her hair as in the pictures of the previous session. The black monster was also present in both pictures. However, this was the first time that Mary put shoes on the figure that represented her in that dream and she also, for the first time, included a stuffed toy tiger in her pictures of this nightmare.

The last painting that Mary had done in the previous session resonated the most with the first picture that she did in this session. In both paintings, Mary had placed herself in the lower right-hand corner. In the last painting, the little girl was sitting on the large black chair and this time she was standing facing the viewer. The little girl's hands were raised up into the air as if she was reaching for help. There was a sense of desperation and hopelessness inherent in the little girl's body posture and facial expression. Blue tears were streaming down her face and body. Her mouth was closed and she was just standing there. The little girl's stillness was in stark contrast with the black, raging figure in the background. It also had its arms stretched out – not in a pleading way but in a threatening manner. The monster's arms and body almost took up the whole page. Its arms reached from one side of the paper to the other as it jumped through the air. There was red paint spouting out of its head as if it was lava from an erupting volcano. This red mass gave this figure the appearance of burning rage that was threatening to engulf everything. The words "FAT-HURT-HATE" were written in black over the red paint that was spewing out of its head uncontrollably. It was difficult for the viewer to decide if the black monster was just as helplessly trapped by its rage as the little girl was by her fear and sadness. Was the shadow really the "other," the one that torments, the monster who terrorizes the little girl? Somehow they both seemed to be victims.

Mary had painted her stuffed toy tiger floating on the invisible ground next to her left foot. Its shape echoed the stretched-out arms and legs of the monster but, unlike the monster, its body posture symbolized supportiveness and comforting. The question comes to mind as to whether the toy tiger, with its softness and its big smile, signaled both a potential for and longing for a tender and rewarding relationship with others that was the opposite of that which was represented by the black monster. The tiger's yellow coat echoed with Mary's little girl's yellow hair and its black stripes resonated with the black monster's furry coat. The visual connection that the monster and the tiger had, besides the black stripes, was that they both were monsters; one was comforting and the other was threatening. This stuffed tiger seemed to be the only comfort that the little girl had in this picture and it belonged to her. Its furriness was comforting not threatening. However, the tiger was floating through space and appeared to be in no apparent relationship with her or with the monster. It appeared outside of their awareness.

In her second painting Mary, as in the previous one, painted the black monster, the toy tiger with its smile, and herself in the same-colored dress. All the same elements were present in this painting but their positioning, shapes, and sizes had changed, which also then changed their relationship to each other. The toy tiger's shape again echoed the monster's shape. As in the previous paintings, the monster seemed to be the shadow side of the friendly and cuddly stuffed tiger, which was floating now in the right-hand corner below it. The whole sentiment of this second picture was different and echoed the loneliness and abandonment of her earlier painting.

The main difference between this painting and all the earlier ones was that Mary, for the first time, had painted herself in full figure in the center of the page in a way that she took up almost the whole page. She was much larger than the monster, which was now floating in the upper right-hand corner in the far background. Similar to the painting with the black chair, the monster in this painting had also moved more into the background but here Mary was no longer a child. Thus, the monster seemed no longer as threatening and the contrast between the two figures was striking. In this painting, the figure did not appear to be aware of the power she had through her size, and the same helpless stance was still present in this figure. There were still many similarities to the little girl. Both had yellow hair and their skin tones were the same. Tears were running down both their faces but the young woman's facial expression seemed to portray an even more intense sense of sadness and loneliness that was accentuated by her large and bloated body shape.

Although Mary was now in the center of the picture and her green dress was like a big tent that had been blown up with air to take up as much space as possible, she did not recognize her new power but seemed trapped by it. She seemed to have become immobilized. In this painting, Mary also used the same blue-dotted outline as in her earlier pictures to symbolize boundaries between her and the world. Here again the blue line was symbolizing a buffer between herself and the world. Unfortunately this boundary and way of becoming safe from the monster also stopped her from getting close to anything around her. The way Mary had drawn the blue boundary, by making an outline around the large, green dress, encased her whole body. This boundary protected her from the monster but at what price? This picture echoed some of Mary's body posture and way of being in the group, which gave us much to explore during group discussions. Although in this picture Mary had symbolically reclaimed her space, it appeared not to have made her happy. Setting healthy boundaries, as Mary had indicated in her first session, was still a very difficult, painful, and costly process.

Looking at both of the paintings that Mary had done in this third session, it became clear that they continued along the themes of her earlier work. These themes appeared to be propelled and shaped by many internal and external forces originating in the past and connecting with the present. The two images seemed to be in a dialogical relationship with each other, which became the foundation for later works. The themes that were emerging were that of abandonment, extreme terror, the body as boundaries to the world, and the sense of self in relationship to a hostile and empty world. In this world, people were treated as objects floating in space. Positive emotions such as love, happiness, and connectedness, as they were symbolized by the toy tiger, were in stark contrast with overwhelming negative emotions such as fear, terror, loneliness, and sadness as they were represented by the black monster and by her tears. Was the black monster her shadow and the tiger her positive emotions? Both floated disconnectedly through the air outside of her body. During group discussion, Mary indicated that these images resonated strongly with her memories of her brother, who she remembered as having terrorized her as a small child in many different ways. To Mary, the second image represented her sense of self and being in the world after the alleged abuse had occurred. As the dialogical image/word process unfolded, this theme of disembodied emotions was carried over into the subsequent paintings.

Mary was able to let the images unfold within the safety of their symbolic representation and to give external shape to the shadow side of her inner being. In this way, Mary appeared to be able to release the trapped energy of forgotten and well-hidden memories so that they could be processed in a way that she could learn from them. Through the symbolic realm of the image-making process, the unconscious cycle of traumatic re-enactments could be transformed so that it would no longer affect her life in the same way. Bringing memories into her awareness through the dialogical image/word process helped her to see how they had been influencing her way of relating to the world. She was then able to develop different ways of being in the world.

A remembered past that was given shape through images could become transformed in the present and gradually opened. New experiences could then be added that would provide many opportunities for a transformative process to unfold. The frozen images of Mary's nightmares gave way to the expression of the unexpressed. This opened the door for Mary to see, experience, and remember herself and her way of being without becoming trapped in her past. Hacking (1995) writes: "Each of us becomes a new person as we redescribe the past" (p.68). Through these images Mary was symbolically able to express and act upon feelings and impulses that she had not been able to in the past. Thus, in her images of the nightmare, unexpressed aspects of her being found external expression and were shared within a community context, where they could be felt, externalized, released, and transformed rather than remaining in isolation. Through this process, the fear, terror, sadness, and loneliness of these earlier pictures were gradually being replaced in her later paintings with fantasies of rage and anger and images of retaliation.

Fourth Session

In her fourth session, Mary did three paintings that showed this progression from fear and loneliness to rage and anger and back again. In these three paintings, Mary used a wide range of iconographic styles, which ranged from abstract expression back to her more usual representational style. In her first painting, she used a large paintbrush and black and red paint. Mary began by painting a black square in the upper left-hand corner. She then applied the black paint by stabbing the paintbrush again and again onto the large piece of paper so that it made a loud noise and caused the paint to drip down the page. The smaller, black paintbrush marks gravitated more toward the center of the picture, leaving some open spaces around the edges of the paper. There was directness in the way the paint was applied. One could sense the force with which the paintbrush had been pushed against the surface. Mary appeared completely absorbed by this process and it looked as if she was trying to stab the black square that she had painted in the left-hand corner where she usually had placed the black monster. Mary finished the image by splashing red paint over the big areas of plopped black paint. The red paint appeared as if it was coming from beneath the black. The drips of the red paint resonated with the way the tears had been painted in her earlier works. Here, the red paint evoked a sense of being wounded, yet the victim was not visible. In this painting, Mary's usual timid and shy stance was replaced by the emotions of anger and rage, which appeared to have freed her from her earlier, frozen stance.

This was her first abstract painting and it gave a strong message to her and others. The image signaled the presence of very deep pain. The manner in which this painting was created made reference to the depth and intensity of her feelings of pain, anger, and rage. In a sense, this painting was symbolically reflecting a turning point for Mary. The painting, with its archaic and primitive qualities, gave voice to feelings that had been deeply buried underneath the pleasant surface of Mary's usual presentation. This painting was the embodiment of feelings of rage and anger that now overshadowed the earlier feelings of terror, fear, sadness, and loneliness. Mary was able to deal with these feelings through the symbolic space of the art materials but it was questionable as to whether she would be able to hold them within her own body and whether she would be able to talk about them with the group.

In her second painting, Mary went back to her more usual representational style. This painting conveyed, through its more realistic shapes, her revenge fantasy and her imagined attempts to free herself from the black monster. In this way, it incorporated some of the feelings of her earlier abstract painting. In this second picture, Mary gave form to a fantasy where she was no longer a small, helpless victim but a beautiful young woman who was able to defend herself. In this painting, there were two figures and a tombstone. All were floating again above an invisible ground. The figures were now about equal in size. Mary had painted herself in the same green dress as before but this time as an attractive young woman with a well-formed body. She now was a beautiful young woman with a slender figure and a competent posture holding a gun in her right hand. On the other side of the paper, almost the same size as herself, was the black monster with red paint running down its body. The gun dangled in her hand as it pointed toward the invisible ground. For the first time she had a smile on her face. The monster had taken on a more human figure and no longer appeared to be as frightening. The way this figure was painted echoed the earlier abstract in the way the red paint was dripping down the black figure. The black monster was painted with the same energy and embodied brushstrokes as in the abstract painting. However, this time the black was not an unrecognizable shape but it was in the configuration of the monster. The big puddle of red paint at its feet gave an ominous quality to the painting.

The rendering of the self-portrait was much more controlled and realistic in this painting. It reflected a very different stance. Although Mary had kept many elements of the rendering similar to her earlier works, her self-portrait had changed drastically in its appearance. It seemed that through the dialogical process of her earlier works she was able to gain a sense of being able to defend herself. She now no longer needed to protect herself through the oversized body, which had immobilized and isolated her from the world. However, the symbolic violence portrayed in this painting was almost equal to that of the raging black monster in her earlier images. It appeared that Mary needed to be able to have a sense, at least on the paper, that she could defend herself before she could give expression to her memories. In a strange way both of these images were speaking of self-empowerment. But there is a fine line between self-empowerment and becoming an abuser. Through the symbolic realm of the image-making process Mary was able to move through this phase and to gain strength to look at some very difficult and painful material without becoming stuck in the abuser role. Through the two images and the very different painting approaches, Mary was able to integrate her feelings with her thoughts and to give voice to both so that they could become embodied again.

In her third painting, Mary went back to the earlier types of renderings of the nightmare. In these paintings Mary's rendering of the nightmare became even more representational and realistic in nature. In the first painting, Mary again had rendered the black monster but this time he had also more human features. She again had painted herself in her green dress with yellow hair. In this painting, her body was very thin and frail. The black figure was no longer floating above her body but was lying directly on top of her. There was no blue boundary separating the two figures. There was a second self-portrait in this painting that consisted of Mary's face. This was a round face with eyes wide open in terror and her mouth covered with a thick black line preventing her from speaking. The face was floating in the upper right-hand corner where she could look upon the scene below. Her yellow hair was barely visible and almost covered with the blue and black paint that had become mixed in with the yellow paint to create her hair. Her eyes were wide open in terror. It appeared as if all the emotions were trapped in this floating, round head, which gave the two figures an ominous overtone. This self-portrait was in stark contrast to the thin, faceless, stick figure below that was lying helplessly underneath the larger, more dominant black figure.

Mary had painted all three images without interruption and with a greater emotional intensity than in the earlier sessions. During our group discussions, Mary reflected with the group about the process and content of these three paintings. When she first viewed them she had a strong, visceral reaction that led to a recognition and memory that had not made much sense in the past. During this reflection Mary could not shake the question of: "Why was he on top of me? I didn't know what it was then but now I know that he was having sex with me." However, the paintings are somewhat more ambiguous in this matter and although we need to honor the somatic, emotional, and cognitive response to these pictures that Mary shared with us we still need to raise the possibility of a different reading. In order to build a space where group members can find an authentic way of being, we need to create a space that allows for the metabolizing and transformation of remembered, lived experiences so that they become integrated as well as transformed into new ways of being in the world.

Through the dialogical image/word process we begin to create an open text that embraces uncertain and new possibilities; however, we need to face the remembered past as part of our subjective way of being in this world. In this process, we need to be able to own our visceral responses and urges to not deny the reality of what these images allude to. We need to own the terror and outrage at what they speak of as well as to own the feelings for retaliation, for in retaliating we risk becoming what we most despise. Through the dialogical image/word process and the symbolic realm of the art materials powerful and potentially dangerous energies can be channeled and harnessed without the person becoming swallowed up by these feelings. In this way, the energies are not simply expelled but become embraced in such a way that they provide the foundation and energy for future transformations – transformations that can hold both the light and dark and that reflect the complexities of human existence.

When Mary shared these images with the group, she once again was self-contained and showing very little of the affect that was embodied in her images. Yet one could sense that a shift had taken place within her. The group had been listening in supportive silence as Mary had spoken of her experience of creating these pictures as well as her associations to them as she looked at them now. A few group members responded by making connections with their own experiences of their past. For everyone, there remained many unanswered questions. Most of the group members could relate to the longing to want to know what really happened, as if this could take away the pain of these experiences. Mary and the group were struggling very hard to come to terms with the reality that all we had to work with was their experiences of the past as they manifested themselves in the present. The way they remembered these memories influenced their ability to see a future. It contributed to how they would be able to transform and integrate these experiences in a creative and constructive manner. This was a process of reclaiming the present and one's creativity in order to awake to dreams and hopes for the future in a reality-oriented and empowered manner. This dialogical process was aimed at bringing them an awareness of a more authentic way of being in the world. These images were the beginning of a transformative journey as they honored their lived experiences.

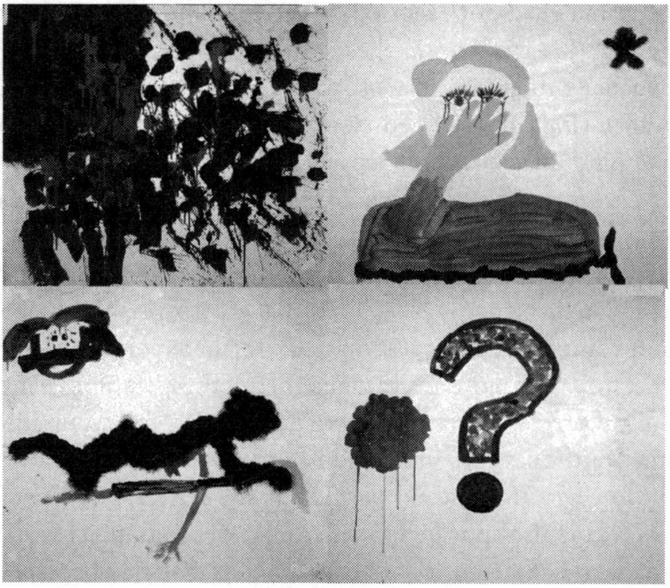

Figure 7.2: Mary's second Interpretative Quilt

Fifth Session

In her fifth session, Mary again continued with the theme of the nightmare by painting two more large paintings. One was an abstract painting of a large, colorful question mark and another was a self-portrait with the black figure far in the distant upper right-hand corner. This self-portrait filled up most of the page and the black figure was now very small. She was again crying and covering her mouth with her right hand. She was wearing the green dress, which echoed the green in her eyes. Her hair was again bright yellow and the shape of her head was wide and round. It echoed elements of the floating head of her previous painting. There was a black rope tied around her chest and the rest of the body was again off the page and invisible to the viewer.

The tears in this painting symbolized on one level the experience of the self as a person who was filled with the awareness of how her personhood could be damaged through abuse. On another level, the tears reflected Mary's mourning for her brother and the person that he had become. The tears could also reflect Mary's sense of abandonment by her parents during their divorce and how they had failed to protect or comfort her during times of great distress. The tears also spoke of a loss of a life that perhaps could have been different if the trauma had not occurred. When looking at this self-portrait in relationship to Mary's earlier works these tears could also reflect Mary's guilt and shame and her difficulties in embracing her own feelings of rage and anger. This self-portrait also echoed elements of the earlier renderings, yet there was something different about this image. It seemed to embody a sense of maturity and a sadness filled with a deepened awareness. In this painting, the tears were not the tears of a helpless child but they were the tears of an adult grounded in deeper understanding where pain, fear, and terror have become contemplated.

The second painting of the question mark further spoke to Mary's deep, contemplative stance. The more abstract qualities of this painting seem to open up to different ways of representing experience. During the group discussion at the beginning of the session, there had been many strong emotions shared and according to Mary this was, in part, what she had responded to in her paintings. However, it also appeared to reflect another shift in her work. It was as if Mary had taken her memories of her brother as they had become filtered through the nightmare and through the dialogical image/word process to a point where she needed to bring something new to them but she was not quite ready to take that step yet. Mary realized that she still needed to stay somewhat longer with her feelings of loss and anger in order to honor them and her experience of her past as she remembered it before she could move on. In order to integrate this material within the context of the present, Mary needed to relocate herself in relationship to what had been shared and made visible. The context in which Mary had shared her experience of this nightmare was different from that of the past and it could provide her with the support she needed for her to take this step. The dialogical image/word process and the symbolic realm that was created through the art materials provided many opportunities for discovering a different way of experiencing herself and the world.

In this picture with the question mark in it, Mary used soft pastel colors to paint the inside of the large shape and she used a dark blue color for its outline. The dot of the question mark was painted in black and she positioned it, similarly to the self-portrait of the earlier painting, in the center of the page. On the right side, Mary had painted a white disk and on the left she had painted a red one. There was red paint dripping from this red disk that was very similar to the way Mary had applied the paint in her paintings of the previous session. During the group discussion Mary's reflections on this painting spoke to her hopes that she would be able to move from this place of darkness and be able to bring something positive to her paintings, something that would indicate a change to a different, more hopeful future. She was not sure what this would look like at this point and the white disk symbolically expressed this ambiguity to her. The red, dripping disk represented to her the feelings of pain associated with the remembered past. The question mark, with its many soft pink, green, and blue colors, reminded her of how she had used these colors in her previous pictures. At this point, they represented confusion to her but they also represented hope and there was a sense of deep questioning that could provide the way to new images.

As a group, we found ourselves responding to the images and to each other on many levels and in many different ways. It is painful to remember. It is painful to face uncertainty and potential disbelief of that which forms one's identity. To embrace the power of emotions and see one's potential for retaliation and then feel the doubt of that reality is difficult. It feels so real when it becomes remembered, but it is this uncertainty that allows one to embrace different possibilities and gain a deeper awareness of one's own being as well as that of others. It helps one to appreciate the complexity of being human and to honor one's experiences. As a group, we would never be able to ascertain what really took place between Mary and her brother but this was not our purpose. The need to know gradually gave way to Mary's will to restore and create her future, a path to her authentic way of being in this world.

Sixth Session

In her sixth session, Mary chose oil pastels and a large piece of paper for her first rendering. In this image, Mary depicted again, using a more representational style, four full figures and two portraits. The first figure on the left-hand side was a self-portrait, the next was a portrait of her mother, which was followed by a representation of her father, and the last figure was again the black monster, which was now representing her brother. In the upper right-hand corner, Mary had drawn a portrait of herself and her brother as children before the abuse had occurred, both of them appearing as normal and happy. The four figures below, except for the black monster, were all equal in size. They all were well shaped with confident postures and smiles on their faces. The black monster that was right underneath the children's portrait was smaller now and was throwing its hands up in the air in an almost helplessly pleading manner.

The other aspect that stood out in this picture was that Mary had drawn herself in a similar manner as in the picture of her revenge fantasy. Mary again had rendered herself as a well-formed, attractive young woman dressed in a sexy green dress. However, in this image she was holding in her right hand a briefcase instead of a pistol. The tombstone was not present in this image and, in the place of the stuffed tiger of the earlier works, Mary had now painted a small cat that was standing next to her left foot. Mary had drawn a rectangle-like box around herself to mark her boundaries. She filled the box with golden and silver stars that surrounded her self-portrait. The box was drawn in the same kind of dotted blue line that Mary had used in her earlier pictures, particularly those of her first session.

There were also similarities in theme to the earlier picture in that Mary had made use of two other figures when facing a conflict with a third person. This time it represented a conflict or way of relating to her brother rather than to her friends. The two figures that represented her parents were facing in apparent solidarity in the same direction as she. They were not looming above her in an oppressive manner like her friends did in her first drawings. They were smiling with her. However, there were small thunderbolts that separated them from her and from each other that would indicate there was still some turbulence between them. In this picture, the thunderbolts were golden and silver instead of black, as in her previous drawings. They did not appear threatening and none of them were penetrating her boundaries. In this picture, Mary was reaching into the future, a future that went beyond what she had experienced within her family in the past and that found a different way of them relating to each other as adults.

According to Mary, these golden and silver lightning bolts represented some of the conflicts that still existed between her family and herself and they related to Mary's experiences of the past. They were the transformed residue of the pain related to her parents' separation and how that had affected her and her brother in their subsequent lives. As Mary explored this image with the group, she also became aware of some existential issues that were related to the fact that we are all separate individuals with our own ways of being and that sometimes these ways of being in the world can be painful or hurtful to one another. The lightning bolts in this picture had many elements that could symbolize different opportunities for change, transformation, and growth.

One golden and one silver lightning bolt was connecting the brother and the father, and then the other two figures with the father, in a way that could symbolize transformation through synthesizing rather than through exclusion or dissociation. In this way, the black monster was in some ways reintegrated with the rest of the family and with Mary's sense of herself.

Seventh Session

In this session, Mary again created two drawings on the large sheets of paper, using oil pastels. Mary used oil pastels because they gave her greater control and kept her more connected with her thinking rather than with the feeling part of her being. In her first picture, Mary drew another self-portrait portraying herself from her shoulders up. She was wearing a pearl necklace and her green dress. The necklace indicated that she had grown up and that the darkness and pain of her past had produced this beautiful pearl necklace. As an adult, she had different choices than when she was a child. In this way, she was able to grow beyond the trauma of the past and begin to embrace some of the positive elements of her own history in order to develop a stronger self-image. That is to say that she was able to envision herself as a beautiful young woman without feeling guilty or shameful about her sexuality or appearance. The green dress that she had used in all her pictures resonated this gradual change in self-perception. It had become a symbol of her identity and her way of being in the world. The dress and the necklace symbolized an embracing of her femininity that opened new possibilities for her in the future.

In this picture, the green of the dress echoed the green in her eyes. There were small, gray lines radiating from her eyes as she spoke through the images in this cartoon-like bubble of all the things she remembered her brother and his friends having done to her. In this portrait, her mouth was no longer covered but open and she was able to speak about her memories and experiences through the images that she had drawn inside the green bubble. Mary had drawn this green bubble coming from her mouth in the same way that one encounters thought or word bubbles in cartoons, except that in her bubble there were hardly any words but mainly images depicting the remembered abuse. The bubble also contained these images and in a way protected Mary from slipping back into the past where she would feel these feelings in the same way as she did as a small child. In this way, she was firmly grounded in the present and she was able to speak about these memories without being overwhelmed by them.

Inside this bubble, there was an image of a naked young girl, who was running away from some snakes, which were followed by some dark figures. The words "Ha, Ha, Ha, Ha" were written as if they were emanating from these black figures. The green dress and the toy tiger were floating in space beneath the naked body of the young girl, who was screaming as she ran away from these figures. Above this scene, there stood the same black figure with its arms stretched out in the same threatening manner as in Mary's earlier renderings of the nightmare. These images in the bubble had the same feeling as the pictures of the nightmare and spoke of the same terror and torment suffered at the hands of others. There was another image of a black figure trapped inside a box. The figure inside this box appeared to be trapped as it was kneeling on its hands and feet. There was black stuff on the bottom that gave the inside of the box a very unpleasant feeling. There were more boxes stacked on this box, which enhanced the appearance of the figure being trapped.

During group discussion, Mary described the content and meaning of this picture. For Mary, this terrorizing scene resonated with her memory of having to run naked in front of her brother's friends. The scene represented a memory where her brother had stuck her in a box. He and his friends had then buried the box underneath some more boxes. Mary remembered this as a terrifying experience and she had no idea how long she was in the box. All she remembered was that there was something very disgusting at the bottom of this box that had a terrible smell and feel. The images drawn inside the bubble were in stark contrast to the self-portrait that reflected calmness and self-confidence. She seemed to be protected from the content and the bubble by the green lines. It seemed as if Mary's earlier pictures and the subsequent dialogical process had helped her to reach this point where she could talk about her experiences in a way that acknowledged their impact but that allowed her not to be controlled by them as she had been in the past. The last images that Mary created reflected that she gradually was seeing herself again in a more positive and confident manner and that she was again building a trust in the world and in herself, in spite of what she had experienced in the past.

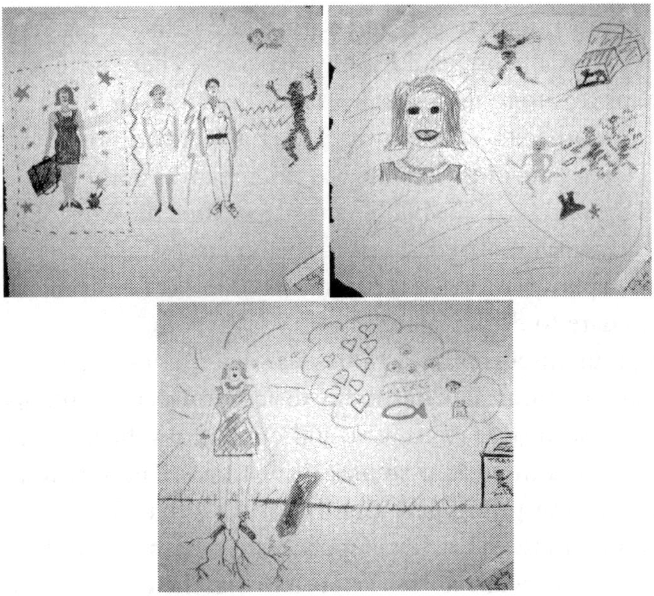

Figure 7.3: Mary's third Interpretative Quilt

Eighth Session

In her last session, Mary drew another portrait of herself and of her dreams for the future. In this self-portrait, she depicted herself in the green grass with green ballet slippers and her pearl necklace. Again, she had illustrated herself as a beautiful young woman, looking at the viewer with confidence and openness. This was the first time Mary had included a ground in her images and it was a central focus in this picture. This ground seemed to have a very strong, symbolic meaning to Mary and she had planted herself deeply within it by drawing her feet underneath the surface of this ground. In this way, the figure of the self-portrait was almost like a plant that drew its strength from underneath the ground through its roots. In this image, Mary's feet were planted in the ground where they were growing roots from her ballet slippers as if they were growing from bulbs. Using again silvery lightning bolts Mary attached a green sign saying "HOPE" to these roots. Through the pictures that she had done in the previous sessions, she had been able to reconnect with her own history in a way that allowed her to gain strength and self-confidence.

Mary drew another bubble in this picture, in which she placed images of things that she hoped for in the future. There were lots of hearts representing love. There was a ring, a house, and a portrait of a man that represented to Mary her hope for a happy and healthy marriage. There were also four children's portraits representing her hopes of having children in the future and of being able to mother them in a way that could provide them with joy and happiness. The outline of the bubble was not green, as in the previous picture, but silver. In the middle of the bubble she had written the word "SUCCESS" in silver. This picture symbolized a hope for being successful and moving beyond what she had experienced in her relationships with her family of origin and for being able to dare to dream again.

During group discussion it became clear that Mary still had some healthy concerns about her future and her ability to accomplish these things in her life. These concerns seemed very realistic and one did not have a sense that this image represented a flight into an unrealistic future. The way Mary explored her picture with the group gave one the feeling that she was not moving blindly into the future. What was important to note here was that Mary was able to dare to dream again about a future and that she was willing to share her dreams with others by talking about them with the group. This sense of realism was symbolized, to some degree, in her picture by her depiction of the black monster that she had drawn on the right-hand side of the drawing. The monster was well contained within a green box, which was marked "TRASH." He was very small now and in a way this image of him in the box resonated with Mary's depiction of herself as being trapped inside a box. Perhaps, symbolically, she wanted him to experience some of the pain that she had gone through when he had trapped her. His stretched-out arms in this picture looked as if he was pleading for help. When Mary reflected on the picture with the group, she noted that perhaps the box symbolized a recycling bin and that there may be still some hope for him in the future as the recycling bin was also firmly grounded on the same ground in which Mary had drawn her roots.

In her last session, Mary wanted to honor her journey and transition from the group by sharing her images. This sharing allowed her to take one, last, reflective pause within the safety of the group – a pause that acknowledged her past, connected her with the present, and allowed her to embrace the future. This pause allowed her to connect to life and to embrace the world with all its uncertainties and ambiguities. During this reflection, Mary consciously tried to stay focused upon being able to acknowledge the work she had done without becoming pulled into that world.

When Mary reviewed all her pictures at the end of her last session, her journey became much clearer to her. Although she had already explored all of her pictures with the group at the time that she had created them, to see them up altogether allowed for a very different dialogical process to unfold. Looking at all her pictures one more time gave her an opportunity to see which pictures still had strong visceral, emotional, psychological, existential, and spiritual resonances for her. Exploring her visual journey with the group for one last time allowed her to get a sense of what she would like to do with her images. Depending on what resonances the pictures set off, she was able to evaluate how to treat them before taking them outside of the safe container of the group. Sharing her visual journey with the group also allowed the group members who had not been in group with her since the beginning to see the evolution and change and this helped instill hope in others who had just begun their journey.

When looking at all of Mary's pictures together, one was able to observe a natural progression where each image seemed to flow and build upon the themes and feelings of the earlier ones. Having watched Mary create all of these pictures allowed me to observe that she had not consciously planned this progression and that it appeared to be an authentic reflection of the process that she had gone through. In this process, it seemed as if her earlier paintings of the nightmare had allowed her to get in touch with many different feelings of fear and sadness, anger, and rage, which she then was able to gradually transform through the dialogical image/word process. As she moved through this process, within the safe container of the group, her experiences could be given a voice and transformed in a reality-oriented and integrated manner. It was interesting to note that, as the healing flow unfolded, the art materials that Mary chose and the number of paintings that she created during each session appeared to reflect the different processes she was engaged in at that time.

The last three drawings that Mary did toward the end of her stay reflected a movement away from allowing the depth of her unconscious to emerge through her images and through her expressions of the nightmare. Instead, she was now moving toward a more focused and deliberate way of engaging in the image-making process. In this sense, Mary's journey was similar to those of other group members and it was not unusual to see, particularly in those group members who had the opportunity to stay for eight sessions, a movement away from free expression of feelings and unconscious experiences toward a gradual coagulation of earlier themes into more stable forms as the members approached their discharge from the group. In her later images, Mary began to ground herself more in the present and to look toward the future by drawing more representational illustrations of different possibilities. Within the safe boundaries of the group and through her images and the unfolding dialogical process, Mary was able to learn that, in spite of her past, she had the capacity to make real connections with the other group members and that she was able to dare to dream of a better future – a future that built upon its past and accepted all its darkness while providing the ground where resilience and creativity could be discovered. It was also a future that would help her to move beyond her old patterns in a constructive and healing way.

The word "HOPE" in her last picture symbolized the connections she had been able to make with herself and with the other group members through the dialogical image/word process and the therapeutic and supportive context of the program as a whole. Her journey that was described in this quilt patch had taken her to many places. Her images had taken Mary deep inside of her internal landscape and shown her fragments and split-off parts of her past so that she could integrate them with her present in order to envision her future – a future that was full of hopes for making real connections and for creating an authentic way of being grounded in the world, in self-reflection, and in awareness.

CHAPTER 8

A View into the Activities in an Art Therapy Session

In the previous quilt patches, the healing flow was explored through the description of two fictionalized characters and their journey with the image-making process. The imagistic pauses and the fictionalized text that explored Sam's, and Mary's, journey gave the perspective of the dialogical image/word process as it unfolded from one image to the next and from session to session. These two individual journeys brought forward different themes and styles of engaging with the dialogical image/word process and brought to life some of the contextual backgrounds that may have influenced and propelled the healing flow.

In this chapter, the process of art toward healing will be explored as it unfolded within the context of one fictionalized art therapy session. The two characters, Sam and Mary, who were introduced in the previous quilt patch, were carried forward into this fictionalized account of a session. They provide continuity and a bridge between the richness of the previous perspective and the exploration of this same process from the perspective of the collective group dynamics that were involved within this art therapy session. In this way, the following quilt patch is to give voice to the complexities and range of activities that were part of the dialogical image/word approach to an art therapy group process as it was observed within a specific, clinical context.

The Preparation Phase

The co-therapist and I met in the art therapy studio to prepare the room for the upcoming session. We orientated ourselves by reviewing the pictures and our notes from the previous group. The focus of the last session had been on creating safety and establishing trust in the art therapy process in relationship to working with trauma-related issues. In the Thursday session five days before, two new members had started the group. This disrupted the group dynamics and the dialogical image/word flow to some degree. A greater part of the last session was spent on assimilating the two new group members into the group. Therefore, after some deliberation we decided that we would not hang up the patients' images before the group and that we would give the individuals a chance to let us know how comfortable they were with their pictures being shared with the group. We also wanted to see if the images were still relevant to them in today's session. In this preparation we were considering different possibilities that could provide a bridge between the experiences of the last session and the one of today. Some of the clinical themes from the last session had been related to trust and safety issues on the interpersonal, emotional, and psychological level. Another theme that had evolved was finding a comfort level with the unfamiliarity of processing, disclosing, and exploring therapeutic issues through images and group discussions.

In that Thursday session some of the new members had looked with trepidation at the sandbox and the large sheets of white paper that were hung on the walls. Rosalyn, who had not attended the orientation session, had started that session in a rather defensive stance. She had been somewhat insulted by the sandbox and the toys. Rosalyn stated that she was not allowed to play as a child so why bother starting now. Cindy remarked in the previous session that she was here in this treatment program in order to deal with very difficult problems and that she could not see how playing with toys and art materials could be of any benefit to her. The co-therapist and I responded to both of their concerns by first acknowledging and validating them. We also used some of the group time to go over the group goals, structure, and parameters again in order to help them enter the process more freely.

During that Thursday session the group members had an opportunity to introduce themselves and to initiate the new members into the group by sharing images with each other. Thus, the new members learned about the process from the group therapists, the other group members, and the using of the materials. The individuals, who had been in the group for a number of sessions, shared their experience of how making images and reflecting on them with each other had been helpful for them. By the end of that last session both Rosalyn and Cindy had appeared somewhat more open to the process. The group had ended with a brief reflection period on the experiential component and on what had been created through the materials. Some group members had explored their images in more depth while others acknowledged them only on a non-verbal level by leaving them up on the wall where everyone could see them. We had left the last session by saying that we would come back to some of the images that we did not have time to explore.

In the last session, feelings of anger and fear had been expressed through the art materials but had not been fully acknowledged by the group on a verbal level. For this reason, the co-therapist and I decided to bring out the pictures from the previous session to make them available to the group. However, we were going to leave the choice of how they wanted to reflect upon this material up to the individual members. Before starting the session we wanted to get a sense of where individuals were in relationship to each other and to their own subjective state of being in the world so that we could guide the unfolding of the dialogical image/word process.

Since we were aware that most group members had already formed some relationships with each other through the other parts of the program, we knew that we were working with a group that had already established group dynamics. This had been particularly visible in the last session where the interpersonal dynamics were played out in different ways and, to some degree, influenced the unfolding of the dialogical image/word process. However, it was not unusual for the group dynamics to shift from one session to the next. Within the five days between last Thursday and today's session many events could have transpired that might have changed various aspects related to the inner and interpersonal dimensions. This was particularly true because of the nature of the therapeutic milieu that patients lived in and the therapeutic works that group members would be exposed to in the other parts of the program. Thus, in the days between sessions, an individual patient could have moved into a very different place and could potentially have very different responses to the material generated in the previous session. For example, what was an issue in the last session may no longer be as relevant in the next meeting. Therefore, we needed to see if some of the issues and conflicts still needed to be addressed or if we could move directly into the dialogical image/word process by looking at the images from a slightly different perspective in order to help the group stay focused on the process without getting sidetracked from the healing flow.

In today's session we were not taking any new people into the group. Therefore, we were expecting the same eight group members as in last Thursday's session. Sometimes we had people closing on a Tuesday and as part of saying goodbye to the group they could review their work with the group. However, as far as we knew, most people were continuing in today's session. We had arranged ten chairs in the circle around the sandbox and the walls were covered with white sheets of paper. We left some of the toys scattered in the white sand of the sandbox. This concluded our preparation phase and we opened the room to the group.

The Orientation Phase

The studio was gradually filling with voices as the group members entered the room. Sam and Brenda were chatting informally with each other, while Mary and Nina were more quietly looking around the studio. Nina seemed somewhat more nervous today. Lois was going over to the other end of the room in order to look at the materials laid out on the tables. She looked as if she was ready to start using the materials and she appeared reluctant to join us in the circle to begin our check-in. As there were no new members starting today, we did not go over the introductory material again and we were able to proceed with our group discussion and orientation phase. Cindy and Rosalyn, who had started the group in our last session and who had been struggling with the concept of using art materials and toys as part of their therapeutic treatment, seemed somewhat less apprehensive today. Gradually we all found a seat in the chairs that were arranged around the sandbox. Naomi was joking with Sam about something that had happened at lunch while Mary and Rosalyn were playing in the sandbox pretending that they were at a beach. Sam looked at me and then at the other group members to see if we were ready to start the session. Some informal smiles were exchanged before the mood in the room shifted toward a more serious and reflective mood. There were a few moments of silence that indicated to the group that they were preparing themselves for the upcoming process.

We were now almost ready to begin the session with our orientation phase. The co-therapist and I, after briefly summarizing some of the themes from the last session, invited the group to identify what they wanted to explore during today's session through either the use of group discussions or art materials. One by one the group members gradually let each other know about their needs and what they hoped to gain from the session. As individuals spoke we began to get a sense of the group and how its members were connecting with each other and with the material from the last session. We were getting a sense that some positive changes had occurred since our last meeting and that the group seemed to be more cohesive.

While we were talking, Lois picked up a box that was filled with toys. She quietly searched through it. She found a gangly, green, friendly-looking dinosaur that she had chosen in previous sessions. This figure seemed to have taken on a special meaning for her. As in previous sessions, she again placed this small figure in the sand and added more pieces around it. The overall scenario seemed to change slightly from session to session but the core figures were always the same. She hardly ever drew much attention to her figures in the sand but rather appeared to use them as a portal into the symbolic world of painting. It also appeared to help her focus and to become more comfortable in the group. Today, Lois placed the figure in the sandbox near the corner where she was sitting. She turned it so that it looked upward and openly out at the group. This gave it a more open and playful appearance. Lois passed the box of toys to Cindy who was sitting next to her. She invited Cindy in an encouraging voice to search for something that might look interesting.

Mary was an attractive and bright young woman in her early twenties who was somewhat overweight. She had joined the group four sessions ago with Brenda, Nina, Sam, and Lois. Mary interacted in a caring and sensitive manner with other group members and offered support to anyone who looked like they could use it. However, when conflict arose within the group, she would become very quiet and almost invisible. The criticism that the two new members had brought forward in the previous session in relationship to the use of art materials and toys as therapy tools seemed to have made her somewhat uncomfortable. Mary glanced at them during the check-in phase, assessing for any potential conflict, but she did not acknowledge her apparent feelings and concerns on a verbal level.

At times, it can be difficult for group members to voice their concerns or feelings at the beginning of the group, as they may not feel comfortable enough or they may not be consciously aware of them. Therefore, besides the verbal aspects of the orientation phase, there are many non-verbal dimensions that can give signals to the therapist in how to direct the healing flow. Through using the art materials some of those non-verbal dimensions could be given voice. Hanging up patients' work at the beginning of the session so that they could become included in the dialogical process could help to integrate feelings and thoughts across all the different dimensions. I sensed that at this point the group was mainly working on connecting with each other on a more superficial level. It was not unusual for group members to test in many different conscious and unconscious ways the therapeutic boundaries of the group before moving into exploring some of their deeper and personal issues through their images and group discussions. During this orientation phase, patients were also invited to ask questions of each other and to share their fears, hopes, and goals.

The way a person would participate in the group also depended on the individual's comfort level and personality style. Cindy and Rosalyn had not yet shared much about themselves, yet the pictures that they had created and the defensive stance that they had taken in the previous session had given them much power within the group. However, behind this confrontational style seemed to be fear and discomfort. In spite of these apparently different interpersonal styles Cindy and Rosalyn had something in common with the other group members. They all, to various degrees, had difficulties dealing with feelings of uncertainty and vulnerability within an interpersonal context. During the last session it was quite apparent that it would take some time for the group to become more cohesive and to get more comfortable with each other's personalities. We, as the group therapists, were aware that we needed to work in a way that respected everyone's strengths and weaknesses while utilizing the unfamiliar process of using art materials and toys. To some degree, all of the group members would need continuous reassurance and information about the dialogical image/word process so that the various expressions of the healing flow could be kept within respectful and therapeutic boundaries. In this way, trust and confidence in the group, and in the group therapists, could develop over time.

During the previous session, Cindy and Rosalyn were able to experience that we, the therapists, did not have any expectations of them to create artwork; the focus was on self-discovery and finding their own voices through the use of art media in a way that was different from the more verbally oriented groups. Nina had always been very shy and quiet during the group discussions. However, today she was encouraging the new members by saying that while she did not understand how the process worked, it seemed to help her to express herself in a way that she was not able to do through talking. Nina added that one did not have to be an artist in order to benefit from the group.

In the previous session I talked about how it was not unusual to feel apprehensive at first but that after a while most group members found the process helpful and even enjoyable. Brenda replied in this session that in her first drawing she had surprised herself with what had come up on paper. She shared that when she first applied the paint to the paper, she had no idea what she was going to do. However, when she sat back in the chair and looked at her picture she realized that she had disclosed more than she had intended. This had initially made her feel frightened and exposed. These words seemed to resonate with Rosalyn and Cindy. As they listened to Brenda they appeared to get somewhat more apprehensive again about the process of exploring images with the group. It looked as if they were already struggling with accepting unwanted and rejected material that was emerging from their unconscious and that they were not sure if they wanted to use this group to explore these frightening images any further. Although it was very likely that these internal images had influenced their lives in many ways, it was still frightening to pull them out and see them expressed on paper for everyone and themselves to see. For some group members like Brenda, it was a relief to express her internal world on paper and to have it validated and explored by the group. Others preferred to keep their internal world more to themselves and to try to work it out on their own in isolation as they had done for so many years. Brenda continued to assure them that once she had started to talk about her images she realized that she had many choices about how she would explore them, and that she had found the group responses very helpful and supportive.

It was not uncommon in this patient population to experience the unconscious as a frightening place filled with nightmares and flashbacks of horrible images and memories. At this point, the idea of venturing into this frightening place was very terrifying to them and the group needed first to get connected and comfortable with each other as well as with the image-making process in a way that made them aware of their inner strengths. Seeing journeys of other group members could quicken this process of venturing into trauma-related material. Thus, it was the role of the therapist to guide the process carefully through the use of the different interventions.

We briefly went over some of the material and options presented in the introduction session in order to help some of the group members, who appeared to be struggling, to find their way of entering into the process. We reminded them of the reasons why we were using art materials in this group and that the experiential component was an essential aspect of the dialogical/image word process. In order to enter into this process one had to experience it, as learning occurred via doing. We had learned through many different sources that, in order to harness the power of this creative energy, we needed to bring it alive within the context and social structure of our physical world and within our community. The use of the art materials was a channel that provided us with an external object upon which we, the group, could reflect upon the experiences in a more integrated manner. Therefore, one of the main ways we learn about the healing flow is by allowing it to be experienced, by letting feelings, thoughts, and associations emerge through the creation of lines, shapes, and colors, and by moving from sensations to feelings to thoughts and back again. In this way, perceptions could emerge through the evolving images and unfold within the safety of the symbolic realm of the art materials.

We also again assured the group that, as far as we were concerned, there were no right or wrong ways of using the different materials. However, since we were working in a group context we reminded the individuals that their actions, verbal expressions, and images would all affect each other on some level and would influence the healing flow. Within the group, individual members had much freedom in how they would use the materials as long as they were respectful of each other's personal space in a way that was not destructive to others or themselves.

The co-therapist and I communicated in many verbal and non-verbal ways again and again that although images could elicit strong emotions, there were no such things as "good" or "bad" pictures and that the relationship and dialogue that one had with what was created could bring forward self-understanding and a sense of empowerment. It had been our experience that patients could work with many challenging experiences through the symbolic realm of the images. Within this symbolic container the group in general was able to embrace and hold many different feelings at the same time and to gradually work and explore them through the dialogical image/word process in a way that expanded the material beyond the entrapment of the traumatic experiences.

By making reference to her previous sessions and without going into many details about what she had shared, Brenda continued by saying that it had been surprising how easy it actually had been for her to set boundaries within the group around her verbal sharing of her images. She found when she talked about her experience of making the pictures that she was able to make many choices about how she could share her images with the group. She could focus on the shapes or colors first, then gradually move to feelings and thoughts, and if she felt safe enough within the group she could talk about some of the personal meaning and content of the pictures. She continued by saying that the sharing and feedback that she had received from the group also helped her to learn that other people had very different associations to the material presented in these images. This realization had helped her to move beyond the historical entrapment of the pictures.

Other patients who had been in the group with her shared briefly how they had been able to discover that their unconscious was not only filled with frightening images and nightmares but that it had many hidden resources that could become visible as the creative forces were freed up. Lois decided that she did not want to talk about the painting that she had created in the previous session. She felt that she had spent most of the morning listening and talking and that it would be more beneficial for her to start by using the materials before reflecting on her work. She added that perhaps she would share her pictures at the end of the session. Naomi was in a very different place from Lois. She felt that she wanted to start today's session by sharing her pictures so that Cindy perhaps could become more comfortable with using the paints on these large pieces of paper. She added that she was not an artist but that she enjoyed creating these pictures. She also felt that by looking at the images from the previous session she could become connected with where she was at that time and see how much things had changed for her since then.

We took a few moments to reflect upon the pictures that the patients had chosen to hang up at the beginning of the session. All were images from the previous sessions that we wanted to revisit. Even if individuals did not want to talk about what they had done, it was at times helpful simply to look at them again. In this way, depending on how the group discussion evolved, material from the paintings on the walls could spontaneously enter the discussions. Sometimes there were only a few comments made while at other times many different themes were stimulated by the images. Thus, by having the paintings up on the walls, the dialogical image/word process could unfold more freely.

Naomi had painted three large abstract paintings in the last two sessions. The first image had a tremendous energy about it. She had applied bright colors to the page using different brushstrokes. There was a rich texture that was created by the thick layers of paints. The colors were radiating around a circular shape in a free and spontaneous manner. There was a joy and freedom expressed in this image that was still contained in a harmonious balance. Naomi shared a bit about her process with the group and how the colors and shapes seemed simply to have fallen into place. She liked what she had done in this image and it was a big change from the dark and sombre abstracts that she had created in the previous sessions.

After looking at the three images that were hanging on the wall for a while, she remarked that she recognized a long and forgotten part of herself in them. This part of her had been gradually covered up through life events; the playful and free aspects of herself had become split off from her life. As she looked at her images, she could feel a sense of freedom gradually rising up within her. She recognized this aspect within herself and she was excited by this discovery, but at the same time she was afraid of this free playful spirit that resonated so strongly. Somehow this free spirit had become associated with darkness, shame, and feelings of guilt. She was able to see that this part had never been able to mature. In some ways, she feared this wild and uncultivated force. She had learned to blame it for many things that had gone wrong in her life. But now she felt ready to reclaim and integrate it back into her life in a constructive manner.

The second picture was in stark contrast to the first one. It was also an abstract yet it had very different qualities about it. She had still used bright colors, but this time she had applied them carefully using a small brush. The brushstrokes were concealed and every shape was contained with a solid black line. She had drawn this line carefully with the thick, black oil pastel after the paint had dried. It had the appearance of a stained glass window. We looked at the paintings in silence for a few moments. Then someone remarked that the third picture appeared to be a synthesis between the more spontaneous feelings from the first picture with the more structured and defined aspects of the second. In this third picture, she appeared to be able to bring together the two opposing emotional and structural forces.

In this third picture, Naomi had again used bright colors to create an abstract design out of shapes and colors. There were some similarities to how she had used colored patterns in her second picture. However, this time the shapes were smaller and more spontaneous. Instead of being framed by a black outline, each shape was surrounded by the white of the paper or it was allowed to touch the other colors freely without running into them. She had completed the painting by splashing white, black, and some red paint over the overall design. This had given the painting the spontaneous, free quality presented in the first picture, which she had here successfully combined with the more deliberate manner of a formal design, used in the second picture, to create a synthesis of the two. In this way, the picture symbolically reflected the journey that Naomi had identified and her struggle with integrating her free and spontaneous side with a more planned and deliberate aspect of herself.

Some group members looked as if they were searching for ways to put their feelings and thoughts into words. There was some shuffling in their chairs. One group member stated that she liked the free and spontaneous image better. There was silence in the room again, which allowed us to focus on the images on the wall. After this reflective pause, Mary sighed and remarked that she wished she could paint like this. Cindy, who had been apprehensive about the process, started to interpret the second image by saying that she saw two figures and that they looked like they were fighting with each other. She said that the one on top appeared to be winning. It looked as if Cindy was very comfortable and excited about interpreting Naomi's paintings. I was not sure if behind all of this interpretation there was not perhaps some attempt on Cindy's part to avoid working on her own issues. I decided to continue listening to her interpretations in order to see whether she would make some connections with her own life experiences.

It was not uncommon for individuals to start to get familiar with the dialogical image/word process by interpreting or responding to the other group members' images. Perhaps the interpretation of someone else's pictures provided a safer avenue for Cindy to express her thoughts and feelings. Only if Cindy was to own her responses to the images in a way that grounded them within her own life experiences and way of being in the world could this dialogical exploration provide a portal into her own therapeutic process. This aspect of the dialogical image/word process differentiates it from when it unfolds outside the therapeutic relationships. Within the context of the art therapy group, the therapist's interactions shape and propel the unfolding process toward certain therapeutic goals that keep the focus on self-exploration and understanding within a community context.

I asked the group if they could relate to the thoughts, feelings, and experiences that these pictures evoked. Looking at Cindy, I continued by saying that perhaps some of these feelings, thoughts, and perceptions could also be explored during the experiential part of the group. I wanted to help the group members to remember that we were not limited to exploring our experiences through group discussions but that we could also reach into the non-verbal, symbolic realm through the use of the materials.

Naomi responded to Cindy's interpretations by saying that, although she had not been aware of it when she was painting this picture, it was related to conflicts in her life; she could see it now after she looked at her second picture again. It seemed to resonate with some of the struggles of the conflict that she was experiencing in her marital situation. Sam, who had got to know Naomi quite well through the other parts of the program, thought that the second image was almost like a stained glass window and that the bright colors actually disguised the true light that lay behind it. For him, he said, this connected with his experience of Naomi. He felt that her pleasant personality concealed and covered up some of the pain and suffering inside her. He also felt that the first and third picture expressed more of an openness and freedom.

Sam was able to give Naomi this feedback because of the relationship that he had formed with her through the many other aspects of the program. Any interpretation or feedback that group members gave about a painting would usually reach beyond what was visible in the picture and speak to their experience of and relationship to that person as a whole. Many times it seemed that an image was just a catalyst for the exploration of the themes that had emerged for the individual through the many aspects of the program. This is not to take away from the importance of the image, but it speaks to the essential role of context and its effect on the dialogical image/word process. In this sense, there are no right or wrong interpretations as each is context bound and embedded in relationships that either support or reject what is being offered in the interpretation. Thus, feedback and interpretations of images created in the group can affect the unfolding of the healing flow and the relationships between individuals and the group.

Brenda focused more on the developmental aspect of the pictures, which echoed some of the earlier statements. She felt that Naomi had undergone some kind of transformative process that was reflected in the images that she had created since the beginning of her stay in the group. She had observed through Naomi's images that she had been able to move through the darkness of her past, which was expressed in her earlier pictures, by discovering a free and playful aspect of herself that found expression in her present pictures.

Brenda continued by saying that she could relate to this experience and that the sexual and physical abuse that she had suffered at the hands of her father appeared to have robbed her, too, of this carefree and playful spirit. Without going into more details about her past, Brenda focused on some of the qualities of Naomi's second picture. She commented on the clear and defined boundaries of this image and that she had also reacted to her own traumatic experiences by concealing and confining them behind pretty colors and strong black boundaries. Brenda really liked the third picture. It symbolized to her a rediscovery and integration of this free and playful spirit in a balanced and contained manner. For Brenda, the third picture synthesized all the components from the earlier paintings to form a new and balanced whole.

In these reflections, Brenda worked with her own multidimensional existential and ontological struggles. These images allowed her to find a balance between the different aspects of her life. This gave her an opportunity to gain a sense of self that was grounded in her lived experience but that was not trapped in the repetition of old maladaptive or pathological patterns. Brenda's natural way of working with the image-making process tended more toward a detailed, descriptive, representational style. Most of the work that she had done in the previous sessions had been related to being able to talk about her memories of abuse so that others could see what she had experienced. The core of the therapeutic work that she had been doing in the program was related to working through these memories and being able to have a sense of self that reached beyond the trauma of her past. Naomi's paintings, with their abstract nature, allowed Brenda to see and perhaps move beyond some of the representational and content-laden constraints of her own images. It appeared to be a positive sign that Brenda was able to relate so well to Naomi's pictures and that she was able to identify with them by drawing upon her own life experiences.

The group discussions that came out of the exploration of Naomi's paintings generated many possibilities for the different group members. Their abstract nature invited a broad range of responses that allowed for the exploration of many feelings, thoughts, and experiences. In the previous sessions, Brenda's images had evoked more specific context-bound thoughts and feelings and had led to serious existential and ontological questions. It was important to acknowledge all of the different dimensions that were expressed in these images and the potential meanings that were latent within them. We, as therapists, always attempted to keep the dialogical process moving through the different aspects of being and not to become trapped within certain existential or psychological dimensions. In this approach to an image-oriented therapy, the essence of transformation needed to incorporate all levels of existential and ontological reality. Therefore, the images that were created during the sessions needed to be expanded beyond the content and struggles of the past in order to open up new possibilities of being in the world that were grounded in the present and that reached into the future. After acknowledging the importance of what had been shared, the group's focus shifted toward some of the other images that had been hung up on the walls.

Brenda seemed eager to share her little paintings with the group. I remembered the pictures that Brenda had done in previous sessions and the intensity of feelings that they had stimulated. Therefore, after looking at Brenda's images for a few moments, I stated again that, although the images may in very graphic ways represent to the individual their internal world in relation to their experience of traumatic memories, this meaning is not that apparent to other people who view the images. I looked at Brenda and said that unless she would tell us about what these images meant to her, we would only be able to respond to them from our own personal and historical backgrounds; her personal/ historical symbolic meaning would not be visible to the rest of the group unless she revealed it to us. I said this to open the possibilities for her and the group members to respond to the images and to the reflective process by drawing on different levels of experiencing and processing. These levels included the kinesthetic and sensory, the perceptual and affective, the cognitive and symbolic, the social/external validation levels, as well as the creative/spiritual dimensions.

There seemed to be a greater cohesiveness in today's session and most of the group members appeared to have moved into a more open place. The co-therapist and I felt that some of the interpersonal difficulties that were expressed in the session of four days ago had faded into the background and that we were getting signals from the group that they were ready to work on more difficult issues. In spite of the new members' initial reluctant attitude and suspiciousness of the process, the majority of the group wanted to move on to work on deeper issues. Brenda, who only had two sessions left in the group, asked for some time where she could share some of her images and experiences from the previous sessions. She said that they were related to her sexual abuse issues and how these issues had impacted on her current relationship with her daughter. She looked around the room at the other group members to see their response to her request. I reminded the group that it was important to check internally to see how ready they felt to listen to Brenda's experiences in an empathic way.

I also asked Brenda what her hopes had been for sharing this material with the group and to think about how she could stay connected with us while sharing these emotional latent experiences. At this point, I was not as much concerned about Brenda's ability to share with us but rather about some of the group members' capacity to stay empathically connected without getting overwhelmed. The co-therapist and I again stated the importance of listening and respecting one's own needs and abilities. We also reinforced the choices that each group member had in listening when Brenda was sharing her images.

I was aware that when a group member was about to share their pain and suffering in a way that could involve detailed and graphic descriptions, there was always a risk for a traumatic re-enactment to occur. The material could be too intense for other group members to handle and could trigger feelings, thoughts, and issues related to their own abuse history. Thus, the person who was sharing this very sensitive material could interpret the others' responses and inability to listen as rejection. At this point, the therapist's role was to help prepare and guide the group through this process by raising their awareness of the potential risks and benefits involved in sharing, and to regulate the healing flow through the different therapeutic interventions such as educating, supportive encouragement, interpretations, reframing, confrontation, supportive witnessing, and the use of metaphors or stories. The images that were created during the sessions mediated and triangulated this process, providing another way to work with the healing flow. Although images sometimes brought up material from the unconscious that was related to past trauma, the focus of the therapeutic work was always on experiencing this material in the present and integrating or transforming it within the context of the person's current life situation. It was the processing of the material in the present, not the actual telling of the experience, that brought about relief from the entrapment of past memories.

I reminded the group that it was not the details of the shared material, but rather the integration of feeling and thoughts into one's being through the dialogical image/word process that mattered. I knew that the options that patients had in how they listened and responded to each other's verbal and non-verbal sharing depended to some degree on the individual's internal resources, personality style, and the group dynamics. As the therapist, I could provide guidance and set an example for ways of sharing and being with each other that could lead to connection rather than to isolation and rejection. I could think of many different verbal and non-verbal ways of working with the group as a whole so that material could emerge through images and group discussions in a way that was considerate of the different individuals' needs and abilities. However, once the process unfolded it became a continuous balancing act of keeping the healing flow at healthy and therapeutic levels.

Before exploring her pictures, Brenda made some reference to the previous works she had done. Some of the group members who had been in the group with her shared a bit about their own past experiences and how they had been able to work with the material that had come up for them from the unconscious through the symbolic realm of the images. They spoke a bit about how reflecting on the images had helped them to gain an understanding of their own ways of being in the world and their relationship to their personal history.

Retrospective View: A Therapist's Reflections on Previous Sessions as a Tool to Guide the Healing Flow

At any time during a therapy session, I was aware of the person's work from the previous sessions and my interventions were based on my experience of them as a whole. I remembered Brenda's images that she had shared in the previous sessions. They all had been related to traumatic memories. I remembered how she had been able to move from naming and identifying what she had experienced in the past on an intellectual level toward a greater integration of feelings. It was the integration of feelings with what was remembered within the social support of the group that had helped Brenda to move beyond the isolation caused by trauma and to expand her identity beyond these experiences. Brenda, when she had spoken about her pictures in the past, tended to include many details about the remembered abuse. I had been aware of and had attempted to modulate the quality and amount of sharing related to the traumatic experiences so that Brenda could learn to integrate these experiences more on an intellectual as well as on an emotional, psychological, social, and spiritual level without getting stuck in one mode where content was disembodied from feelings.

I remembered her sharing in a way that reflected a need to talk about her traumatic experiences. It had become important for her to break the silence and to address the guilt and shame that were attached to these memories. In previous sessions she had always, before starting to speak, looked at the other group members to make some connections with them. While she was speaking she had been looking at the two small drawings that she had done during the session. The drawings had been relatively realistically rendered illustrations of what she had remembered about the abuse. I remembered how in these earlier sessions she had spoken about the content of her first picture. Brenda had said:

> This is a picture of me on the farm in my bed. Dad is naked on top of me. I'm laying face down and he is sodomizing me. I'm grabbing the sheets tightly and I'm crying very quietly. Dad resembles a hairy animal because that's what he felt like to me. A big fat, hairy animal that smelt! I drew Mom standing farther away from the foot of the bed than she actually was because I wanted to illustrate how well the room was lit around me by the flashlight. My sister was hiding in her bed all curled up under her sheets and covering her ears. My brother was hiding in my closet curled up against the wall covering his ears and crying quietly. Mom was wearing her skimpy lingerie. She was smiling.[1]

In that session the group members had been quietly listening. Most of them had known each other from the other groups and had been familiar with Brenda's story. Still, the words and the small image brought up many intense feelings within them. First, there had been a tense silence and a sense of wanting to move on and to turn their attention to something different. The content of Brenda's first picture had been very difficult to stay with and had been, on some levels, too intense for some of the group members to fully embrace. However, it had been surprising how much support the group was able to give her at that time because many of them had been able to relate to what Brenda had shared. On some level, the group members had seemed to be relieved that someone was able to talk about the experiences that they had lived with in silence for so long. Nevertheless, when an individual shared material in this descriptive manner there was always the potential for group members to become overwhelmed by the experience and to lose the empathic connection. However, during these past sessions the group members had formed enough emotional connections with Brenda through the other components of the program that they were able to stay with her so that the experience was therapeutic for both Brenda and the group.

At that time, after acknowledging the pain and suffering that was expressed in what Brenda had shared, I shifted the focus toward the different qualities of the image. I commented on the way she had depicted her room and that there appeared to be no walls enclosing it. It appeared to be just fading into the darkness. After looking at the picture for a few moments, Brenda had acknowledged that this might have signified that there was darkness and danger all around her. She explained that:

> I felt as though I had no boundaries – even walls wouldn't have given me boundaries. They would have been crossed anyways. The light that was surrounding me from the flashlight was in the shape of a balloon. It was huge, trapping me and exposing me totally. I felt degraded and just totally exposed.
>
> I remember telling the police that while I was being sodomized I couldn't breathe – I was choking and gasping for air. After drawing this picture, and seeing myself trapped within this balloon shaped light, I have to wonder if that's why I was gasping for air. From doing this picture I realized how alone I was during the assault. Mom, Dad, [sister], and [brother] were all there. They were all taking care of their own needs. I was completely alone.

When Brenda had spoken she seemed to be somewhat more in touch with her feelings but she was still relating to the material on an intellectual level.

I remembered that Brenda's sharing had brought up many responses within the group. On a gut level, there was an initial outrage and anger about what she had shared. On an intellectual level there was some sense of disbelief about what she had brought forward. This was not as much a questioning of the authenticity of what she had shared but rather a type of protection against the pain and injustice attached to what she had described. We, as therapists, never really know what actually happened to someone in their life. All we can respond to is what the individual is sharing with us through the image and other non-verbal and verbal expressions within the here-and-now context of the group.

I felt that in this situation it was important for me to stay empathically connected with Brenda and with what she was sharing without becoming lost within her life experience. As the therapist, I needed to be able to stay grounded in my own experience of the world in order to connect with the multitude of possible existential and ontological realities without becoming lost in them. This was important in order to help her to move beyond the entrapments of the traumatic experiences and to embrace future possibilities of being differently located in relationship to the world. Through the facilitating of the dialogical image/word process, we were able to guide the healing flow. I needed to be careful not to get stuck in the frozen moments of traumatic memories and to see how I could find a relationship to the image that allowed me and the group to move through it into the symbolic realm, where the creative energy could be expressed in a playful and self-affirming manner.

From these earlier sessions, I also remembered how Brenda had spoken about the images that she had created in her following sessions and how her focus had shifted from her experience of the abuse toward examining patterns of re-enactments. As she looked at her work from this perspective, she was able to explore ways of seeing how patterns of abuse had found their way into her and her daughter's life. In these sessions, she had shared with the group through her images and words the following experience of how trauma had affected her and her daughter's life. She wanted to share her images and associated experiences with the group, as this helped her to break her sense of isolation, shame, and guilt. I remembered that in the following session Brenda again had carefully checked with the group to see if she could take some of their time in order to examine the picture. She started to explain her image in the following manner:

> This is a picture of my daughter's life prior to her abuse by Dad and the result of what happened to her. It starts off with [her] playing on her bike (she has a halo over her head) with her friend. This picture shows her roller skates, skipping rope, swimming pool, swing, pail, and shovel. The house was full of love for her and was secure. She was happy. The next picture shows her on the train with a friend on their way to her house. My daughter was happy, felt loved, looked pretty.

In the next section of the picture Brenda had drawn a different aspect of her daughter's life that indicated a continuation of the abuse into her daughter's life. Brenda continued:

> Then her and this friend are in the car on the way to Grandpa's [my parents'] house. [My daughter] is nervous and asking who Grandma and Grandpa are. Why did she have to go? She'll miss us. This friend assures her she'll like them and that she'll be missed. In the picture a sign ahead of them says "HELL 20 miles" (Direction to Grandpa's).

After Brenda had finished speaking there had been a brief pause of silence. The question of why her daughter was visiting Brenda's father hung in the air. But nobody asked it. We could sense Brenda's feelings of anger, frustration, and guilt about how she could have let this happen to her daughter. There was also a question of how her parents could have engaged in such horrific acts toward their own daughter and granddaughter. However, I also had the sense that for the most part we, the group, wanted to hear from Brenda about her thoughts and feelings, to learn to understand her experiences that were so graphically represented through her images. After a brief pause, Brenda continued to talk about the next picture:

> The next picture was enclosed by a red barrier (dangerous) – this is the hellhole that Grandma and Grandpa lived in. Trees and the lake surround it. It is clear there is no way out of this hell. The room on the right is the family room where I have drawn all the weapons he used on us and where he and Mom performed belly dance sex. The other room is the room my daughter slept in. It shows her in her bed. Dad is kneeling on the floor beside her and he is touching her. Mom is standing in the doorway watching with her arms folded. She does nothing – just watches.

There was another long pause that allowed us to reflect silently upon what had been shared and to sit and honor the feelings that had emerged. I noticed that some of the group members were having strong emotional reactions to what had been shared. However, I had the sense that they were able to handle their feelings as well as being able to focus empathically on Brenda's experiences. Brenda looked at the pictures and then at the group members before continuing to speak:

> The next picture shows dad driving my daughter back home. He looks like a DEVIL. He's reminding her to keep it a secret. She's full of wonder as to why this happened and agrees to keep silent. In the next image she has come back home. She stands next to a sign that states how she feels now after her abuse. She is very sad, angry, and empty. She doesn't feel loved. Her heart has shrunk and her hair is a mess. She's crying.

As Brenda had been describing the picture tears had come to her eyes. Someone had reached for the Kleenex box and passed it to her in a supportive gesture. It seemed that she felt terrible about what had happened to her daughter but she did not seem to have the same compassion for her own suffering. The question had implicitly arisen again of why Brenda had not protected her daughter from that known danger. It was a question that she obviously had been struggling with for a long time. She commented on how her actions had been grounded in a sense of disbelief that had made her question her own experience. Seeing her husband's family and parents interact so positively with her daughter, combined with the wish to see her own parents in a more positive light, had clouded her perceptions over time and caused her to build upon the small hope or dream of a different reality. Thus, in spite of her own experience, there had always been the hope that perhaps things could be different this time and that her parents could perhaps be more like her husband's family. Perhaps they had changed? Maybe now they could be the parents that she never had. It often is these kinds of hopes and fantasies that in so many cases bring the victim back to re-expose themselves and those around them to a continuous cycle of traumatic re-enactments. In this sense, Brenda's struggle resonated with many of the group members' experiences and most of them could relate to her on some level.

Hopes and fantasies of a better future or a different outcome generally help us to make positive changes in our life patterns. However, there is much clinical evidence that many traumatic re-enactments can put an individual or others at risk of being retraumatized or hurt. In this book the theme of traumatic re-enactments and fragmentation through dissociation have been connected with different aspects of the creative process and the human ability to adjust to many different life situations. However, in a traumatic re-enactment it appears as if the creative process has gone astray and is not able to move through the different phases of the initial gathering, the incubation period, the discovery, the evaluation, and the resolution phase in an integrated manner. Thus, in spite of the individual's efforts and hopes of avoiding situations that are similar to the original trauma, they actually end up, as if pulled by an invisible force, being drawn into situations where traumatic re-enactments can occur over and over again. In this replaying, quite often the victims expose themselves unknowingly over and over to similar, traumatic situations. This dynamic appears to be the driving force behind the continuous cycle of traumatic re-enactments.

The creative energy that has been a theme throughout this book, and this strong and at times invisible mechanism that appears to pull individuals on unconscious or conscious levels toward a replaying of the original trauma, have been connected. The creative and adaptive forces described in earlier chapters propel many positive developmental and evolutionary aspects of being, but somehow they can become entrapped and concretized through traumatic experiences. Thus, Brenda's struggle was, in part, grounded in a healthy and creative process that helps one to move toward a better future and that allows one to seek out ways to move beyond the scripts imposed by traumatic experiences. However, if these ways of coping with the traumatic experiences are not grounded in one's experience of the world, but rather are ways of unconsciously or consciously avoiding or escaping from the pain and implications of one's lived experience or reality, there is a great risk for re-enactments to occur. The individual needs to be able to find some way of returning back to his or her lived experience and regaining the ability to embrace life within the context of their emotional, psychological, social, and spiritual reality. One way of facilitating this process was by providing a relatively neutral place where the individual could reflect and contemplate upon this lived experience in an integrated manner, where feelings and thoughts had an equal voice.

Within the therapeutic context of the art therapy group, individuals can play out the different scenarios through the symbolic and transformative realm of the different art media. It appears that within this symbolic realm individuals can find a way to begin to break through the trauma-related patterns and begin to accept and understand themselves separate from the traumatic experiences of their past. By accepting what her subjective reality is and by reflecting upon it within the supportive structure of the group, Brenda may be able to examine old fantasies and replace them with more adaptive and creative ones. Within this space, she may be able to expand into the symbolic realm and begin to accept new possibilities, through insight and awareness that will allow her to embrace her life in all its different dimensions. In this way, the creative energies can become redirected toward reality-oriented patterns that open up to different choices and life patterns.

As I reflected upon the therapeutic work that Brenda had done in the previous sessions, I remembered her speaking about her daughter's abuse almost as if she was speaking about her own memories and experiences. In these sessions I had noticed many parallels between what she had depicted in her first picture and her subsequent images that were related to her daughter's abuse as well as to her own. When Brenda had explored her images with the group for the first time, she had focused mostly on the content of the experience and had not been able to connect with the emotions involved. However, in the subsequent sessions she was able to gradually express and be in touch with more emotions; particularly when she spoke about her daughter's pain, for which she seemed to have greater empathy than for her own.

It is important to note at this point that the process of writing out these reflections has, to some degree, changed the dynamic multidimensional flow that happens during an actual therapy group. The shifting back and forth between my internal reflections on the work from previous groups and the current group activity happens on a more intuitive/embodied level where interventions are based upon the embodied clinical knowledge described in earlier chapters. The dialogical image/word process unfolds quickly and simultaneously on many levels. In order to help group members learn to work more in an integrated manner, the therapist must also be aware of his or her connections with physical sensations and feelings as well as with the intellectual dimension. Thus, the therapist's way of reflecting and guiding the process of art toward healing is multi-modal and complex in nature, yet it may take only a few seconds or minutes in real time. As I looked at Brenda's pictures in today's sessions, the question went through my mind as to whether she would pick up on some of the themes of these earlier works in the next images.

Shifting the Focus back to the Group

After these internal recollections and reflections of Brenda's earlier work, my focus shifted back to the group and to Brenda's pictures that were taped up on the wall. Lois, who had mentioned earlier on in the session that she was eager to start using the art materials, was getting somewhat restless. Our orientation/check-in phase had been somewhat longer than usual. However, it seemed important that Brenda had some time to reflect on her work, as she was unable to do so in the previous session. Brenda, noticing Lois's restlessness, asked the group again if they would mind if she took a few moments before the experiential component of the group in order to talk about the images that she had done. The group members, who had seen her earlier work, seemed to be very interested in finding out about these images. Also, Rosalyn and Cindy seemed to be open to her request. The group was now quietly focusing on the small and detailed images. Some group members stood up to take a closer look at the pictures. Then there was a brief pause before everyone settled back into their chairs again. The images included many details and Brenda had again used a representational, descriptive drawing style but this time the image seemed to shift and begin to incorporate more of the symbolic realm. Brenda started to speak:

> This is the story of my life. This picture starts at the left and works its way across to the right. I have visualized myself as being an innocent baby being dropped from the clouds when I was born. I was dropped right into a ball of fire (Mom and Dad's arms). I was scarred for life. As I try to crawl away from the fire and get away, I cry.

> Just as I stand up and think there's hope, a ton of firebombs drop on my head and burn me again and drop me to the ground again. Again I lay there crying, burned, and hopeless. I work hard at finding some hope and at working up the courage to try and break free again.
>
> This time I kneel for a bit and wait anxiously for the next bomb to fall. Nothing happens. So I stand up and BAM a huge fireball falls on top of me and I'm trapped. I say NO as it's coming but it comes anyways.
>
> One thing that stands out to me is that the fire on the left is huge and it left several scars on the first three babies. Then as I move along to the right, it appears that the scars have disappeared and that the flame of the fire has gotten much smaller. Also, the fire is over the baby, which means she can escape if she crawls along very slowly towards HOPE.

There were a few moments of silence. Nina said that she could relate to the image and that it reminded her of her struggle of trying to protect her husband and children from the abuse that she had suffered as a child. Nina also acknowledged, with some pain, that in spite of her efforts her past had impacted her ability to relate openly to her husband and children. She continued to explain that through her stay here in the program she had discovered that her way of protecting them from her past had actually contributed to her becoming isolated from them. Some of the other group members' body language showed that they could relate on some level to Brenda's picture and to what Nina had shared. Those group members who had been in the session with Brenda were able to make some connections between this picture and the ones she had done in previous sessions. Sam pointed out that there appeared to be more hope in this picture than in the previous ones. Brenda responded to the feedback in the following manner:

> When I finished this picture, I looked at the previous picture of my daughter's story and I realized there was a connection between the two. I have felt as though I was dropped onto earth into hell and have lived there all my life. Then I looked at my daughter's picture and realized how responsible I feel about her abuse because I feel as though I took this beautiful innocent child and dropped her into the same fire in hell (my parents' arms) that I've tried so hard to get away from. I felt angry with myself for this. Doing these second pictures helped me realize that I am not responsible for her abuse. Dad and Mom are. These pictures also helped me see that I have been grieving and carrying guilt and shame for [my daughter's] abuse because I can relate to her story so well and I have resolved my own guilt, shame, and grief.

As Brenda spoke, there seemed to be a different quality to her voice, which was also reflected in her body posture. She seemed to be more in touch with her own feelings of sadness and pain than before. However, I had the sense that she had just begun the process of forgiving herself and that the memories that she had depicted through her images were only a starting point for the feelings that she had not yet fully assimilated into her whole being. Naomi, who was sitting next to Brenda, took the Kleenex box and passed it to her. After a few moments, Naomi said in a quiet, encouraging voice that it had not been Brenda's fault and that the abuse should have never happened in the first place. Other group members responded to what Brenda had shared by reflecting upon their own experiences and how they had been trapped in different types of traumatic re-enactments that were grounded in denials and fantasies of a life that they had never had. Many group members felt that it was hard and painful to come to terms with one's history of abuse but it was probably better to go through that pain rather than to continue on in the way that they had been living in the past.

Although most of the group members were connecting with Brenda, I noticed Lois still fidgeting in her chair and playing with the toys in the sandbox. She seemed somewhat in her own world yet still listening. In previous sessions where we had spent more time using the art materials, Lois had been able to utilize the image-making process by painting two or three large paintings at a time. It had been much easier for Lois to express herself through the art media. However, it was much more difficult for Lois to speak about her feelings and to take a reflective pause, as this required her to sit with her feelings in a conscious manner without dealing with them by doing things. Painting had allowed her to channel and express her feelings in a more direct unmediated stream of consciousness. Playing in the sandbox allowed her to tolerate and stay with her feelings and with the group to the degree that she was able to at this point without having to escape into dissociation or to physically leaving the group. Each group member had slightly different needs. Some would need more time using the art materials while others needed more time to process verbally. Thus, the dialogical image/word approach is considerate of these individual differences and interventions are based on helping the group as well as the individual members to learn to regulate the healing flow in a more integrated manner.

I also noticed a shift in feelings within the group as a whole from sadness to anger that appeared to be facilitated by the dialogical process of the images that Brenda had created. For a few moments this anger had increased in intensity and became redirected toward a verbal outrage over how children in general were treated and betrayed by those who were supposed to protect and care for them. For a while this discussion took place on a more general level, focusing on how poorly children are treated in the world. This allowed a safer way of handling feelings related to the content of the materials shared. It took only a few refocusing questions by the therapists to get the group members again to relate to each other on a more personal level. This more general discussion then shifted to a different level. The group members again contemplated, on a more personal level, about how easy it was, even if one had the best intentions, to be pulled into a traumatic re-enactment or to get stuck in the victim triangle. Group members described how they had noticed, since they had been in the program, that it was very simple to unknowingly or unconsciously slip into a traumatic re-enactment and to get stuck in the rigid scripts of being the victim, the rescuer, and/or the abuser without being able to move outside of these roles in order to live or react to the world in a more integrated manner.

Mary said that feeling and staying with the feelings without getting overwhelmed or dissociating from her feelings or body was the most difficult thing to do. Feeling the pain associated with different aspects of lived experience seemed almost worse than when the trauma had actually occurred. Cindy said that dissociation had become a way of life for her and it had allowed her to tolerate many difficult and painful situations, but it had at the same time robbed her of the ability to connect with others and to experience joy and happiness. It was hard to break through the dissociative coping style and to embrace the hardships, struggles, and monotony of everyday life in an integrated manner. However, the long-term costs of avoiding feelings and disconnecting from them appeared high. It seemed to be connected with a sense of fragmentation and isolation within the self and within the relationship to the world. Cindy said in a half-joking manner that it was too bad that we had to feel all the different feelings and could not just stay with the good ones like happiness and joy. Sam said that although he was learning that feelings could be helpful in the way they inform us about the world and our needs within this world, it was sometimes difficult to see them as friends.

The questions and feelings that arose from what Brenda had shared did not have simple answers and each group member was trying to locate themselves in relationship to their own experiences of the world in connection to their past, present, and hopes for the future in the best way they could. Mary asked why, when we hear each other's stories and experiences, they have so much more of an impact than when we see all the horror of the world on television news reports. Naomi responded by saying that we probably have become so disconnected and numbed out from what we see on the news that we never really stop and think about what this means to us personally. Through the reflective dialogical process the experience of hearing a painful story was qualitatively changed and made more personal.

The different concepts, like traumatic re-enactments and the victim triangle, were helpful in providing some intellectual understanding of the underlying dynamics, which then could open up new options to the patient. However, these concepts alone did not take away the pain and suffering. The challenge of working through some of these experiences in an integrated manner that included mind, body, and spirit still remained. The symbolic realm of the arts, if it was propelled and shaped by the creative life forces and a reflective dialogical process, could help individuals to come to terms with and to transform old patterns and to begin to travel along different trajectories. In this group we, as therapists, needed to do relatively little guidance of the healing flow. However, the group's dynamics and ability to shift and work on all the different levels in an integrated manner determined the types of interventions used to facilitate the dialogical image/word process and the healing flow so that they could unfold in a more integrated manner.

Cindy suddenly pointed toward the picture that she had done in the previous session. She seemed to be very excited about something that she had discovered while we were exploring Brenda's drawing. She said:

> I had tried to make a picture of a beautiful peacock and the harder I tried to achieve likeness the more the image began to look like a turkey. At the time I had attributed this to my inability to draw or paint anything. I thought my failure to reproduce exactly what I had in mind was simply due to my painting skills. However, as I looked at the picture today in the light of what others have shared I began to realize that this simple attempt of painting a turkey resonates on a much deeper level.

Mary responded to Cindy by saying: "Is it not strange how the unconscious works when you try to put something on paper?"

Cindy felt that for the greater part of her life she had tried so hard, like when she was painting this picture, to see her family as this beautiful peacock but that she now realized that this had been an illusion. In a half-joking manner that pushed away the sadness and disappointment she said: "I know now that the family I grew up with were really not beautiful peacocks, but they were all turkeys." I was aware that there was much pain behind this statement and that it would take some time for Cindy to come to terms with the implications of this new realization. I hoped that she would be able to explore this in the future through her images and more group discussions. Before returning the focus back to Brenda's images we took a few moments of silence in order for the group to assimilate some of the feelings and thoughts related to the insight that Cindy had so spontaneously shared with the group.

After this pause, Brenda continued to speak about her second picture:

> This picture shows my desperation at trying to get closer to [my daughter]. She is the blonde standing behind a brick wall with her arms crossed. She's angry with me for not being there for her when Dad abused her.
>
> I am kneeling outside of the wall begging for her forgiveness. I have tried every conceivable object to break down the wall and I can't. I've used a hammer, drill, chainsaw, bulldozer, fire, and helicopter dropping a rope. It just won't break.
>
> I feel as though I can never make it up to her for not having been able to protect her from Dad. I feel as though I was as bad as Mom because she didn't protect me from Dad either.

There was another brief pause that was followed by some discussion that echoed earlier themes. Some of the group members, who had seen Brenda's earlier works, pointed out that she was not there when her daughter's abuse had occurred and that she mainly knew about it through her own experience with her father. This feedback seemed to help Brenda to step back into a more reflective mode of thinking. Brenda continued by saying:

> After doing this picture, I felt differently. This feedback that I just received helped tremendously. It helped me see that I was different from Mom. I didn't know about my daughter's abuse happening. If I had of, I would have protected her. I've done this now by reporting Dad to the police. Once I knew about it, I did stop it! Mom knew about it, helped him, and abandoned me.

Someone in the group noticed that the way Brenda had rendered the bricks in her second picture showed that the wall was not completely solid. This indicated to Naomi that this could perhaps mean that Brenda would be able to reach her daughter at some point in the future. Rosalyn wondered if perhaps Brenda's own guilt was what was keeping her from reaching her daughter. Brenda's response to this comment was to question whether it was actually her own feelings that had created this brick wall. In the picture it looked as if her daughter was actually approaching the wall with perhaps the intention of coming through. Brenda stated: "Maybe I'm still so full of guilt, shame, anger, fear, and pain. Maybe once I resolve these feelings I can let the wall down." As Brenda looked around the room it appeared that maybe it was time to start using the art materials. There was a sense that our verbal explorations had reached their limit and that creating more images in response to what had been uncovered could perhaps be more fruitful at this point.

Brenda appeared relieved that she had been able to share her pictures before starting the experiential part of the group. She felt that it really had helped her and that she was now ready to work on some new pieces. Brenda concluded that she had noticed when she was not able to share her work with the group during the previous session they appeared to have affected her in a much longer and in a more negative way. In some strange way, the images and associated feelings had contributed to her worrying about what other group members were thinking about her in relationship to what she had drawn. She felt that this had made it harder for her to return to this session. It was almost as if the images had become more powerful over time because she was not able to process them verbally with the group. This had left her with feelings of vulnerability and fears. In order to deal with these feelings between the last session and today's session, she had written some of her thoughts down in her journal, which had helped her at the time. She wanted to let the group know that talking about the images in today's session had helped her to process some of the feelings and to deal with her sense of being exposed or misunderstood by others in a way that she had not been able to do on her own or through the other parts of the program. The group responses had also helped her to understand that she judges herself much more harshly than others do.

The co-therapist and I again reminded the group of the many choices and supports that they had in the here-and-now context. Within the context of the group, each group member could learn to use the symbolic realm and reconnect with their imagination through the art materials and toys in a way that could facilitate awareness, acceptance, and growth. We again explored how using the different art media could help to expand associations related to traumatic experiences and to develop them beyond this narrow context. We also briefly went over different choices of using the art materials so that they could facilitate a sense of becoming more grounded and connected with the physical world and the here-and-now context of the group. Patients could also use the various art media such as paints, Plasticine, clay, charcoal, and pastels in a way that could help with affect modulation. The image-making process could provide an avenue to becoming more aware and being able to tolerate and work with feelings in a more integrated manner. The co-therapist and I also reminded the group members that we would be available for them if they needed our help. We let the group know that we would like to leave about half an hour at the end of the session for verbal reflection and contemplation time and it did not take long before everyone got up to start to explore the materials.

The Experiential Phase

There was a moment of silence before most of the group members got up to use the art materials. It did not take long before most of them had settled in and were deeply involved in their own process. Only Cindy remained in her chair. She noted that when it came to expressing something about herself there seemed to be a big void. After a brief time of watching the other group members, she moved over to sit at the table with some of the other patients. Cindy gazed at their work and then at the empty piece of paper that she had placed in front of herself. Mary made some encouraging remarks and then went back to working on her image. I made myself available by walking over to the table and sitting down next to Cindy. I had the sense that more instructions about how to use the materials were not what she needed. A blank piece of paper can have a lot of meaning. We both sat quietly looking around the room. After a while, she said that she always was told what to do and how to behave. It was very frightening to be given the space and freedom to find her own voice when she was not even sure who she was. Tears came to her eyes and she cried for some time. They were tears of acknowledgment rather than tears that cry for help or attention. She needed time to grieve in silence. In the group it was all right for a person to be outwardly inactive when they needed to take an internal pause.

My gaze was now turning toward Mary who was working on a large piece of paper close to the end of the table. Using paints, Mary was continuing to work with the theme of the nightmare that she had explored in her previous images. Rosalyn was also working on a large piece of paper but at the other end of the room. Rosalyn started to build a yellow-brick wall using Plasticine and paints. There was a sense of determination about her manner of working that seemed to be grounded in her sense of an intuitive knowledge of what she wanted to create. I noticed Sam out of the corner of my eye. He was also using Plasticine and paints as he had in the previous sessions. He seemed deeply engaged in his image-making process and hardly noticed Naomi who was creating another abstract on a large piece of paper next to him. Nina was using finger paints and two pieces of paper that she treated as one very large piece. She was splashing on paint freely, creating many different patterns, and she also seemed completely absorbed by the process. I walked over to the other end of the room to cut some more pieces of paper and to refill some of the small paint containers that were sitting on the table.

My focus then shifted toward Lois, who had also chosen to work on two large pieces of paper, using black and gray paint. She was again working with the theme of bringing together the kinesthetic and affective with the cognitive and symbolic aspect of her being. Each paper seemed to become a container for either the affective or the cognitive symbolic domain. In the one painting she created, in a very stylized manner, a figure carrying a large and heavy black weight on her head while walking painfully but steadily along a dark road. On the other page, she had created a painting by splashing on paint in a free and spontaneous manner to create random, dripping patterns. Using two very distinctly different painting styles, Lois was able to externalize and work with her struggles of bringing together her opposing forces of emotions and intellect. Lois and the other group members seemed not to need any help so my gaze fell upon Brenda who was sitting at the table not far from Lois. She was working on another detailed drawing while Cindy had moved back over to the circle and was now playing in the sandbox.[2]

It was interesting to note how quiet the room had become during the experiential phase. Even the noises from outside the room seemed to have faded into the background as everyone focused on their own work. One could almost sense the intensity of the process and it was nearly magical how images emerged so quickly and spontaneously through the different art materials. Cindy was now playing quite freely in the sandbox and it seemed that in a playful manner she was processing some of the feelings that had come up for her. This was a big step for her as only one session ago she had been quite apprehensive and suspicious of using art materials and playing in the sandbox. To allow herself to play with the toys in the sand without being task orientated was something completely new to her. The sandbox was also a challenge for her because she did not like to get her hands dirty. In many ways she was able to challenge many old patterns and ways of thinking by simply playing in the sand. During this quiet time, while I was watching the group, I had some time to reflect upon the process and to get a sense of the group as a whole.

My thoughts drifted back to the images that Brenda had shared during the orientation phase. Because of the way the image-making process appeared to evolve for Brenda, as well as because of her present-life circumstances, it had been important for her to have her images and story witnessed and acknowledged by the group before she was able to continue with creating further pictures. However, this witnessing was not to make what was presented in these pictures more concrete or real but rather to allow her to learn how to experience them within the fluid, dynamic symbolic realm and the community context of the group. Through the dialogical image/word process the meeting and experiencing of these images could be expanded and transformed.

The material that Brenda shared had had the potential for bringing up many different feelings rather quickly, which could potentially have retraumatized individual group members. Therefore, the co-therapist and I were keeping a close watch on the group as a whole in order to help to guide the healing flow. Brenda also had been very present and conscientious in her sharing and exploring of the images and had been able to maintain a sense of openness and connectedness with the group. The group mix also seemed to have supported a contemplative process that led to a sense of subjective empowerment through the symbolic realm of the image-making process. Thus, the experience appeared to be therapeutic and healing for Brenda as well as for the group.

Throughout the different phases of the art therapy group, the therapists have many choices of how to help guide the unfolding dialogical image/word process. In order to regulate the healing flow, therapists can keep patients' focus on the here-and-now situation of the group and the interpersonal relationships that have developed between the group members. By keeping the focus on staying consciously connected with the group, the physical reality of the room, and the options that the art materials can provide, the shared process can become one that is grounded in a multi-modal dialogical exchange rather than one of purging traumatic and unwanted memories in a way that might lead to revictimization and isolation. It was not unusual for patients to start out with the fantasy that if they purged their memories through visual and verbal expressions, they would free themselves of them. The other fantasy that was quite common was that patients felt that if they could find the answers or truth related to their memories they would be relieved of their pain. Through the group process and the experiencing of the dialogical image/word process, patients gradually were able to let go of these fantasies and to replace them with more creative, regenerating and reality-oriented thoughts, feelings, and experiences.

The art materials and the image-making process provided a safe container for feelings and thoughts to emerge. These images could be related to themes that were resonating with different traumatic experiences but they were not limited to them and could expand beyond this context. The symbolic container of the images could provide a triangulation between the patient, the group, and the therapists. The images or art objects could hold many different projections, experiences, feelings, and realities, which could be reshaped and transformed through the dialogical image/word process. Thus, the symbolic realm of the transitional object created through the image provided many opportunities for projections to be mediated and various transferences to be worked with. The physical reality of the image permitted the owning and the transforming of these experiences within the social context and community of the group. This reality-oriented, multi-modal process helped the patients to become more connected with the world around them and to gradually let go of fantasies that were hindering them from connecting with the world. In this way, they could begin to reclaim their experiences of themselves independently of the traumatic memories. Through this process individuals could practice, on an experiential and verbal level, integrating or transforming these experiences rather than unconsciously re-enacting them. Within the microcosm of the art therapy group, patients could begin to alter unsuccessful patterns of discarding unwanted and painful material. Thus they could start to break the continuous cycle of traumatic re-enactments.

The art materials, with all of the possible choices that they offered, the container of the art therapy room, as well as the social support that the group members and therapists provided, allowed this transformative process to unfold along certain therapeutic trajectories. The nature and multidimensional aspect of the various art media allowed for the modulation of the healing flow within the physical reality of creating external objects that at the same time inhabited a symbolic and transformative realm. Within this transitional space, experiences of the world could be given physical and external shapes within the transformative and symbolic domain. The physical size and shape of the paper, the types and texture of paints, and the thickness of brushes all affected the dialogical process between the self, the physical quality of the materials, and the emerging image. They all contributed to how quickly the images and related feelings and thoughts could emerge. Thus, the choices that the different art media provided, the interpersonal dimension of the group, the timing and level of sharing through the verbal and non-verbal explorations, and the therapists' interventions all affected the unfolding and modulation of the healing flow and the material that could emerge through the images.

During today's experiential phase the therapists' attentive and mindful presence was all that was required for the most part as the majority of the group members did not need much individual guidance. However, it was difficult to predict beforehand how the healing flow would unfold for the different group members and how their images would affect each other. Therefore, it was essential that the therapists be aware and alert to the process as it unfolded in order to determine when or what kind of therapeutic interventions would be needed in order to guide and modulate the unfolding healing flow. For this reason, the therapists' self-knowledge and intuitive and explicit familiarity with the image-making process and the process of group therapy was an essential part of the dialogical image/word approach to art therapy. This integrated approach to art therapy and the process of art toward healing required a broad base of knowledge in art therapy, psychotherapy, related clinical areas,

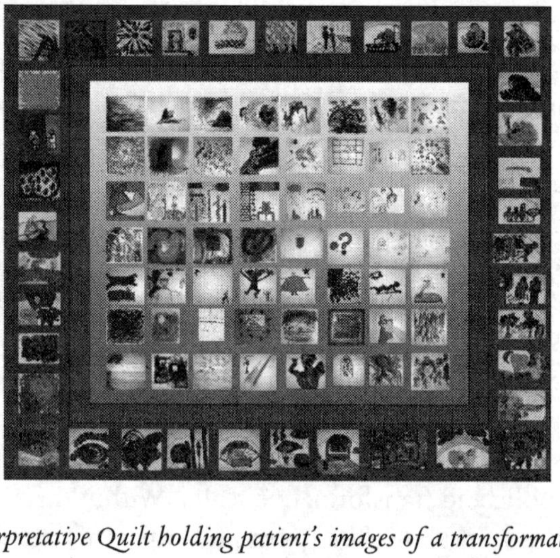

Figure 8.1: An Interpretative Quilt holding patient's images of a transformative process (completed in 2001)

psychology, the arts, as well as an awareness of the existential and ontological issues discussed in earlier chapters.

As I looked around the room, I noticed that most of the group members were now coming to a natural endpoint within their work. They were putting final touches on their pictures as the experiential phase of the group was slowly coming to an end. Sam and Nina were just cleaning their brushes while Mary had already returned to the circle of chairs to join Cindy and myself. Lois was hanging up her picture from the previous session together with the pictures she had made in today's session, as she had not yet taken an opportunity to talk about her work from the previous session. This allowed us to reflect upon them together and to acknowledge the flow and transformation from one session to the next. This was a transition time, a time that allowed the group to shift their focus from working on their individual images backwards toward the group as a whole. Now individuals were coming back to sit around the sandbox in order to process their experience further through the verbal, reflective phase of the group. Before we started the reflection phase, the co-therapist and I helped some of the group members to hang their pictures closer to the circle so that we were better able to see them.

Notes

1 The quotations used in the previous and following pages that make reference to Brenda's involvement in the group were based upon written feedback that I received from one of the patients who had been in the art therapy group. This patient, who I have named Brenda in the fictional art therapy sessions, had given much written feedback about her experience in the group as well as given me her written consent for her images to be photographed in order to be included in the visual database. In this feedback she had also included a detailed, written description of her images and the process that she had been through. This written exploration had come unsolicited and I have chosen some of the quotations from this text in order to include patients' voices in this inquiry not only through their images but also through their words.

2 In order to obtain another view into how the dialogical image/word process could unfold for different individuals within this clinical context, the reader can explore different journeys of patients' images and the different fictional characters provided in the other quilt patches.

CHAPTER 9

Verbal Reflection Phase of the Healing Flow of Images and the Quality of the Dialogical Image/Word Process

The transition from the experiential phase to the verbal reflection period always involved a noticeable shift from a physically active yet contemplative stance toward a more reflexive, dialogical process. During the experiential part of the group, individuals were able to focus more upon themselves and the unfolding dialogue between the self, the art materials, and the image. In the verbal reflective period the focus was shifted more toward a dialogical process that included other group members' images and the group as a whole. Coming back into the circle and seeing all of the works that were created during the experiential phase made it obvious how the room had become transformed.

The empty pieces of papers that had been pasted upon the wall at the beginning of the session were now filled with many images and powerful symbols that had been generated during the group. Seeing these images and symbols could sometimes be quite a powerful experience, as many feelings and thoughts were simultaneously brought into awareness through the images. During this reflective phase, the internal worlds of all the different group members had been made visible all at once. In a way, it was as if everyone had been able to give voice to some part of his or her internal world through the image-making process and now we were able to see and experience these worlds as they resonated within our own, internal being. The circle of chairs, the sandbox, the small clay sculpture in someone's hands, all had become containers for the many different types of experiences and were reflective of a dialogical process between self and the world. Even if no one spoke, there was still so much communicated through these images on a somatic, emotional, psychological, intellectual, existential, and ontological level. It took some time to orientate ourselves to the images and to absorb what had unfolded before we were able to attach words to the experiences.

We, the co-therapist and I, started the verbal reflective phase by inviting the group members to take a few moments to examine the experience of coming back together as a group and to acknowledge the feelings and thoughts that they had as they looked around the room at the pictures that had been created. We also reminded the group that it was important to honor one's experience and to respect each other's boundaries when exploring the image-making process and the pictures that were hung up on the walls. It was also important to remember that it was up to the individuals to determine how comfortable they were in sharing their feelings about the process they had gone through and the picture or sculpture that they had created.

We acknowledged that each of us was affected, on one level or another, by the different images but that it was essential to own one's feelings and responses to a picture and that feedback was more helpful when it was grounded in one's experience of the world and one's knowledge of and relationship to the person who had created the image. We also reminded the group that it was OK that each group member might have a very different experience of a painting and that this was not to negate someone else's view. In the verbal exploration of each image we needed to respect different views and that it was important to learn to evaluate and tolerate discrepancies and incongruent perceptions without losing one's own sense of the experience. Therefore, we invited the group to keep the focus upon each person's own experience of what had become visible and to relate it back to each person's own existential and ontological reality. In this way, the dialogical process that could unfold during the reflective phase through open-ended questions could propel the healing flow within an atmosphere of honesty and more authentic ways of being in the world.

The verbal reflections started slowly with Rosalyn volunteering to talk a bit about her experience. She remarked that it was interesting how, once she had started to create her painting, using Plasticine and paints, she had hardly been aware of the other group members' activities and the noises in the room. Rosalyn also shared some of the meaning that had arisen for her while she made this picture and she made reference to how this experience had been very different for her from the one in the previous session. She received feedback about her image and the questions that the yellow wall had raised for some of the group members. After Rosalyn had finished exploring her picture, Brenda volunteered to talk about her two images.

It was good to see that Brenda was taking responsibility for exploring her images with the group and not finishing this session, as she had done in the previous one, without having taken this opportunity. This was particularly important because Brenda had already realized how not processing her pictures with the group before leaving the group had negatively impacted on her in the past. Processing her images within today's session also allowed her to challenge some of her old patterns of being invisible and not taking up other people's time. Brenda began by sharing the following description with us:

> When I did this picture, Dad was supposed to be arrested within a few days. I was feeling pretty positive about it.
>
> On the top left-hand corner I drew a picture of the OPP [Ontario Provincial Police] cruiser. In it is an officer announcing on his radio that he's bringing "the bastard" in.
>
> Behind the car is the OPP detective arresting Dad and putting on handcuffs. Dad is furious and blushing with embarrassment at the same time. He's threatening to sue them. "It's all a big mistake. She's crazy." Mom is standing next to Dad crying and also blushing and furious with me. She also blames me and is worrying about herself.
>
> My sister is kneeling on the ground in front of the officer crying and begging him to let Dad go. She also blames me. She's angry with me and blushing too.
>
> Under the rainbow's cloud are rays of healing light shining over all the people who have come together to free us all from Dad's abuse and Mom's neglect. My other brother is standing under the rainbow, but he is not holding our hands. This is because I don't know if I want him in my life yet because he raped both my daughter and I. My feelings are very confused. I'm grateful he came forward to report his own abuse by Dad to support us, but I'm angry that he also abused us.

> Holding hands with me are all my other brothers and sisters and my daughter who supported me.
>
> Outside of the rainbow stands one of my other brothers, all alone. He doesn't know where he belongs. One minute he's telling the police about how Dad abused him; then he's wanting to retract it. He's scared and alone. The rays of healing light are reaching out to him so that he can hold onto them and join us when he's ready.
>
> When I did this picture, I was really surprised to see how much support is there for me if only I could learn to reach out and ask for it. I realize now I'm not so alone. It is up to me to change that.

After sharing this description of her first drawing with the group, Brenda again looked around the room to invite feedback before continuing to describe her second drawing. Rosalyn connected very much with this picture and she said that she imagined that it would be wonderful to have this kind of external validation and how this was so different from her own continuous struggle of trying to get her mother to believe and accept responsibility for what had happened to her and her brother. Rosalyn also wondered how it felt to know that her father was finally facing some legal action and, she hoped, consequences for what he had done to Brenda, her siblings, and Brenda's daughter. The group explored these views for some time and gave voice to their feelings, thoughts, and hopes in speaking about their experiences in a way that they felt believed and understood by each other. Brenda replied that to some degree it felt good to have had this kind of external validation and that there were finally some consequences to her father's actions but that this did not take away all the pain and damage her father's actions had done to her and her daughter's life. Brenda felt that this aspect of her experience was addressed more in her second picture.

> When I painted this picture, I started off by drawing a pretty, pink balloon in the sky. I have no idea why I did that. Then I painted a big tree with long branches. It started feeling familiar. Then I painted the sun with a happy face. Then some background sky and birds. Before I knew it, I was painting onto the string from the balloon.
>
> Down below the ground is covered in fire. My bed is standing in the fire. Mom is standing at the edge of the bed holding the flashlight over Dad. Dad is naked, laying on top of me, sodomizing me. However, I didn't paint myself in the bed.

> I realize that this painting illustrates my experience of leaving my body while Dad abused me. It was *so* painful and frightening that I used to leave my body and go up into the trees and play. It was so beautiful up there that I never wanted to come back. Every once in a while I would peek down to see if it was OK to come back. I could see the fire burning, so I'd go back up into the trees.
>
> Looking at this picture helped me realize that even though Dad thought he was "getting" me, he wasn't. I left my body and went to a better place. He just got an empty shell. I can see now how smart and creative I was to be able to escape into a safe place and be happy.
>
> I also was surprised to see that unintentionally I painted the branch right over my bed as if to help me get up into the tree to escape. That's exactly how I remember it happening. I climbed onto an old trunk and followed it up into the thick leaves.

I made the observation that Brenda had also painted a balloon in her first drawing and that she was using it here again but in a very different way. Brenda replied:

> This seemed to mean that the balloon (the light over my bed) was over my bed. At the time I drew this picture, I felt too much guilt and shame to have allowed myself to grab onto the balloon and escape from the hell. I see my last picture as progress because I pretty much drew the same scene (Dad sodomizing me in my bed with Mom standing there holding the flashlight) except that I kept myself out of the bed and I was holding onto the balloon in the tree.

Nina thought that some of the newer elements of this picture could perhaps indicate that Brenda had been able to let go of some of the guilt and shame since she had been working so hard to stop the cycle of abuse on a personal level through her therapy and on a community level by pressing charges against her father. This picture seemed to represent a shift from a more literal validation toward a more symbolic, emotional transformation. This was reflected in the overall more symbolic quality of this last painting where Brenda had unconsciously reframed the experience of her abuse. In this way, the lived experience that was represented in Brenda's pictures showed a trend toward the expansion of symbology that helped to process the painful memories and that opened her awareness and connectedness with her own creative, transformative power. Thus, the process of art toward healing was propelled by the dialogical image/word process and made visible through the continuous flow of images.

During this group exploration, Brenda had shared more about her work than in the previous sessions. It appeared as if the material that Brenda had worked on through the images in her earlier sessions was gradually coming together and that she was more open about sharing her process with the group. When Brenda had started the group, she had been very quiet and tended to let other group members go first when exploring the images. She had always been afraid about taking too much time away from other group members who perhaps needed it more than her. It was good to see her use the group discussions more to explore her own work, particularly because she was coming to the end of her stay in the program. It was also important to note that when Brenda had explored her pictures with the group in today's session, there was more of a confidence and openness in her voice than during her earlier sessions. She seemed to have transformed the initial image and come back to the same material as in her first picture but with a very different, embodied awareness.

Although many more questions were raised, it was by working with the images in an open-ended manner and by staying with the image-making process that the gradual transformation was able to take place. In this multi-modal dialogical process, nothing had changed yet everything had. Brenda's journey had begun and she was in the process of reclaiming a future for herself that was different from that of her past and from what she had learned from her parents' way of being in the world. What had been shared within the group had been affirming for all of us but what was most important was that she had been able to learn and embody a process that allowed her to harness her internal resources and creativity in order to deal with life's challenges. The group was able to share some of this transformative process with Brenda, and this experience, it was hoped, would stay with her through her images and memories in such a way that she could access this process after she left this therapeutic context.

Brenda thanked the group for listening again and then inquired about Sam's picture. Sam's earlier paintings had always evoked strong emotional reactions from the group. Their abstract and symbolic nature had usually generated many deep existential and ontological questions. Sam's journey over the past few sessions had changed from one of searching for the "truth" about his childhood abuse to dealing with issues of identity and self-understanding.

It reflected the gradual acceptance of his existential vulnerability and the dialogical image/word process between Sam and the group was able to unfold more freely once the group's concerns about his physical safety were addressed. Only after the group had been assured by Sam that he was not in any immediate danger of hurting himself were they able to explore the images on a more symbolic level. Once the potentially destructive forces were contained within the symbolic realm of the art materials, the dialogical process, with its creative energies, could unfold more freely and in a more integrated manner. The picture that he created in today's session was a portrait that was much more open than the previous ones. The group commented on this change and on Sam's overall more positive stance. Rosalyn and Cindy commented on how Sam and Brenda's work had given them the courage and the hope to work through their own pain.

Mary volunteered to go next. She shared with the group the two pictures that she had created during the session and talked a bit about how the image of the nightmare had gradually changed over the past few sessions and had become more and more like a depiction of her relationship with her brother when she was a child. To some degree, Mary attributed the quality of her current interpersonal relationships with her friends at the university and her difficulties with setting healthy boundaries to these early experiences. Mary's continuous fear of other people's rage and anger in response to her requests, needs, and wishes had been holding her back from making decisions that were the best for her. Even when dealing with small issues, she had always felt that it would be better to let friends walk all over her rather than risk their abandonment of her or their potential for angry outbursts. This had made it quite difficult for her to express her feelings and thoughts, which had also been visible to some degree in how she had interacted within the group.

Within the art therapy group and through the dialogical image/word process Mary was able to gain some understanding about these fears and to re-evaluate her interpersonal patterns within the safety of the group context. Mary's sharing of her images with the group allowed other group members to see her internal struggle and allowed her to look at interpersonal issues in a less threatening manner. The images provided a triangulation between Mary and the group where she could address her fears within the symbolic realm of the image-making process first before exploring them more directly with other group members. Rosalyn asked Mary if the way that she had interacted with her in the previous session had been an example of this pattern. With the help of the group and the pictures, both were able to clarify their experiences with each other. Through the dialogical image/word process, Mary was able to move to a different understanding of herself where she was able to address interpersonal issues more easily within the context of the group.

There was just enough time for briefly hearing from a few more group members before we would end today's session. Mary, who had been aware of Cindy's struggle during the experiential phase, invited Cindy to speak about her experience. Cindy said that it had been difficult for her to start using the materials and that she simply did not know where to begin. After having made the picture of the turkey she had come to the realization that most of her life she had been following someone else's dreams and wishes. Her family had treated her like a commodity or object that they felt that they could use to satisfy their own needs. This had led her to a place where she really had no idea who she was and what her needs were. Cindy said that all that she knew was that she did not want to be one of these turkeys. She said that at first she had a sense of an overwhelming sadness, which was followed by an intense anger. Cindy continued by saying that all these feelings had gradually faded into the background as she was playing in the sandbox and that she actually experienced a few moments of being at peace with herself while she was playing. She felt that this was rather ironic, given her initial response toward the sandbox and toys. Lois, who loved playing in the sandbox, asked: "Isn't that wonderful how this works?" And then Lois went back to playing in the sandbox while the group discussion continued on.

There was so much that the image-making process had generated and not all eight members had the same opportunity to explore their work at equal depth. However, we always had the possibility of coming back to the images in the following session. Not all group members had the same needs for verbal exploration and some appeared to have used the experiential part of the group more. Depending on the session, the patients' personality styles, and their needs for verbal feedback on the image-making process, the three different phases of the group could vary greatly in quality and length. Lois generally felt that the experiential phase was too short and she was not as interested in talking about her experience as others were. She tended to let other people speak while she would explore the toys and the sandbox but she was usually paying attention, even when she was playing in the sandbox, and every so often she would give some very good feedback to other group members and add great comments to the overall group discussions. However, when it came to exploring her own work she would be quite willing to let someone else talk about his or her images and experiences.

Although group members could benefit by sharing each other's pictures, it appeared that there were times when it was very important to acknowledge the images without directly verbally exploring each one by applying the same type of contemplative, dialogical process. This seemed particularly true of transitional images as their meaning shifted and needed to remain open for the non-verbal shift to occur. Quite often these images needed to be explored more through an experientially focused process until they reached maturity. Only at that point could the full shapes open up to more verbal articulations. I have found that pushing for meaning during this phase of the creative and transformative process could force the dialogical interplay too quickly into cognitive and verbal domains before the kinesthetic, emotional, and spiritual dimensions could become honored and assimilated. This shift into the cognitive, intellectual realm could potentially freeze up the healing flow if it did not include connections to the non-verbal and felt aspects of being. If this happened, there was a risk that this shift could not occur and thus the person would reinforce the traumatic experience and their sense of fragmentation into the incongruent verbal and non-verbal experiences that are so frequently associated with symptoms of Post Traumatic Stress Disorder.

Traumatic experiences tend to fragment the integration of one's being and one's connection to the world and oneself. If an individual did not have personal, cultural, and/or collective ways of transforming and metabolizing the traumatic experiences, there was a greater risk of the continuous flow of one's existential and ontological reality and being in the world being disrupted. In this way, an individual could easily become disconnected and trapped within the repertoire of the traumatic experiences. Culturally, there is a greater tendency to focus on the intellectual aspects and to perhaps ignore or split off from the other visceral, emotional, psychological, and spiritual domains of the victim's being, thus limiting his or her ability to access internal creative and transformative energies. Within the symbolic realm that is created in the art therapy group, these experiences could potentially be expressed, transformed, and integrated by allowing the dialogical process to unfold within the needed domains until it reached verbal, symbolic maturity. In this way, verbalizations and intellectual explanations could become attached without dominating and concretizing one's lived experience. Therefore, even if the images were not spoken about, they still were part of the dialogical image/word process. Thus, all images, whether they were verbally explored or not, had some effect upon the group dynamics as a whole and the healing flow.

Therefore, it was important to remember that the dialogical image/word process could take many different forms, depending on the individual's characteristics and needs. The healing flow could unfold through the different stages of creativity in many different ways. It was important to be sensitive to the situation in order to choose the therapeutic interventions that could help to propel the healing flow through verbal and non-verbal expressions in a way that it would not become stifled or released in uncontrollable externalizations without needed, reflective pauses. By choosing the interventions carefully, the therapist could help channel the expressions and promote opportunities for insight and processing of lived experiences in a more integrated manner. In Lois's situation, it appeared that she was at the stage of the creative process where she had a greater need to use the art materials rather than to explore her work verbally on an intellectual level.

However, it was very important for the therapist to be able to assess whether or not a group member was in a traumatic re-enactment or a place where he or she was not able to access the therapeutic opportunities offered during group. In Lois's case, I came to the decision, which was based on the work that I had seen her do in the previous sessions and the information that I had obtained from her clinical records and team meetings, that it was probably better at this point for Lois to process her existential and ontological issues more on an experiential level rather than be pushed to verbalize these experiences too quickly and in too great a depth before she was ready for them.

We had almost reached the end of our session and Lois, Nina, and Naomi still had not yet taken the opportunity to talk about their experiences and their images. Nina said that she did not need much time to talk about her pictures as she was simply playing with colors and shapes that at this point did not have much deeper meaning to her. The only thing that stood out for her and that resonated with some of the group themes was the issue of boundaries and balance. This issue was an ongoing struggle for her. Naomi said that she also did not have much to say about her painting besides that she really enjoyed the contemplative process and the peace of mind that it provided her. However, she would be quite happy to reflect upon the painting during the next session as she always found that she needed some distance from her work before she could meaningfully talk about it. Then Naomi looked at Lois, who was still playing in the sand, to invite her to speak about her pictures.

Lois looked at Naomi, then at the clock, and then at me with a question in her eyes, before saying, "I guess I should go next especially since I have not yet talked about my picture from the previous session." She continued by saying, "I'm really appreciating hearing the rest of you speak about your work, but as you all probably know I'd rather spend time playing in the sandbox or painting images than talking about them." Then Lois proceeded to comment briefly on her picture from the previous session and how it had been an experiment with colors that was a continuation of her earlier work of exploring a wider range of shades of colors to symbolically move away from her usual black and white approach to life. Through her pictures, she was also challenging her fear of being messy and allowing herself to be less organized and defended.

Lois said that the two paintings that she had made in today's session were also a reflection of these attempts and that the picture of the old woman walking along the road carrying all her garbage on her head represented to Lois her way of dealing with the world by habitually loading up and hanging on to things that only made her journey harder. Lois felt that she was getting to the point where she needed to let go of some of that stuff that she was carrying before she could go on with her life. Lois said that she was able to do this symbolically in her next painting where she had splashed black and gray paint on the page in a free and spontaneous manner. She said that making this second picture brought up a lot of intense feelings but that the overall process was a lot of fun. She continued by saying, "Perhaps this was the beginning of unpacking and reorganizing all this old crap." Naomi responded by saying, "Maybe you will find a pony in all this shit." The group laughed and I said that this might be a good time to stop as we had finished our time together and the group had moved to a point of saturation.

I looked around the room one last time, at the images on the wall, the sandbox, the group members, and the co-therapist. There was a sense of connectedness and completion and there was a sense that we could now let go of what had been unearthed during the group. There was a felt sense that although much more could have been said or done, it was time to end the therapy session and to leave the images behind in their safe place.

The co-therapist and I thanked the group for their honesty and willingness to do this very difficult work and urged them to symbolically leave what had emerged during the group within the containment of this room. In this way, they could carry with them the internalized process but not the content of the trauma-related material that might have emerged in their images. We reminded the group to focus on leisure and other relaxing activities that the program had to offer in the evenings to balance out some of the intense therapeutic work that they had done during this group and to embrace playful and different ways of being in the world.

As group members were leaving the room, each one of them was in some way entrusting his or her work for safe keeping to us until the next session. The art therapy room, the images, and the relationships that had formed within the group had symbolically created a container in which material could be left behind but simultaneously it provided a possibility of carrying the internalized experiences of the dialogical image/word process and the healing flow forward into their life outside this container.

CHAPTER 10

Transition Phase and Closing Ritual as a Container of the Healing Flow

After the group ended, the co-therapist and myself were usually also going through a transition phase where we shifted our focus from facilitating the group therapy process toward reflecting more on our own experiences of the group as therapists and human beings. Although this phase did not involve patients directly, it was as important as all the phases described in the previous quilt patch. In this phase of facilitating the group process, I had found it to be important, even if it was just in a small way, to acknowledge how the group and each member's images had impacted on my own being. With our busy, patient-focused schedules, it was easy to skip over this part and to give it only superficial attention. However, over time I had found that this would affect my own well-being and ability as a therapist to facilitate the dialogical image/word process within the group. During this phase, it was not the amount of time but the quality and depth of reflection that took place on an intellectual, emotional, psychological, existential, and ontological level that was important.

During this phase, I was able to acknowledge and wonder in awe at the trust and the strength that had been put forward by the group members; a trust in each other and in the therapists' ability to guide and hold the many feelings, thoughts, and experiences of their worlds. It was a time to remind myself that this was a very special trust and to be aware of how I responded to these entrustments of their experiences that the group members had put forward through their images and dialogue. It was important for me to acknowledge how I had been able to embrace and work with this material on an emotional, psychological, existential, and ontological level. In order to do this, I needed to also engage in the dialogical image/word process by using the art materials in order to process, integrate, and transcend some of these experiences in a more integrated manner.

The process of earning and maintaining the trust and respect that are so essential to building a therapeutic relationship was not easy at times. In order to facilitate the healing flow through the dialogical image/word approach to art therapy, a well-balanced therapeutic container was essential. It needed to be a situation where relationships could evolve and the group would be able to move forward through the different stages of creativity. The way the individual group members entrusted their images to our care echoed this trust on a symbolic level and happened, in part, because of our professional role as "psychotherapists." This role endowed us with power and an image that, for the most part, allowed the group members to take chances that they would not have been able to do outside of this context.

The trust that was bestowed by the patients in each therapist and subsequently in the group process was on the one hand remarkable, as it came from people who had been, for the most part, badly abused by other human beings. However, it also spoke of their desperate need for hope and for different and more satisfying ways of being in the world. This trust spoke of the human need to connect with other human beings in spite of negative and painful experiences. It is this intrinsic human need that makes group therapy so effective, but it also makes each group member particularly vulnerable to different types of traumatic re-enactments. Because of the power that has been bestowed on the therapist by the patients, the therapist is also at risk of being pulled into these traumatic re-enactments.

If the therapist is not well grounded and self-aware of his or her own existential and ontological responses, this could potentially lead the therapeutic process to go astray and the therapist unconsciously could be pulled into traumatic re-enactments where he or she could potentially misuse this trust. Therefore, the reflective pause described in this section illustrates the importance of the parallel between the therapist's own engagement with the dialogical image/word process in order to deal with the materials brought up in him or her during the group sessions and how this process appears to work for the patients. In this way, the therapist and the patients can use a similar process in order to deal with their own existential and ontological issues in a more integrated, creative, and healthy manner. Although this section will focus more on the patient's images and their work, it will also illustrate the therapist's engagement with these images and make visible some of the therapist's internal processes related to what is presented in this Interpretative Quilt.

I mentioned in earlier chapters how the exploration of the parallel process between the patients and the clinical staff was an important tool for maintaining a therapeutic milieu. This was particularly important when working with victims of trauma, as the images and materials that were expressed through the dialogical image/word process within this population could, at times, evoke strong feelings of existential and ontological uncertainties in the clinical staff. Therefore, what I would like to note again here is that there are many parallels in how the dialogical image/word process can function for the patients as well as for the therapist. Thus, by exploring the process through the patients' work, one is also able to gain insights into how this process could work for others, including the therapist. For the therapist, these explorations of the dialogical process took place outside of the group context and, to some degree, through the therapist's own engagement with the dialogical image/word process as well as through discussions with other team members.

I would like to stress the importance of this part of facilitating the healing flow. It requires that I be knowledgeable and trusting of the process within myself before I can hope to facilitate it in others. I explored some aspects of this reflective process in earlier chapters where I discussed the development of the dialogical image/word approach and the program parameters. In this part of the quilt patch I would like to still keep the focus more on the patients' work and on the facilitation of the group process. Thus, the preparation for and the running of the group, as well as the reflective pause at the end of the sessions, were all important aspects of creating a healthy therapeutic container that was conducive to the unfolding of the healing flow. All the subtleties involved in creating this therapeutic container became a kind of ritual. I use the word "ritual" instead of "routine" to refer to our activity because there was a consciousness and awareness that was put forward in these daily routines that is not usually associated with other habitual activities. In this way, this transition phase or renewal ritual was much more akin to the meaning of ritual as summarized in the following quotation:

> Ritual ushers us into a welcome and comforting rhythm of thoughts and activities. It unclutters our minds by providing structure and boundaries during times of change. The order imposed by meaningful ritual allows us to reflect our values and convey messages to self and the community about who we are and what we are experiencing. Ritual helps us face together those things that are too painful, confusing, or awesome to face alone. Because rituals both come from and create dreams, they encourage the deeper wisdom coming from these visionary levels. (Achterberg, Dossey and Kolkmeier, 1994, p.19)

During this reflective phase or ritual, we were able to fill out the group notes, share our concerns and speculations, and reflect upon the group process as a whole. After the group members had left the studio, we had a chance to experience the images somewhat outside of the therapeutic relationship in which they were created. During this time, we were also able to engage in our own dialogical image/word process with the images and were able to gain different perspectives as well as process our own experiences in a way that would allow us to reconnect with our own way of being in the world. Depending on how the group had gone, we perhaps would comment on our experiences on a more personal level and reflect upon our own feelings, thoughts, and associations. Usually, most of the paintings were still wet at the end of the session and we would hang them up carefully in the storage room where they could dry in a safe and confidential space until we needed them again. The activities of this reflective pause became a form of ritual that helped to connect us with the ebb and flow of the group's development and also helped us to make the transition back to our other responsibilities and to reconnect to the pulse of the larger community.

Over the years it became more and more clear to me that some of the material that the patients brought into my world through their interactions with me changed my way of seeing and being in the world. I became very sensitive to when I was not able to acknowledge and process these experiences in an active and integrated manner and how they could go underground and affect me negatively in many different domains. I was able to observe how my sense of well-being and my ability to spontaneously, creatively, and constructively interact with the world around me was affected if I did not take the time to engage in my own dialogical image/word process in order to keep the healing flow at a healthy level within my own being. Therefore, it was important for me to process the group therapy sessions on many levels that also included the non-verbal aspects of my own being. It seems to be almost impossible to install hope in the face of great despair if one is not rooted deeply within one's own existential and ontological reality in an integrated manner. Just as the patients were, I was also at constant risk of splitting off and separating from material that was unacceptable or emotionally difficult and of pushing it underground through intellectualizations and a false sense of professionalism. Thus, to trust and effectively facilitate the healing flow in others, I needed to be deeply rooted in it through my own continuous engagement with this process.

As I have explored extensively earlier, the therapist's/researcher's active participation with the dialogical image/word process and his or her experience with the healing flow were essential in maintaining an integrated approach to research and therapy. In this way, this at times invisible or taken for granted aspect of facilitating the healing flow could be acknowledged and brought to awareness here. Therefore, the reflective pause that is described in this section is there to create a bridge between the patients' experiences, which were explored in the previous chapter, and the therapist's/researcher's experience of this very same process. The content may be very different but the process is not dissimilar.

This reflective process or ritual was particularly important and appeared to be more visible when working psychotherapeutically with victims of trauma. The images that had been created during these groups could leave residues in one's being and touch one's life potentially in a way that to some degree paralleled the patient's experience of the world. As one attempts to help and facilitate the dialogical image/word process in others, there will undoubtedly be times when one will experience similar feelings of hopelessness, fear, terror, and intense sadness. It is essential to acknowledge and work with these feelings outside the context of the therapy session as they otherwise could negatively affect one's functioning as a therapist and a human being.

During an art therapy session there were many non-verbal, powerful messages communicated that one needed to be sensitive to. If one was not aware of the impact of these experiences upon one's being, the effects could very easily go underground and take on a life of their own. However, through one's engagement in the dialogical image/word process and one's own reflective phase, these experiences could be worked at on many levels and brought to the surface where they could be integrated and transformed. Thus, as already mentioned above, patients' work could parallel that of the therapist and could give insights into how the therapist could maintain and facilitate the healing flow within the art therapy group.

The images that were created during the art therapy group, such as Brenda's, Mary's, or any of the other works described in the previous sections, offer me a constant reminder that as a human being I must also accept my own existential and ontological vulnerabilities and insecurities. The images that I witness during the art therapy sessions may be, for the most part, out of the realm of my own personal, lived experience but on a deeper level they still impact my awareness of human potential and a collective existential and ontological reality. By constantly recognizing and examining my own reactions on a somatic, visceral, emotional, psychological, intellectual, and spiritual level I am able to examine my transference and counter-transference reactions in a more integrative and constructive manner. This allows me to examine my experiences of the groups and the images in a way that allows me to facilitate the process of art toward healing more effectively in others.

The awareness that I gain through my own reflective rituals provides a pause that allows me to utilize the dialogical image/word process more effectively. Over time, this reflective phase gave rise to a dialogical practice that allowed for the processing of the material that was generated during the groups in a more integrated manner. The knowledge and insights gained from this reflective pause allowed me to bring important elements of the non-verbal domain into the verbal realm where they then could be shared and worked with on a more conscious level. In this way, I was more likely to be able to bring a more holistic perspective to the patients' work and to share it with the clinical team. This reflective pause also allowed me to work with my co-therapist and with other team members within the domain that they were more familiar with and to then be able to use them as a resource in processing different internal residues such as various transference and counter-transference issues. This was particularly important in order not to become drawn into different types of traumatic re-enactments. Thus, the therapeutic work related to conducting an art therapy group does not end when the patients leave the studio but continues on many levels.

My awareness of this important aspect of facilitating the process of art in others was to a great degree embedded in my own reflective pause. During times when I had not been able to engage in this reflective pause due to other commitments, I became particularly aware of how important this ritual was. During those times, I noticed how residues would build up in my body, mind, and soul, which affected my ability to access the creative process. In the literature this has been referred to as secondary post-traumatic stress or burnout (Figley 1995; Grosch and Olsen 1994; Hudnall Stamm 1995; Schaufeli and Enzmann 1998; Skovholt 2001). However, for me it speaks of the importance of living and practicing therapy in an integrated manner where the mind, body, and soul are nurtured and rejuvenated through different daily activities or rituals.

Before describing the transition phase and as part of the interpretative stitching, I would like to make a brief reference again to the general group parameters as they affected both the unfolding of the dialogical image/word approach and the transition phase described in this section. Patients usually stayed in the group either for four, six, or eight sessions. The nature of the group dynamics changed constantly, with patients starting or leaving the group on a weekly basis. Co-leadership was also alternating regularly. As already described in earlier chapters, the group mix and the therapeutic container were in a constant state of flux and depended on the patient community and other aspects of the overall program. In spite of this fluctuation that was dependent upon many factors described in earlier chapters, the depiction of the group presented in this Interpretative Quilt does convey some of the general dynamics and themes of the art therapy group and the process of art toward healing as a whole.

The fictional art therapy session that was described in previous quilt patches did not include a transition ritual *per se* and usually a group where a number of group members were finishing was somewhat qualitatively different from the one described above. However, since this phase was an important aspect of the group process, this transition phase and the closure ritual are described in more detail in the following text. The individual journeys that were explored in previous chapters, as well as the imagistic pauses in other parts of this book, in some sense provide an opportunity for the reader to view the images again from the perspective of this transition phase. In this way these images can further give a sense of the overall healing flow. Thus, by looking at all the pictures together as they were presented in the different imagistic pauses, some essential features of this process can be communicated and can also provide a transition for the reader. In both, one is able to gain a sense of how one's experience of these images has changed from when one first encountered them within the different quilt patches, as the experience can change depending on the context in which the materials are examined. This gives the reader an opportunity to engage in his or her own dialogical process with these images and to gain a sense of how this transition ritual could function holistically on an experiential level.

During a patient's last session and as part of this transition phase, it was customary that group members would reflect upon all the work that the individual had created during the group. In this quilt patch, the reader is also invited to reflect on the descriptions that have been presented so far through this discussion of the transition phase. In this way, the reader, similarly to the patient who is moving through this phase, is able to experience a different kind of processing of the material presented in the different quilt patches. As part of this transition phase, patients share their images with the group in order to process their experience further. This parallels the overall goal of this section which is to provide an opportunity for the reader to process his or her experience of the different quilt patches and the imagistic pauses in a different light through the following text and images.

The individual patient's journey with the image-making process, as well as the descriptions of the different phases of the art therapy session that were explored in the previous chapter, were based on a model situation where the group mix and the dynamics were such that the dialogical image/word process and the healing flow could be made more visible without too many distractions or any extraneous noise. Thus, within this fictional art therapy session, a more rounded perspective was provided with a balanced group mix where some group members had just started the group, some members were in the middle of their process, and others were almost ready to do closure from the group after six or eight sessions. In this way, a sense of the different stages of creativity and the healing flow can be given in a clearer manner.

Over the years, the review of the images of the patients who were leaving the group became the transition or closure ritual that is described in this quilt patch in more detail. This ritual helped patients to say goodbye to the group, helped to instill hope in new group members about the process of art toward healing, and was a way to acknowledge the work that the individual had accomplished as it was externalized through the person's images. It also prepared the patients to take their artwork outside of the protective, therapeutic context in which the images had been created and in which the images had taken on so many different, symbolic meanings.

There were many variations in how this ritual could unfold, depending on the individual's and the group's needs as well as their abilities. However, the essential features and functioning appeared to be similar in that it was a way to help patients to make the transition from the group and to acknowledge the work that they had done during their stay. There usually were group members leaving the group every week or at least every second week. Depending upon the group as a whole, during this transition phase it was not unusual for one, four, six, or even, on rare occasions, eight group members to leave the group at the same time. The individual closure rituals looked very different depending upon the number of group members leaving, the amount of work that they had generated, and the connections they had formed to the group. Thus, the rituals were formed by many factors and the group therapist needed to be conscious of individual needs, time constraints, and group needs in order to help guide the process of the unfolding of the transition phase.

This transition ritual usually included the sharing of all images a patient had created during his or her stay in the group. It was typically left up to the individual patient to decide how they would like to end their journey with the group and most of them chose to share their images by hanging them up on the wall, either at the beginning or at the end of the therapy session. By looking at all the paintings at the same time, the patient was able to see what the pictures evoked for him or her now and what kind of resonances the pictures set off. This gave individuals an opportunity to experience the images again within a slightly different context and frame of mind. In this review, they could explore through the dialogical process how much power the various pictures still had over them on a symbolic level and how closely they were still framed within their lived experiences of the world. It also allowed the patients to assess how these images could be useful for them in the future. Before the individual left the group, this phase provided an important portal into gaining insights about the experience of creating these images and the meaning that these works had for the individual now, as he or she looked at them again with the knowledge of this being his or her last group session. In this way, the transition phase was an important aspect of the dialogical image/word process and the Healing-Flow Model of art therapy.

Many times, the transition ritual was also shaped and influenced by numerous complex factors, which have been, in part, already qualitatively represented in the earlier quilt patches and in the fictional art therapy session. Factors such as group size, the group mix, the commitment and honesty that each group member brought to the interactions, as well as how well the individuals had bonded with each other, all contributed to the quality of this transition phase. Thus, the number of patients that were finishing the group, the number of sessions that each group member had had, as well as the amount of images that each member had created, all affected the nature of the transition phase and the different closure rituals.

If patients had been in the group for only four sessions, their works tended to be fresher in everyone's mind and, for the most part, the review tended to be less content focused. However, those members who had been in the group for eight sessions, as in Mary's case, tended to explain their earlier works in more detail so that the newer members could understand them better. However, it was usually those early works that were experienced very differently during this final stage of a person's journey with the healing flow and this provided a new opportunity for reflecting on older and already transcended materials. The individual's needs and ability to listen and reflect on the images, as well as his or her ability for being actively engaged in the image-making process, further shaped how this phase could unfold. Other factors were the content of the material represented in the images, the quality of the iconographic expressions, and the overall quality of the relationships between the patient, the paintings, and the group as a whole.

In general, this transition ritual was more a process of acknowledgment than an in-depth analysis. It was a pause, a rest from activity, and a time of quiet reflection and contemplation. This phase involved a witnessing within a social context of that which had taken form through the images. It was an honoring of what had been brought to light through the coagulated external forms of the healing flow in the form of the images. The external record was there irrevocably in front of us offering an opportunity to connect through the material form of the images with that which was hidden deep within us. In this ritual, there was no room for critiquing the images according to their formal design and techniques, as is more customary during formal art training. Shapes, colors, and forms were allowed to flow freely and this enabled associations to emerge through the dialogical image/word process.

During the reflective pauses of the transition rituals, there were no right or wrong ways of expressing one's perceptions and there were no right or wrong answers. Some interpretations would increase the flow of associations while others narrowed them down more to specific meanings. Some explorations would take place mainly in the intellectual realm while others took place more on an emotional, psychological, or spiritual level. All of these explorations were part of an integrated approach and the process of art toward healing. It was the role of the therapist to help guide and focus this exploration and to shape the dialogical process of this transition phase along a trajectory that helped individuals to gain a sense of completion without closing the door on a process that, for the most part, had just begun. To help modulate the individual and group practice so that the different dimensions of being were kept within the parameters of the individual's and the group's physical, psychological, emotional, and spiritual capacity, the therapist needed to be cognizant of personal and collective possibilities and limitations.

In spite of this free manner of exploring the images, there was much honesty and deep connections were formed between the images and the group members. It was also interesting to observe that although the goal of making these images was self-exploration and understanding and not to create aesthetically pleasing works, most of the paintings appeared to have their own internal balance and a sense of completion. When viewing the different works of the group members who were doing closure within the group, one almost had the sense that the images had unfolded from one to the next following some invisible yet very clearly present script or trajectory that only became visible when viewing all the works together. Quite frequently the images seemed to complete a circle and tended to loop back upon themselves as they returned to their origin with a different sensibility.

Sam, Mary, and Brenda's journeys all embodied some element of this phenomenon where between the first and the last picture some important changes had taken place on an unconscious level. Through the dialogical image/word process, each image and each reflection appeared to have slowly shaped and made visible this script. Although these changes were not always evident to our intellect, the way we resonated with these works brought us closer to understanding our way of being in the world in a more integrated manner. "The work of art serves as an optical instrument in which one comes to see the unexpressed or unrecognised depth of oneself" (West, 1993, p.5). In this reflective space, no one had exclusive authority over what had been externalized on paper and with each viewing we all learned something new about ourselves and each other. In spite of this aspect of the dialogical process that allowed everyone to benefit from the transition ritual, the focus was more on the patients who were leaving the group. Thus, within this final reflection, it was important for everyone to honor the person's experience of his or her journey as well as to give feedback in a way that was cognizant of the group members who were leaving.

Within this general framework, the format of the transition ritual described so far then took on some unique dimensions that were more characteristic of the individual patient. For example, some patients chose to share their images at the beginning of the session because they could then draw upon this experience to create some new works that would specifically embody what they had discovered in their healing journey. They would then make this last piece of work part of their transition ritual. Other patients felt that it was more important for them to paint another image before they reviewed their pictures with the group, so that this last work could embody more their unconscious and intuitive experience of the process of art toward healing that they had moved through. In general, most patients chose the latter as, for the most part, it was more reflective of the overall group structure to which most of the members had become accustomed and it allowed the translation of their experiences into the verbal realm through the dialogical process, thus allowing them to gain more of a sense of closure.

It also has been my experience that some patients emphasized the verbal, dialogical dimension, while others preferred to use this phase as an opportunity to share their understanding and perceptions of their images and the process as they remembered it. On some level, Sam, Mary, and the other journeys described in the previous quilt patches reflect this dimension and show some of the variations in the individual styles. In this way, the healing flow, as externalized in the images, could show the process of art toward healing and how the images had evolved over time. This helped the individual to create a transition between the therapy context and the community at large. This transition helped the patient to become more aware of the healing flow as it became externalized in his or her images, to summarize some of the earlier themes, and to see the images within a new context that might set up new resonances. The actual paintings gave them an opportunity to take this experience and to physically carry it forward into their life outside of this therapeutic context. This helped them to move this embodied knowledge beyond the boundaries of the art therapy group.

Often, when all the images were up on the walls, they tended to be experienced very differently from when they were looked at individually. This was a good time for the person leaving the group to find out how the images resonated within the person's being, what tender spots they still touched, and how it felt to hear or speak about others' responses to them. This process was slightly different for Mary, Sam, Naomi, or any of the other members described in the fictional art therapy session. The healing flow and the dialogical process needed to be guided in different directions depending on the individual's needs, habitual ways of being in the world, ability to connect with the creative energies, and ability to move through the different phases in an integrated manner. As has been made visible in the fictional art therapy session, the interactions and focus would be different and responsive to the different individual group members as well as to the group as a whole. During this closure phase, the therapist's role would be similar to the way it was represented in the previous quilt patches, with the exception that the focus would be more on seeing how much the different images still had power over the individual and on recognizing what would be the best way to work with this power on a symbolic level to make this ritual meaningful and helpful. Thus, the focus during this transition phase was on allowing the patients, for the last time, to reflect experientially on how they felt about their images before taking them outside of the therapy context and to stimulate a contemplative process about how they might use them in the future.

As was already made visible to some degree in the previous quilt patches, the sharing of images could have a powerful impact on everyone in the group. Therefore, there was also a small risk that during this transitional phase some of the images and material shared could bring forth difficult feelings, thoughts, and memories too quickly. In this case, the therapist needed to shift the focus in order to help modulate the experience in an integrated manner and to facilitate a more embodied understanding. In this way, these feelings could be worked with and contained in such a way that the individuals who were leaving the group had an opportunity to get a sense of closure and completion of their process.

Over the many years that I have been facilitating this process through the dialogical image/word approach and the metaphor of the healing flow, more often than not the overall experience of reviewing the paintings as part of this transition phase was a positive and empowering part of the process of art toward healing. I have also observed that this phase gave the people who were leaving the group an opportunity to acknowledge their work with other group members in a meaningful manner that allowed them to carry this experience forward and allowed the newer group members to get a sense of what the healing flow could offer. In this way, this transition phase brought closure to the experience of integrating diverse conscious and unconscious material within the self and within others through utilizing the creative energies.

This closure ritual, in many cases, marked the last phase of the creative process, which was colored by the individual's style of working, the number of works that he or she had created, and the relationships that the individual had formed within the group. This last phase allowed a space for split-off aspects to emerge and to reach fuller consciousness through the themes that had become visible when seeing all the work together. In this way, the patient could discover during this review the "unthought known" (Bollas, 1987) and bring internal balance to the energy flow of the once entrapped and frozen aspects of his or her being. Images that once made the patient feel helpless and small were now reclaimed, reshaped, and transformed through the process of art toward healing; forgotten and disassociated memories and images of the past that had symbolically been transformed through the physical engagement with the art materials and the group reflections could now be let go of. In the here-and-now context of the group, images could be reshaped over and over again until power over that which had once controlled so many aspects of the individual's life was restored. In this way, this last reflection made it clearer to the individual patient what they would need to do with some of the pictures that they had created and that had become important transitional objects.

CHAPTER 11

Interpretative Border
The Process of Art Toward Healing in Psychotherapy

In the previous quilt patches I focused on describing the surface level of different patients' experiences with the process of art toward healing by looking at what was most easily visible to my own and others' immediate observations. Using the material presented in the previous quilt patches, my aim for the interpretative border of this section is to look underneath this surface and to move more into the interpretative realm. In this interpretative border I will make my experience with the image-making process more visible by referring to my own work as a therapist, researcher, and artist. Through the interpretative stitching this border will attempt to show how these experiences have been guided by the dialogical image/word approach and the conceptual metaphor of the Healing-Flow Model. In this way, the metaphor of the Healing-Flow Model will once again guide these interpretations and give voice to some of the dynamics and experiences that appeared to have propelled the process of art toward healing within the specific clinical context described earlier.

The following section will explore some of the themes and findings of what has become comprehended in this work using an integrated approach that includes my perspective as the therapist, researcher, and artist in a multi-modal manner. These reflections will be looking at the material presented in the different quilt patches by first exploring the material from the perspective of the therapist, then of the researcher, and finally of the artist.

These different strains of thought will be interwoven into this interpretative border through images and text. In this way, I will summarize the findings of this work into predominant themes and essential aspects of the process of art toward healing within the clinical context described earlier.

The manner in which these reflections are interwoven through the dialogical image/word process will further illustrate how this approach can be used as a therapeutic approach and as a research methodology and will show how this expands its use beyond the narrow confines of what has been named the "Arts." This expanded use allows the healing flow to enter into a broader range of human experience and activities. The interpretative border that is created in this manner will include graphic depictions of the emerging themes, their dynamics, and their overall part/whole relationship to the other elements.

Therapist's Reflections on the Dialogical Image/Word Approach to Art Therapy

The many changing factors or forces that surrounded the process of art toward healing over the years that I have worked with it have provided an opportunity to observe the phenomena in a way that has made the essential components of the process more visible. From the analysis of the patients' feedback forms as well as from my and the co-therapist's observations the following aspects of facilitating the healing flow using the dialogical image/word approach within an art therapy group setting were distilled and will be discussed:

- Cultural factors
- The creative process and the role of the voluntary treatment inpatient program
- The therapeutic container
- Number of sessions and group size
- Group dynamic and the dialogical image/word process.

Cultural Factors

Another factor that appeared to be culturally supported was the belief that artistic activities and creativity tended to be done only by a few individuals who were seen by others as possessing unique abilities that most other people did not seem to have. Within this view, creativity was attributed mainly to a few artists and was generally not seen as part of most people's everyday activities. Unfortunately, this view puts the arts into a special category in which the dialogical process between the artist, the image, and the other viewers is stifled and potentially dissociated from other aspects of life. In this way, art is turned into objects rather than being seen as a life-giving process and an essential aspect of being. Thus, one of the most powerful, transformative activities has potentially been rendered impotent and is at risk of disappearing into the empty space that exists in a society that is oriented toward continuous consumption rather than toward creativity and artistic expression.

Within this society, the dialogical process described here has become disembodied and dissociated as the arts are seen as producing only products and entertainment. Within this cultural view, which was discussed in the first chapter, the arts provide entertainment and the sciences provide truth and knowledge, although the endless products of the entertainment industry have a huge impact on how we see and experience the world. However, on a conscious level, we like to believe that our lives are predominantly guided by the knowledge and power of the sciences. In this way, we culturally perpetuate this split between different ways of knowing and the unequal power relationship between the truths discovered by the arts and the ones discovered by the sciences. Because of this, we are at great risk of discounting the truths that we know on an unconscious level but that on a conscious level we view as simply entertainment. At the same time we put the sciences on a pedestal where they are also likely to become dissociated and impotent in their own way.

In the therapy programs, it appeared that the more opportunities individuals had to experience this process within the supportive context of the art therapy group the more they would be likely to be able to connect with it and use it in their healing journey in the future. The patients who were receiving only four sessions within a context of a larger group (8–10 group members) appeared to find it more difficult to enter into the process and they tended to gain only glimpses of the process of art toward healing. In some cases, these brief experiences did not allow the individuals enough time to learn to trust and to honor this new experience within themselves. Yet there was some evidence that individuals had still built up some receptivity and awareness toward the process of art toward healing and appeared more likely to seek it out in the future.

Within the therapeutic milieu and the context of the art therapy group, these cultural factors did, to some degree, contribute to how the individual group members were able to enter into the image-making process. Within the microcosm of the art therapy group, these factors could have potentially created many obstacles for individuals engaged in the process of art toward healing. However, within the therapeutic milieu and within the context of the art therapy groups, this issue was overcome relatively quickly by using an integrated approach and it presented a very small barrier that most patients could usually overcome within the first few sessions. Another reason that may have helped patients to enter into the process more quickly was the fact that individuals had chosen to come into this therapeutic context at a time when they were ready for change and for new opportunities. During the art therapy group, individuals gradually were able to let go of these culturally directed notions. Within the therapy context, patients tended to rediscover their own creative energy and the power of sharing images through a continuous dialogical process that opened connections between the self and the world and that was transformative in nature. As individuals started expressing themselves more freely, they were able to discover their own voice and their way of reconnecting with the world in a more meaningful manner.

The Creative Process and the Role of Voluntary Treatment

An important aspect of this clinical context, as already mentioned, was that the individuals participating in the art therapy groups were entering the treatment program and the art therapy groups on a voluntary basis. Most of the patients had entered the treatment programs in order to alleviate some kind of psychological, existential, and/or spiritual suffering. As already described earlier, patients entered the programs with various degrees of readiness in their ability to gain awareness and insights into their suffering as well as their readiness for making changes in their life. While being in the unique and different environment that the treatment programs provided, the patients were given different educational and experiential opportunities to re-evaluate and modify their habitual ways of being in the world. In this way a pause or opening was created away from their usual life's patterns and they were temporarily freed from their normal responsibilities and the demands of their life circumstances. This all appeared to enhance factors for change.

Within the therapeutic milieu, there appeared to be less of a need for individuals to have their defenses up and they tended to be freer to try and experiment with different ways of being in the world. This freedom provided many opportunities to challenge and to give up old maladaptive patterns and to find creative and more adaptive ways of being in the world. It also provided many opportunities and processes that patients had been able to learn from and to internalize throughout their stay in the programs. Therefore, individual patients who were participating in the various clinical programs were able to enter into the process of art toward healing differently than perhaps individuals in other situations might have.

It was not uncommon that patients who had come into the programs had reached a point in their lives where they were willing to enter into a therapeutic adventure in order to make changes in many important areas of their lives. Although the patient population were, in general, not in an active crisis when entering the clinical programs, many of them had been in enough psychological, existential, and spiritual pain that they had at one point or another either contemplated or attempted to end their lives. Also, many of the patients had long-term, chronic problems related to symptoms of depression, anxiety, an eating disorder, and/or a Post Traumatic Stress Disorder. The pause and sanctuary provided by the therapeutic milieu had opened up a space in which individuals could learn to recover from their suffering. The tragic experiences that many of the patients had had during their lives and which had impacted on them and their families in so many ways were now open to being worked with and transformed within the receptive space of the sanctuary. Thus, within the safety of the therapeutic milieu and the art therapy group, patients were able to rediscover their authentic way of being in the world. The dialogical image/word approach taught them how to access their experiences, express them, and transcend the past negative influences through engaging with the healing flow in order to learn to utilize their own creativity and to apply it to their lives in a very real and concrete manner.

The Therapeutic Container

Another important aspect that influenced the creative process and affected how much members were able to get in touch with and learn about the process of art toward healing was how safe and supportive they perceived their environment to be. The images created in group therapy reflected the internal and for the most part external world of the individual and they, at the same time, were saturated with the themes of the therapeutic context in which they were made. Therefore, in a sense, the images created within the context of the group were also empowered by the relationship with the group. Although, on one level, the images generated within the group belonged to the individual who had created them, they symbolically carried with them elements of the group as a whole and of the multi-leveled dialogical process that had unfolded.

As part of creating and maintaining the therapeutic container safety, confidentiality, and symbolic refuge were essential. Images generated within the therapeutic relationship of the group in a way became part of the group as well as of the person who had created them. For this reason, it was the general practice that group members would keep the images that they had formed during the sessions in the art therapy storage room until they had finished the art therapy group. This created a symbolic and literal place where material could emerge through the symbolic realm of the image-making process within the contained boundaries of the group. In this way, whatever was generated within the group would temporarily stay within the container. This practice allowed individuals to not have to worry about what to do with their images after each session and to symbolically leave behind whatever had come up for them during the session. In this way individuals could establish their own relationship to the images within the safety of the group before exposing themselves and their work to more unpredictable, outside influences.

The person who decided to take his or her images symbolically carried a piece of the group with him or her. It was the individual group members who took ownership over their creations in this way who appeared to have learned to value the images for the meanings that they were able to discover through the dialogical image/word process. In these cases, it became clear that the symbolic realm of the images had allowed the patients to be able to find their own voice and creativity within the greater part/whole relationship of being. Therefore, all the work that a person had created in art therapy was seen as belonging to that individual, in spite of the fact that on a symbolic level the images embodied the part/whole relationship of the individual and the social context of the group. This was important so that the images could become transitional objects that would allow the process to continue beyond the context of the art therapy group.

The reason why patients were strongly encouraged to leave their images within the art therapy storage room while they were in the group was that this was another way of giving the image some special power as a transitional object while at the same time further strengthening the function of the therapeutic container. In this way, the images and the material generated through the dialogical image/word process could be contained and channeled. Being in the therapeutic container allowed the material to reach greater maturity. The availability of their images and the knowledge that the images were in a safe place appeared to facilitate the healing flow. Within this container, as already shown in the Interpretative Quilt, the images could be accessed at any time during therapy sessions and could be processed through dialogical explorations with the group and the materials. This seemed to help with the containment, confidentiality, and closure on the therapy sessions.

The therapeutic container also greatly facilitated the learning and embodying of the creative process by reducing possible interferences from unpredictable factors that could arise from outside the therapy group before the individuals were ready for them. If individual group members took their images outside the therapeutic atmosphere, before they had internalized their experience with the creative process through practice with the dialogical image/word process, they could potentially put themselves at risk and make themselves vulnerable to negative environmental influences. This, in turn, could affect the individual's as well as the group's process. However, there might be times when it could be important for an individual to take an image outside the art therapy context before he or she had reached the closure phase and this was generally explored with the therapist to evaluate the different risks and benefits of this action.

Within the boundaries of the therapy groups, we could generate some of the conditions that Nachmanovitch (1990) had described as the ideal dialogical relationship between artist, image, and audience. "Ideally, artist and audience are close, interresponsive, accessible to each other's minds and hearts" (p.178). These conditions could, it was hoped, be discovered within the context of the art therapy group so that they could be recognized and carried forward outside of this context. Therefore, the way the images were treated and the way they were stored were important aspects of the therapeutic container that allowed for guidance and development of the process of art toward healing that was described in earlier chapters.

Number of Sessions and Group Size

The number of sessions and the group size also seemed to have a great impact on how an individual could utilize the process of art toward healing. Most of the group members had never experienced art therapy before and many of them tended to come into the group with great apprehension about not being able to draw or paint. Also, many patients had had bad experiences during their school years, which had reinforced the notion that they were not creative and had no artistic talent. However, as they attended the art therapy sessions, they gradually got in touch with their creativity and were able to let go of these notions. In general, it seemed that if a group member had more sessions and if they were in a smaller size group of about six members, it was easier for the individual to enter into the process. However, the other factors described in this section, such as group dynamics and personality patterns, also greatly influenced the process of art toward healing.

Group Dynamic and the Dialogical Image/Word Process

As already described in the other quilt patches, group members had many choices of how they would participate in the art therapy groups and how they would enter into their creative process. Within the art therapy group described earlier, individuals could choose how much to participate on a verbal or non-verbal level. Patients had many ways to reflect upon their process and their relationships to others including reviewing the images created during the group. This review was part of a dialogical process that was sensitive to and inclusive of somatic resonances, the symbolic, transformative process of images, as well as verbal group discussions. Using the dialogical image/word approach in art therapy allowed individuals to work on exploring the pictures on a verbal level with the group and the therapist in a way that propelled the transformative process into the symbolic realm of the images. Within this approach, patients could pick freely which art materials to use and how to use them. They could choose what kinds of lines, shapes, and colors to employ. They could also choose how much they would allow the process to unfold on an unconscious level through explorational play or how much to guide it on a conscious, cognitive level through planning and working with the emerging image. The extent to which patients used each approach contributed to how they were able to modulate their feelings and influenced the unfolding of the healing flow for the individual as well as for the group as a whole. Thus, through the dialogical image/word process, group members were able to let the images created by the group influence their experience and then, in turn, to let this experience shape new relationships and ways of being in the world.

It became clear through the description of the fictional art therapy session that the group members would, to some extent, experience their own images as well as those made by other group members on an implicit and explicit level and that this influenced the healing flow in many ways. An image could be experienced on several levels even when it was not attended to explicitly through verbal explorations. All the pictures created in the group would be experienced on a somatic, emotional, and psychological level and were shaped by other unconscious forces. Individual members were not always consciously aware of what the images evoked for them or how much the group had shaped their inner images. They were also not always consciously aware of how they were affected by the dynamic interchange between each patient, their images, and the group. Therefore, it was important for the group therapist to be sensitive to the non-verbal interactions and to use interventions that enabled the group to process what had been brought forth through the dialogical image/word approach by honoring the images created. Thus, the dialogical image/word process included the personal and the collective realm as well as involving the exploration of materials on many levels in an integrated manner.

The different quilt patches of the previous sections illustrated that group members had many opportunities to be a sounding board to themselves as well as to others as they moved through the different phases of the art therapy group. The images shared in the group allowed individual members to discover something about their own perceptions and to see how much these perceptions were shared by others. Group dynamics and personality styles played an important part in how patients could engage in the creative process. The nature of the visual art expression would also be influenced by the use of space, materials, images, and verbal interactions as described earlier. Through the dialogical image/word approach, group members were encouraged to go at their own speed and to discover their own unique language of expression. The social aspect of the group allowed a person to experience how their uniqueness and their creativity could play a constructive part in the group as a whole. The sharing of images, therefore, affected many aspects of the self on a somatic, intellectual, and spiritual level within the interpersonal social dimension of the group.

In order for group members to feel secure and safe, the group therapist needed to facilitate the group process by fostering the expression of opinions in a non-judgmental manner as well as by channeling and modulating the flow of the unconscious material that the image-making process had generated. Group members were encouraged to take personal responsibility for themselves, their feelings, and any of their thoughts that had emerged while they were in the group by identifying them and then exploring them with the group. However, not everyone was always able to do so equally well and the therapist needed to be ready to provide guidance in order to help modulate the flow of feeling and the process of art toward healing for individuals as well as for the group as a whole. Therefore, the therapist needed to be aware and ready to employ various interventions. Furthermore, the therapist's comfort level and trust in the dialogical image/word approach modeled to the individuals and the group how the image-making process and its potentials could be harnessed.

As was shown earlier, the therapist could use the different clinical interventions to help an individual to find his or her way to engage in the image-making process using sensations, feelings, thoughts, and symbols. The use of open questions, clarifying remarks, and the drawing of attention to themes that made connections between different expressions could help facilitate and further the healing flow for the individual as well as for the group. In this way the therapist, like the patients, also had many choices in how to facilitate and work with the healing flow. These choices were, to a great degree, grounded in his or her comfort level and experience with the process of art toward healing, in the therapist's awareness of group dynamics and in his or her knowledge of the individual group members. In this way, the therapist could work with unconscious themes that had arisen out of the dialogical image/word process and help guide the process along therapeutic directions.

When individuals were new to the possibilities that could open for them through the image-making process, there was a risk that they might perhaps self-disclose too quickly through their images and thus express unconscious thoughts and feelings before they or other group members were ready to hold and work with this material on a conscious level. As a therapist facilitating the process of art toward healing using the dialogical image/word approach, I had found that there were times when the embodied messages of the images needed to be explored further in the symbolic realm of the image-making process before working with them through verbal and intellectual explorations. In this way individual group members could gradually integrate this material in a safe way without becoming overwhelmed or retraumatized. This process appears to be similar to how Levine (1995) has described working with traumatic neuroses:

> In the traumatic neuroses, the individual repeatedly dreams about the original traumatic event where he was powerless to act because he was subject to forces outside of himself. By repeating the experience of being

> passive, he becomes active and therefore restores in the act of dreaming, through images, the lost sense of his own power. (p.52)

Creating images in an art therapy session through the dialogical image/word process is a kind of waking dreaming where the different aspects of one's being can come together within the symbolic realm of the image. Within the supportive structure of the group, group members were able to let images emerge on paper while they were in a waking state where they could make conscious choices. In this state, a transitional space was created through the symbolic realm of the images that helped them to contemplate their lived experiences and their ways of being in the world in a self-creating, empowering, and reality-oriented manner.

During the experiential phase of the group, as was made visible in the previous quilt patches, there were opportunities where individuals could spend some individual time with the therapist and receive guidance while other group members were engaged in the image-making process. These times were intended to help individuals, who were struggling, to find ways to engage in the image-making process and to learn how to harness the material that had been brought to consciousness through the dialogical image/word process. These individual moments with the therapist were also to help the group member to find his or her own trajectory and way back to the group. In this way, the therapist had an opportunity to facilitate the process of art toward healing through the dialogical image/word approach that was more sensitive to the individual patient's needs but that did not subtract from the group process as a whole.

Over the years that I have facilitated the different art therapy groups, I have noticed that patients seldom got stuck in a continuous loop of traumatic re-enactments where the images remained untouched by the flow of transformative creative energy. This did happen, however, when the main reason for making images was to get attention from others as a substitute for connecting more authentically with the world. The way an individual patient treated their images and presented their paintings to the group was quite often symbolic of the process that they had gone through and of what the role of the image was for them in relationship to the world.

In the cases where patients used their images in a manipulative way and as a tool for getting attention rather than as a way of learning more about themselves and the world, they were at greater risk of employing the creative energies in a potentially damaging way that could isolate and push them further away from the world. For those patients who in the past had used their images as a way of getting attention and whose artwork was perhaps more rewarded than they experienced themselves as human beings, it was more difficult to enter into the process of art toward healing in a truly self-affirming manner. This dynamic may have led them to see the art object as more important than their own sense of self-worth and thus unbalanced the dialogical process by focusing too much on the art object. In the past, the object may have provided a substitute for affection and now this could perhaps make it more difficult for them to enter the process of art toward healing since they and their relationship to the group members were as important to the unfolding dynamics as the art object that they had produced.

Through the dialogical image/word process, many patients were gradually able to re-establish a balance between their sense of self and the world by entering the healing flow in a more self-affirming manner. However, in these cases there remained always a slight risk that the individuals could use the image-making process in a manipulative manner and become lost, thus not allowing themselves to connect more authentically. In these individuals, the fear of rejection tended to be so great that they found it difficult to take truly creative chances. At first, they might find it difficult to break away from these old patterns and to find more creative and adaptive ways of being in the world. If this dynamic was not identified and worked with by the therapist, the unfolding process could go astray and the individual's ability to enter the process of art toward healing could be hampered.

This dynamic was particularly visible in the dialogical process that unfolded within the group between the patients, in the way they used their images in the group and in the individual's relationship to the group as a whole. In the cases described in the different quilt patches, this dynamic was not emphasized that much and was worked with more indirectly through the group culture. However, this dynamic seemed more prevalent in patients with an art background. This may echo the role art currently plays in our culture. By examining the process of art toward healing within the microcosm of the art therapy group, we may gain some insight into how we can recapture the process of art toward healing on the cultural level.

In my experience, the risks involved with this underlying dynamic were usually brought relatively quickly to the surface and worked with through the dialogical image/word approach and the general group culture that was created within the microcosm of the art therapy group. This process was well described in Rothenberg's (1990) book on creativity. Perhaps this dynamic goes undetected in art education or in the cultural role of the art world because individual artists' suffering and cries for help may be hidden behind the objectification of the art object and the role that art and artists play in our culture.

The other potential risk that I have seen over the years and which in my experience was more easily worked with through the dialogical image/word approach was when patients employed their images as a way of avoiding unwanted material. If the patient had engaged in the image-making process mainly in order to expel rather than to own and reclaim unwanted feelings, thoughts, and images their journey was one of moving away from themselves and the world rather than becoming more connected and whole. In these situations, the images had taken on more the role of the scapegoat and the therapist needed to help the individual to find ways to employ their creativity in order to transform and gain mastery over this unwanted material in a reality-oriented and self-affirming manner that was cognizant of the part/whole relationship of being.

In this process it is important for the therapist not to collude with the patients' fantasies that they will be able to permanently dispel unwanted material through a one-time, cathartic experience. This was true even if the power of this experience is so compelling for everyone who witnesses it that it encourages the belief that this cathartic experience and the way it is mediated by the symbolic realm of the art media can take away pain and suffering on a more permanent level. The symbolic realm is able to provide a safe container in which painful material can be held and responded to and it can initiate a transformative process. Even though the image-making process and the symbolic realm of the art media can have this powerful effect, it does not take away the fact that these cathartic experiences need to be gradually integrated into one's way of being in the world. The different phases of the creative process described in earlier chapters draw attention to these complexities that are involved in the process of art toward healing and illustrate how each phase provides unique challenges that can affect the process of art toward healing. Within the dialogical image/word approach to art therapy, each phase is needed to complete the whole experience in an integrated manner.

The generalization of these peak or cathartic experiences that could occur when engaging in the process of art toward healing was only one part of the creative process. Through the dialogical image/word approach described here, these experiences could be encouraged to move along the different phases of the creative process toward greater integration so that they could be utilized more into one's life. Within the microcosm of the art therapy group, the therapist can guide this process by using the different interventions. However, it is important to note that it takes time and work to move through all of the different phases of the creative process in an integrated manner. A great challenge was to maintain the gains that patients had made during the art therapy group so that they would be able to utilize and integrate the gains into their way of being in the world. Without the support of the therapeutic environment of the therapy group and because of the many stresses of everyday life, these gains were subjected to powerful, unpredictable influences. These influences could push the awarenesses gained during the group into the background and prevent the healing flow from continuing to enrich patients' everyday life after they had been discharged from the program.

This is what makes that last phase of the creative process so difficult and it is often misunderstood or ignored completely. From my observations with the different phases of the creative process, this last phase seems to be a very important aspect of maintaining the healing flow. If this phase is missed there appears to be a higher risk that the gap between the creative energy, with its symbolic realm, and one's everyday reality will become greater. Thus, the process of art toward healing could become impotent, lost, or fragmented from the rest of one's being. Within the microcosm of the art therapy group and through the many therapeutic interventions described earlier, the therapist could help guide patients to work with the images that they and the group had created in a self-affirming and reality-oriented manner that invited transformation and integration of split-off parts in order to become more whole and authentically located in the world. Because patients could take their images with them after they had completed the group, this gave them the opportunity to use these embodied images as transitional objects that could be a creative bridge between their experience within the group and their life outside of the group.

Final Reflection

In conclusion, I would like to say that the clinical observations that I was able to make over the years have led me to believe that not all images necessarily helped individuals to become more authentically connected with the world and at times the images instead became objects to use for disguise, to manipulate with, or to hide behind. I was further able to observe that at times this could interfere with the evolutionary process of self-understanding and transformation and the process of art toward healing as a whole. Thus, the power of the transformative process could potentially become undermined by the individual's conscious or unconscious attempts at getting away from themselves and the world. However, usually a person's habitual ways of being in this world were touched and transformed through the stimulation of the creative energies and the dialogical image/word process that unfolded within the group culture. Furthermore the collective energy flow stimulated by the dialogical process of the group generally encouraged using the symbolic realm to become more closely connected with oneself and others.

The fictional art therapy session and the exploration of the role of the closing ritual described in the earlier quilt patches spoke to how the dialogical image/word process allowed individuals to learn to engage with the healing flow and to use their images in an adaptive way. The closure ritual usually supported this process and marked a transformative shift where the images acted similarly to a transitional object that allowed the individuals to break out of traumatic re-enactments and to shift their perception toward expanding their artwork beyond their original, literal, trauma-saturated meanings. Furthermore, when patients took their artwork with them, after they had completed the art therapy group, the images became transitional objects that could potentially provide many opportunities for the individual to integrate the experience with the healing flow into their everyday life.

Over the years, I have observed that the majority of patients chose to take their images with them after their last session. There were some rare occasions when patients decided to dispose of some of their work as part of their transition ritual. This usually was a symbolic act of empowerment and a sign that they no longer had a need for this image to exist in its material form. However, there were a few patients who abandoned their pieces in a gesture of devaluing the meaning that these objects may have carried for them. After some patients had reviewed their pictures, they realized that because of the power that these images still carried for them they would prefer to leave them in the safe container of the art therapy room. Besides these rare occasions, most patients wanted to hold on to their work as a reminder for themselves of their therapeutic journey and perhaps to share them with their outpatient therapist, family members, or friends.

It will be the purpose of the next chapter to explore further the different functions of the image. What I would like to note here is that although images could become important parts of the individual's journey, they nevertheless also belonged to the group as a whole because their creation was, in part, connected to the overall group dynamics that had affected the unfolding of the dialogical image/word process.

CHAPTER 12

Final Stitching

Closure Ritual and the Transitional Function of the Dialogical Image/Word Process

In the opening chapter, on pages 37–8, I listed ten roles or functions of the image; here they are re-examined in the light of what has been discovered through this Interpretative Quilt. The different themes that were explicated in the various imagistic pauses and quilt patches illustrated some of the complexities and dynamics involved. The continuous dialogical processes between the image, the artist, and the viewers that unfold within the self and the social context of a group are viewed here in a broader context. Within the continuous flow of dialogical processes, the symbolic functions of an image change through the verbal and non-verbal discourse that unfolds. These symbolic functions give rise to embedded meanings, moods, and intensities of experiences. Thus, within the dialogical image/word approach to therapy and research, an image is grounded in a context and in a meaning that is ever-shifting and multi-leveled in its very nature.

In this chapter, the findings are further propelled by this continuous flow and are moved forward by the dialogical image/word process. In this manner, the threads of experiential data are interwoven into an interpretative border that brings to life the different elements of the Interpretative Quilt to create a deeper understanding of the phenomena under investigation. This interpretative border helps to create a more integrated and complete view of the process of art toward healing and, in a way, echoes the stages of creativity discussed earlier by completing the picture in a manner that accents the important elements of what has become visible through this work.

Within the therapy context and when using the dialogical image/word approach, a contemplative exploration of the images is facilitated where self-understanding and connection with the world are encouraged. Sympathetic understanding of the relationships between the person or artist, the image, and the group are essential elements of the dialogical image/word approach and the Healing-Flow Model. The nature of this kind of interaction between the image and the process of interpretation is well captured by McNiff (1989) when he writes:

> The interpretative process involves the person in first establishing a sympathetic relationship to the object of contemplation. There is an opening of the interpreter's consciousness through which the observed phenomenon is absorbed into the sympathetic elements of the soul where it is transformed by the emotions and then expressed in the form of the interpretation. (pp.87–88)

This process was illustrated in the various quilt patches of the previous chapters as they unfolded within the context of psychotherapy. They are now carried forward into the larger context of research and culture.

The contextual or anecdotal meaning of each image and experience is not more important than the interpretative, embodied explications of the image when it is taken out of the context in which it was created, because the image has a life beyond this context. The patients, within the therapy context, were able to reflect on their work through the physical dimensions of their pictures and the somatic as well as symbolic resonances the pictures set off within the viewers, as the experiences were explored in an integrated manner within a social setting. The physical reality of the images allowed the experience to be carried forward. The physical reality also allowed the experience to shift the dialogical process as it unfolded within new contexts. These changes helped patients to understand the transitional aspects of their images and of the dialogical process. Taking their pictures with them after leaving the therapy context allowed each individual to continue the dialogical process within a new context. The pictures in the imagistic pauses can have a similar function for research and on a social and cultural level.

Within the context of therapy described earlier, another reason for patients not to take all or some of their pictures outside the group context was that the pictures sometimes still had too much power over the patient. The pictures embodied the abuse the patient had suffered in its raw and literal form. This could evoke or stimulate flashbacks and traumatic re-enactments for the patient. This froze the images and the patients in time and disrupted the healing flow. In this case, the images could potentially be very harmful to the individual if he or she took them outside the safety of the therapeutic container. In this case, the images tended to have been given more the role of the scapegoat (Schaverien, 1992) rather than the function of a healthy transitional object. In order for the experience to be therapeutic and helpful, these images needed to be treated with care and therapeutic guidance that would help propel the dialogical process into the direction of transformation rather than into the continuation of traumatic re-enactments. We may also be able to observe this process on a cultural level.

Through the transitional qualities of the images and the gradual embodiment of the process of art toward healing, patients had the opportunity to gain mastery and control of their feelings, internal images, dreams, and thoughts. They could find ways of expressing and giving voice to non-verbal or pre-verbal aspects of the self, as well as finding ways to facilitate exploration and communication with unconscious feelings, images, dreams, and thoughts through art materials. The examples used in this Interpretative Quilt, with its different patches, show how patients got in touch with their own creativity in order to metabolize trauma through the dialogical image/word approach to art therapy by restructuring images and making changes in the physical world. This helped patients to break patterns of traumatic re-enactments and gave them an experience of how they could utilize their creativity and become their own tutor. This process may also be part of the function art can have on a cultural level as was discussed at the beginning of this book.

The closure ritual and the transition phase that patients participated in during their last session helped them to reflect on this transitional function of the image and to determine what they ought to do with their work. After this closure ritual and at the end of the patient's last session when they had completed this reflective process, they were asked if they were interested in signing a consent form so that we could photograph their images in order to include them in our visual database.[1] By allowing their artwork to be included in the visual database, individuals were able to expand the meaning of their work beyond the immediate context of the art therapy group into the larger community and to help others to benefit from their work. This allowed for the possibility of assigning a symbolically broader meaning to these images that went beyond the personal significance that they had taken for the individual and the group and allowed the images to speak to the world on a more universal and collective level.

The different imagistic pauses incorporated into this inquiry embodied, to a great extent, many of the themes that became visible in these closure or transition rituals. They also provided a transition between the function and meaning that these images had for the person who created them and the significance that they took on within the context of this work. Each imagistic pause and each picture provided another view into the healing flow and the process of art toward healing within the contexts of both art therapy and research.

The review of images, whether it is at the end of a patient's stay in the art therapy group or at the end of this work, serves similar functions. Within the context of therapy, the closure ritual allows the patients and the therapist to see more vividly the different themes that evolved and to understand how they could perhaps be carried forward. This is very much akin to the reflective process that the researcher uses when applying the dialogical image/word approach to inquiry. The role of the images included in this last chapter is similar to these closure rituals in that the images are to summarize and carry forward the qualitative findings of this inquiry in a dynamic manner that continues the healing flow. They are to communicate, in their unique way, these findings through iconographic themes that were discovered over the years through this work. These diverse themes re-occurred in various forms in the individual group members' images and dialogical journeys with the process of art toward healing and helped to move this dialogical process in order to expand it into the realm outside of this context through the inclusion of their works into the different imagistic pauses.

Themes and Changing Functions of the Image

The ten roles or functions of the image relate to the different themes that were explicated in the various imagistic pauses and quilt patches. The continuous dialogical processes between the image, the artist, and the viewers are examined here in a broader context. Within the continuous flow of dialogical processes, the symbolic functions of an image change and give rise to new embedded meanings, moods, and intensities of experiences. As already stated within the dialogical image/word approach to therapy and research, an image

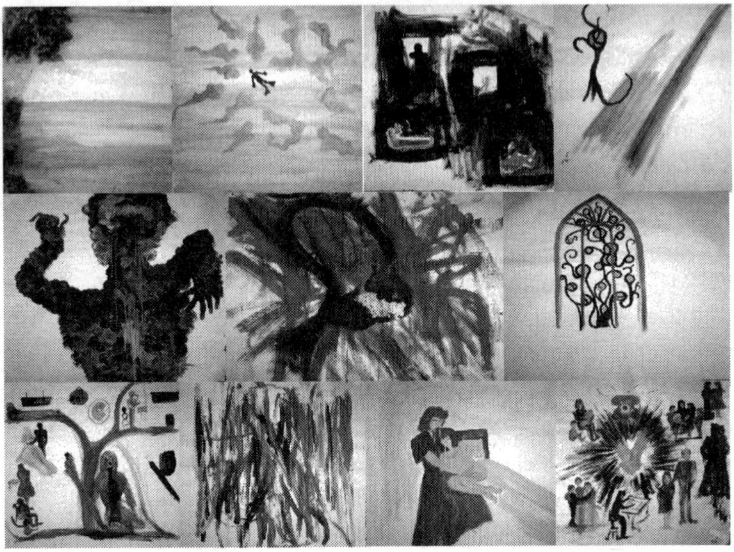

Figure 12.1: Kathy's first Interpretative Quilt

is grounded in a context and in a meaning that is ever-shifting and multi-leveled in its very nature.

The different journeys described in the quilt patches and the fictional art therapy sessions demonstrated the complex dynamics and interdependent nature of the life of an image that is context bound and embedded in relationships that are shaped through a constant dialogical process. Here, the images created within the therapeutic relationships of the group give rise to broader themes. Through their unique iconographic style, these themes are summarized in the following imagistic pauses where they can be contemplated.

This section will take these themes and explore them as they were guided by the metaphor of the Healing-Flow Model in order to take them beyond this specific therapeutic context. The following imagistic pauses are to further enrich the material discussed in this section and to raise questions as to how the process of art toward healing can enter into everyday life. These imagistic pauses are not only to communicate the essential themes iconographically, but they are also the essential features of the transition ritual described earlier. They symbolically and visually show how this last phase could be a helpful way to prepare an individual for the upcoming transition and at the same time to embody and externalize the process of art toward healing through a contemplative pause. Although the experience of the paintings has been altered by the context and by the way the images are juxtaposed and represented in this imagistic pause, the paintings still bring forward themes in a way that may not have been visible if the paintings were viewed individually.

Emerging Themes

1. Solitude and finding a place of peace.
2. Solitude turning into isolation as one attempts to escape from one's lived experience and traumatic past.
3. Dreams turning into nightmares as forgotten experiences are trying to emerge into consciousness.
4. Through the free exploration with the art materials, unconscious forces becoming visible and a connection with the larger web of life formed and affirmed through practice.
5. Spirituality brought to life through contemplation, art, community, and religious practices.
6. The pain of physical, existential, and psychological suffering becoming visible through the art materials and generating fears of exposing one's remembered experience and losing one's self in a sea of memories and imposed secrets.
7. Within the safety of the therapeutic container and the use of art materials, the spiritual energy propelling the transformative process forward in spite of the fears and pains encountered.
8. Within the safety of the therapeutic container and the use of art materials, the tortured self and the crying soul reaching out to rediscover their being, in spite of fear of rejection and existential pain.
9. The crying tree leading the way to self-awareness through a reflection of lived experience and lost potentials.
10. Embodied tears without content and an opening to reintegration of the mind with one's emotions and one's sense of spirituality on a somatic and intellectual level.

11. Acceptance and reframing of what was in order to consolidate and hold the pain of lived experiences and memories and one's true being.
12. To dare to dream of a better future and to envision a different life.
13. The incubation phase allowing the transformative process to unfold and the transformative process being further shaped through the dialogical process between one's being and the world.
14. Life's events continuing to shape this process and propel it in many different directions.

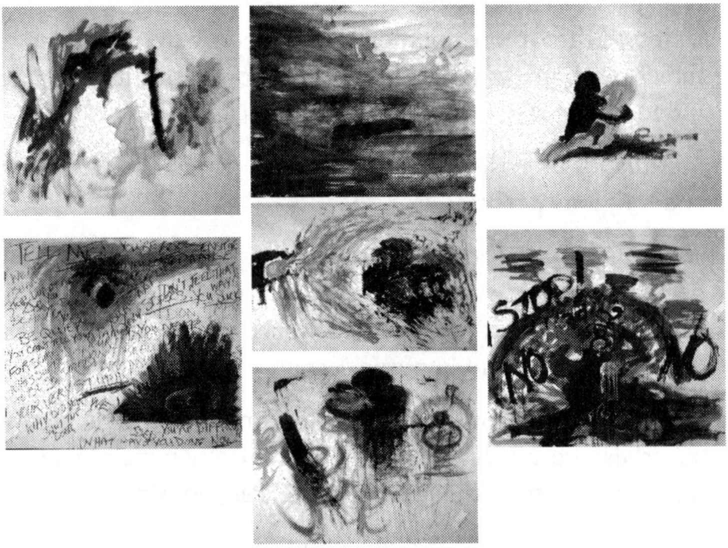

Figure 12.2: Kathy's second Interpretative Quilt

The Re-examination and Further Distillation of Emerging Themes[2]

1. Revisiting and embracing the darkness in order to become whole.
2. Anger and revenge and unbearable feelings of pain and hurt.
3. Feelings of guilt, shame, and regret.

4. Voices of the past that shape and dominate the present and the future.
5. The power of the media and the entertainment industry on the growing child who has no other guidance and the vision and the view of the world they help to create.
6. Stopping the patterns and voices of the past in order to reclaim the present and the future.
7. The tentative sense of self and community emerging through a continuous dialogical process.
8. Opening a space where the mind, body, and spirit can become reconnected and validated in the external world.
9. The ever-changing function of an image being context bound and being brought to life within the person who creates the image and the viewer who experiences the image within her/his being.

The function and meaning of an image are uncovered through the dialogical process and change over time. The way an individual moves through the different phases of the creative process affects the nature of the dialogical process. It is also influenced by whatever aspect an individual brings to the image. Again, it is the therapist's experience with the healing flow that allows her or him to be sensitive to and aware of the different possibilities and potential risks involved in engaging with the creative process and the healing flow.

The image-making process and the part an image played for each individual within the therapy context, as it was observed in this book, varied greatly. Many times, images that were created during therapy reflected some great strength that seemed to bypass the individual's pathology or maladaptive patterns. The strength could be brought to the foreground through the dialogical image/word approach and the guidance of the healing flow. The ten different functions of images listed in Chapter 1 could be present concurrently to various degrees and could shift, depending on how the multi-leveled dialogical process unfolded within the intra and extra personal dimensions of being.

When an image connected more with an individual's pathology than with his or her more adaptive aspects of being, it was the role of the therapist to guide the process and to bring the other dimensions of the image and the healing flow into play. Independent of how much or how little the image resonated with the individual's suffering, it was the fostering and nurturing of the adaptive function of the creative process that seemed to have the most curative effect. Thus, the pathologizing and freezing of the image, caused by the therapist focusing too much on verbal definitions and intellectualizations, sometimes greatly hampered the integrated dialogical process. This caused the effects of the curative and the adaptive function of the creative process to sometimes get lost. That is to say, if too much power is given to interpretation and intellectual exploration, the balance between mind, emotions, body, and soul can be disturbed and the portal that an image can provide for transformation and integration may be lost.

The dialogical process between image and viewer consists of balancing and bringing into play the multidimensional aspect of an image in its various dimensions. This continuous balancing and fluctuation of function of an image is an essential part of the Healing-Flow Model and the dialogical image/word approach to therapy and inquiry. It is important to note that although the evaluation and validation phase of the creative process can be thought of as having an inherent analytic and pragmatic aspect, it goes beyond interpretation. This last phase needs to be an embodied experience that includes aspects of the body, mind, and spirit. The intellectual and analytic aspect should not be given greater value, as this would disturb the balance of the different elements and the healing flow with its many part/whole relationships would be disrupted.

There is a parallel between the process that propelled this research and the process of therapy that is described in this book. Within the context of psychotherapy, the different interventions portrayed earlier have been found helpful in facilitating the process of art toward healing through the dialogical image/word process. The role of the therapist and the role of the researcher are similar in many ways, when using the dialogical image/word approach. By describing one, one learns about the other. Through the dialogical process the researcher creates an Interpretative Quilt. Interpretative stitching parallels the therapeutic interventions described earlier and the final image is continuously propelled further through the dialogical image/word process.

Within the context of the therapy described here, individuals were able to move through the different phases of the creative process and usually by the time patients were leaving the therapy group they were able to look at their images from a different and transitional perspective. During their stay in the therapy group, they had many opportunities to internalize the process of art toward healing and to learn to respect both their images and the gains they made while in the therapy group. Through the individual's experience with the dialogical image/word approach, the images became objects that had embodied and integrated meaning. They were not pieces of decoration to be shared in a careless manner. This is paralleled by the function of the images used in this work.

The group process also allowed individuals to discover their own creativity and gave them a voice to express themselves with, in a manner that could include the personal, the social, the collective, and the universal realm of being. The experiences that patients had during their stay in the group made the closure ritual more meaningful for them and the group. After the closure/evaluation phase, most patients decided to take their images with them as symbols of their work and their relationship with the group, and as a bridge to their journey outside of the context in which the images had been created. The images that were used in this book play a similar role in that they have become embodied with meaning that is unique to the dialogical process that gave rise to the Interpretative Quilt.

On a symbolic level, the images that the patients made during the group embodied the insights that they learned during their healing journey. Taking their artwork with them opened possibilities for them to continue the dialogical process that they had learned and for them to incorporate the healing flow into their life. When individuals were able to reclaim their work and bring their images into new relationships, they could explore these images further in order to form new connections that were unique to this new context. In this way, the dialogical process was able to continue. Individuals could carry on working with the residual effects of their images and continue their engagement with the process of art toward healing outside of the therapy group context. The images that were used in the imagistic pauses also allow the dialogical process to be propelled forward in a similar manner to further provide understanding of the process of art toward healing.

Within the transitional space of the closure ritual, some patients would discover that they were not ready to take their picture outside of this context and they decided to leave their work for safe keeping until they had a therapeutic or safe container outside in the community to which they could bring these important transitional images. Reconnecting with their images could take place later or during a subsequent admission to the hospital. I have had patients come back after one or two years to reclaim their images. Sometimes the messages that the images initially had carried were transformed, and frequently, when patients saw their work after some time had passed, they experienced the images in a different light. The passing of time and the changed group context appeared to have altered their perceptions and associated feelings. Thus, the subjective state of the individuals or artists, as well as the context in which they were viewing their work, seemed to color the experience of the image and the subsequent dialogical process. This subjective experience could at times be so strong that it could change the associations of the images tremendously from how the individual remembered the picture. Thus, the dimension that one connected with an image could shift and the function of the image could change.

This is very similar to the function that the images of the imagistic pauses went through as part of the dialogical process that unfolded throughout the years that this work took to complete. Over time, different experiences that were propelled by the dialogical process between images and text gave rise to a deeper, embodied understanding that could hold the different functions that the images could take. Out of this dialogical process, meanings could change, depending on the context in which the images were viewed. This gave rise to the creation of the Interpretative Quilt.

There are always many layers of verbal and non-verbal experiences connected with the images that are intertwined with the context and the state of mind of the viewer. Depending on the individual, sometimes it takes more time for her or him to gain a fuller, embodied understanding of a work. This understanding and self-awareness can only be gained through the continuous flow of the dialogical image/word process that unfolds over time. Time, mindful contemplation, and an active engagement with the dialogical image/word process allow the Interpretative Quilt to reach greater maturity and depth.

When the symbolic underpinnings of an image are too incongruent with an individual's conscious understanding and their habitual way of being in the world, then the unfolding dialogical process may take more time and further guidance from the therapist. Over time and through engagement with the dialogical process, individuals may learn to integrate their internal truth with what they have come to believe about themselves and the world. With the passing of time and through the stimulating of the internal creative energy within an individual, the seeds of change and embodied understanding can be nurtured and the healing flow encouraged. Through time, active engagement, and contemplation, one can connect with the different symbolic meanings and learn to live with one's deeper internal truths, while at the same time being linked with the broader web of life. These connections are formed and strengthened through the continuous dialogical flow between art materials, self, and the world and they are propelled through a continuous flow of images within a social context. The creation of images and the contemplation of these images within a receptive social context allow the healing flow to unfold.

Within the dialogical image/word approach to art therapy, the images or transitional objects that were created are treated with respect. Even if patients never actually reclaimed their images, there was always the knowledge that the images were in a safe place and were treated with respect. Here in this work, this receptivity and respect is carried forward in order for the emerging themes and functions to continue with the dialogical process that the imagistic pauses generate. This helps to create the Interpretative Quilt that allows the deepening of our understanding of the process of art toward healing.

The pictures in the next imagistic pause embodied that transformative process of the healing flow. They illustrated how patients' images became part of and were embodied in my interpretations and view of the world. Through the dialogical image/word approach, I was able to synthesize my experiences as a therapist. Patients' images reflected a transformative process. Through a dialogical, contemplative process, experiences could be transformed and utilized, informing the patients as well as my work as a therapist, researcher, and artist. In the process of interpretative quilting, each quilt patch and each border or background color contributed to the greater whole in its unique way and was directed by my engagement with art materials, therapy material, and the world.

In the following section, I will explore the dialogical image/word process by using images that I have created over the years. This allows me to engage with the images in a different manner and from a different perspective, as when reflecting on images that patients have created in therapy with me. Another reason for using my own images in this last chapter is to make visible the basis of interpretations in my own experience and historicity.

The process of interpretative quilting emerged out of the need to find a way to summarize patients' work and images in an authentic yet interpretative manner. First, I started with the individuals' images. Then, I added the experience of the individuals' flow and movement through their paintings, which I then placed into a quilt-like pattern in order to create a more cohesive whole.

The visual patterns created and stimulated different somatic, emotional, psychological, cognitive, and spiritual resonances and at the same time communicated the finding of this inquiry and so propelled the dialogical image/word process to further interpretations and verbal expressions.

Each quilt patch of patients' work, as well as my own pictures as they were placed within the context of the quilt, created different perspectives and illuminated the ground in which the interpretations were embedded. Thus, bringing my own images and the images created by patients during the art therapy groups together into one quilt allowed a different image to emerge. The outer rim of the quilt patch in Figure 12.3 holds the images of my journey with the healing flow that I had created over the years during and after my art training. The images in this outer layer embed and frame the pictures that were created by patients during therapy in a way that is very similar to the way my experiences as a therapist/researcher/artist frame my interpretative process. Thus, the quilt patch in Figure 12.3 symbolizes the dynamic relationship of the dialogical image/word approach between subject, observer, and interpretation. The changes that occurred through the dialogical process on each viewing colored the quilt patches in a way that paralleled the interpretative process. These changes illustrated how they could alter the original experience in order to create a new understanding that brings forth deeper levels of knowledge. Thus, each layer of abstraction enhanced the original experience and gave it a deeper meaning that embodied contemplation and the continuous dialogical process. The final stitching of this chapter adds another dimension to what was described in earlier sections by placing them more directly into the context of the creative experience and the language of the creative arts.

Nine Dialogical Entry Points to an Image

The decontextualization of images into different parts can be helpful, as it facilitates greater awareness and the distillation of the specific into more universal themes. However, we cannot simply leave the fragments. We have a responsibility to put the pieces back together in order to create a whole. When using a somewhat more formalistic approach to reflect upon images the meaning of an image or artwork "is found in the formal relationships between elements of the work itself. A valid interpretation of the work, therefore, involves the elucidation of these formal structures" (Wilber, 1997, p.109). This

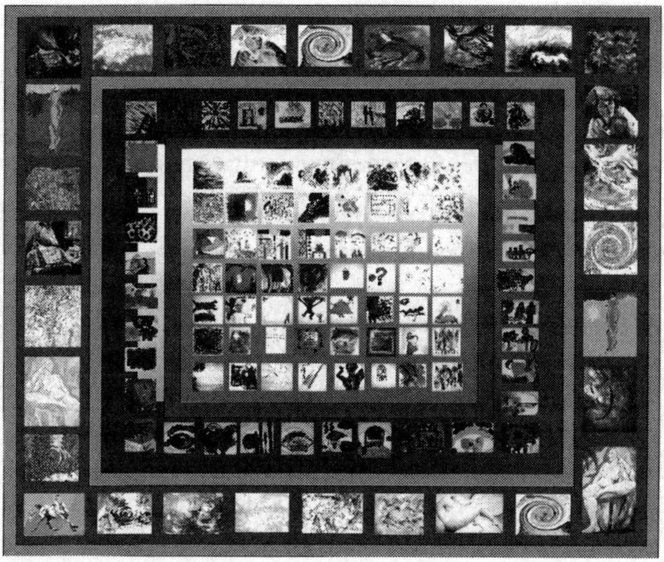

Figure 12.3: Interpretative Quilt of patient's work framed by the perceptual lens of images by the participatory researcher/therapist (completed in 1999)

is not to discount that we most frequently encounter an image first in its wholeness. Only after contemplation do we begin to see its different physical and symbolic dimensions. In this initial encounter we tend to respond first on a more unconscious, visceral level with our whole, subjective being. Through reflection, embodied contemplation, or a meditation such as the dialogical image/word approach, we can bring forth the different elements, associations, and internal resonances that the pictures evoke in us.

The different, imagistic pauses incorporated into this book depicted some of the following themes in a holistic manner through their *embodied iconic abstractions.* These elements also echo my experiences as an artist. They may be helpful to look at in more detail. A picture can be broken down and responded to on the following levels:

1. formal physical qualities of a picture such as the quality of lines, textures, and shapes, the nature of brushstrokes, colors, designs, and patterns, etc.
2. overall mood and Gestalt that set off visceral/somatic, affective, psychological, social, and spiritual resonances

3. nature of the representational style or schools of representations followed
4. quality and technical skill level of the interpretative style
5. embodiment of feelings, sentiments that are somatically grounded
6. quality and truthfulness of the associations of subjective, dialogical resonances/processes that created the image
7. symbolic/intellectual resonance and universal themes such as forces of light and dark, good and evil, beautiful and ugly, powerful and weak, big and small, oppressor and the oppressed, etc.
8. cultural and temporarily related elements
9. spiritual and soul-affirming qualities.

The imagistic pauses of this inquiry embody the personal as well as the universal. They can be examined and engaged with using these dialogical entry points. Focusing on the different aspects of an image will shape our experience, the dialogical process, and the awarenesses that we will gain. The themes that emerged over time are grounded in the images that were created in the art therapy groups over the years, as well as in my own experiences with the image-making process and the pictures that I have created. The different imagistic pauses visually and symbolically communicate the embodied knowledge that emerged over time and they invite a reading that goes beyond the art therapy context. The interpretative stitching is there to give the reader the opportunity to see the elements and themes that emerged through this work independently from the individual patient's journey. A meditative process that involves the different dialogical entry points, as well as an experience of the images as a whole, can lead to a more embodied understanding of what has been comprehended in this work. As the reader or viewer lets the images resonate with the metaphor of the healing flow that was introduced in the water dream at the beginning of this book an understanding of the dialogical image/word process can grow deeper.

One of the main premises of this book has been to maintain the balance between the part/whole relationships of all elements. I will now look at some of the themes by examining the different elements of the images as they relate to the Healing-Flow Model and the dialogical entry points previously listed.

Like the visual quilt patches, where an image was changed a number of times in order to create something new, an experience became transformed through the dialogical image/word process, and the understanding and impact of the original experience or painting was changed. This process is similar to what it is possible to unfold within the context of an image-oriented psychotherapy, but it should not be limited to this context. If we expand what we have learned through this work into the broader realm of experiences and examine the images from a cultural level, we allow them to inform us through a dialogical process that might help to reintegrate and transform personal and cultural wounds.

This process can be very similar to the one that I described earlier in this book, where I explained the process of breaking down one of my paintings through the use of computer graphics. Through this process, I was able to allow a new understanding of the subject matter to emerge that was based on an authentic, embodied, dialogical process. Using the nine dialogical entry points previously listed, we can explore the imagistic pause by allowing the images to resonate within us. By observing the healing flow through images, one can become aware of the trajectories that reflect more universal themes. One can learn from these images by engaging in a dialogical process that opens one up to new possibilities. The integration of split-off parts of oneself into a synthesis that then again gets broken down into parts allows for change and growth within certain parameters. Within the Healing-Flow Model we have free choice within given enabling conditions. It is the acceptance of and the working with these enabling conditions that allows the energy exchange that can transform the trajectory of each of our lives and allow for the evolution of being. In this sense we can learn to take responsibility for that which we have control over, thus exercising our freedom of choice within a range of possibilities while accepting and being able to come to terms with that which cannot be controlled or explained.

Thomas Moore expressed in his conversations with Gablik (1995) that: "Our lives are fashioned, not by our intentions, but by responding to these invitations that come from fate, and from other people and events, mysteriously" (p.409). This reflects some of the limits of reason and control over our own destinies. It also shows how the arts can provide a vehicle that can help us to understand and transform our human experiences in a collective and integrated manner, in order to come to terms with the mysteries and tragedies of life. Gablik (1995) writes: "...what art can do that reason can't do is to provide us with images that help us contemplate these mysteries" (p.409). The insight and embodied knowledge that we can gain by externalizing and giving material form to that which was outside of our conscious awareness provides new possibilities.

The contemplation of that which is outside of our control gives strength and meaning to our being-in-this-world. It allows us to embrace our existential vulnerability and frees us from fighting what can only be accepted and transformed through art and rituals. However, by taking control over the things that we are able to, we do not remain victims of our world, but instead become active participants. "Artistic creation is frequently an exercise in experiencing a subjective sense of freedom" (Rothenberg, 1990, p.75). An engagement in the arts can provide us with many opportunities for transformative and healing ritual (Bloom, 1997; Dissanayake, 1988). This book gives voice to how this transformative process took place for some individuals and how it can be guided through a dialogical image/word process and the Healing-Flow Model.

Within this model it is believed that an active participation with images and the dialogical process that will unfold over time can help one to gain awareness of one's trajectory. It can also create an opening where one can come to terms with one's existential and ontological struggles. The process of making images can create a space where material can take shape and evolve, gradually making the gap between the known and unknown smaller. Through the dialogical image/word process this gap can become bridged until one's conscious being is ready to embrace and utilize the unknown or forgotten aspects of being. It is not always important that we become conscious of all aspects of our being. Embodied experiences can become transformed on many levels. In the shadow of our conscious awareness they can gradually become assimilated into our being, leading to a sense of having always known something but not being able to describe how one has acquired this knowledge.

This intuitive way of learning and knowing, if trusted, can give new energy to our life's trajectory. In order to deal with a sense of chaos and of being out of control, we can use the process of art to restore a sense of our possibilities and to bring us back into being-in-this-world. David Plante speaks of this in his conversations with Gablik (1995):

> ...by giving one a sense of the possibility of what there is outside of one's control, outside of one's intentions and in the darkness, it offers the possi-

> bility of grace. I believe grace is possible, and I believe that writing and art can inspire grace. (p.164)

During art therapy the feelings expressed and externalized through the images can free up energy and allow for reintegration, transformation, and ownership of one's experiential, existential, and ontological reality. However, as discussed earlier, an image that is intended to expel lived experiences and draw attention may trap energy. Thus, the energy may not be available to the person or to a social group in order for the transformative process to unfold. There is always a risk that the image-making process can become part of a traumatic re-enactment where the individual or the social group re-enacts the same theme over and over again in order to expel it. The main difference between transformation and expelling unwanted material is that in the transformative process the material is owned as part of one's experience. In the transformative process one can learn to come to some kind of understanding that allows one to move on in the world in a reality-oriented and authentic manner.

As already described, when a person or a social group is trying to expel lived experiences through images without owning part of them, there is a risk that the experiences will re-emerge in new images, over and over again, until they have been owned and transformed. Without some guidance this process

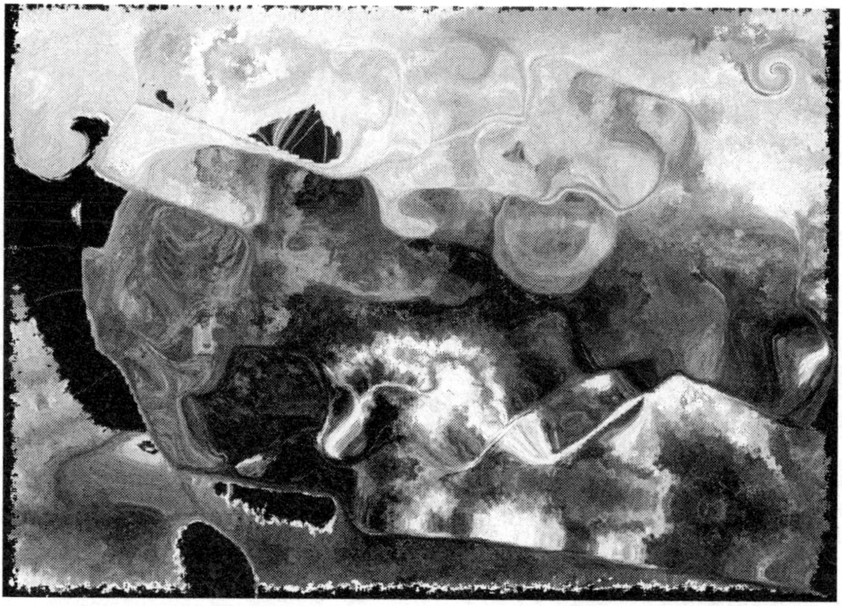

Figure 12.4: Another opening into a new dialogical process (completed in 2003)

may, instead of bringing relief, actually increase the pain as each time an individual or group of people attempt to dissociate themselves from the unwanted material, the risk of becoming dissociated from the world and the self becomes greater. Thus, an imbalance in the part/whole relationship is created which causes further pain and may lead to pathology.

The knowledge gained through this work may help us to find ways to expand our new understanding into the larger context of art and culture and to find ways to utilize the Healing-Flow Model in a wider context. I have attempted to raise possibilities that invite further examination. Through the metaphor of the Healing-Flow Model the process of art toward healing can be studied in different contexts. The previous imagistic pause is to invite further dialogue and to bridge back into the world of images and the arts.

Notes

1 Not all patients who were in the art therapy group during the time of this inquiry/book were asked if they were willing to fill out a consent form in order to be included in the visual art database used for this inquiry. Consent was only secured during certain time periods.

2 A depressive episode re-emerges as life experiences discombobulate one's way of being in the world. As a person enters the dialogical image/word process within the art therapy group for the Core Program, a very different dialogical process unfolds during a second admission.

CHAPTER 13

Modernity, Spirituality, and the Process of Art Toward Healing

Ontological and existential realities are part of the realm of the arts and psychotherapy. The study of the process of art toward healing touches on many aspects of human experience. The subject invites exploration from many different perspectives that are inclusive and authentic to its process. It demands a diverse conceptualization of the phenomena and of how one understands creativity, art, and the use of art in therapy. The very nature of the subject is holistic and interdisciplinary. It defies being imprisoned within the conceptualization of one discipline. This creates in itself an interesting dilemma in that the literature related to this subject is vast, diverse, and interdisciplinary in nature. One can find many different and contradicting theories and research findings. This presents a challenge, while at the same time it also allows for a more integrated understanding. The metaphor of the Healing-Flow Model helped to organize the diverse material into a cohesive whole through the continuous interplay between lived experience, images, and texts. This dialogical process gave shape to the theoretical conceptualizations and to a more embodied understanding.

Wilber (1995) states that one of the greatest contributions of modernity is that it has created a clear differentiation between sciences (it), morals (we), and art (I). It has divided them into the "Big Three," where each could establish its own methods, research, and truths that were independent from each other. This has led to great advances in each area but it also has contributed to an imbalance and dissociation within the different aspects of thinking and being. "It was this *dissociation* of the Big Three that, more than anything else, allowed the sweeping advances of the natural sciences (the it-domain) to overwhelm the interior, subjective, moral, and cultural domains (I and we)…" (Wilber, 1995, p.416). This is what Wilber refers to as the reduction and taking over by "the path of objective it-language (the representation/reflection paradigm, and its converse, production paradigm, and the overall validity claims only of propositional truth and/or functional fit)" (p.416). This overwhelming dominance and dissociation of the "it" domain of the sciences has helped to create "the flatland world of monological, empirical-analytic, positivistic 'its,' where only the entities studied by empirical-natural sciences are 'real' " (pp.416–417). Wilber argues that the sciences have become strongly associated with "truth" and are quite often given a higher value than the other two more subjective domains. This, as he shows in his writings, creates many potential risks.

Dissanayake (1995) points out that Literacy and Modernity may foster "detachment and separation in part because writing makes it possible to see a world as a thing, separate from its referent" (Dissanayake, 1995, p.206). She reminds us that when we look at human history, writing and scientific methodology have only been part of human life for a relatively short time:

> For eight-ninths of their history, humans could not read at all. Reading and writing did not begin to play a significant role in general society until the invention of the printing press five hundred years ago, a mere twenty generations back… Thus, only about 20 generations out of a probable 1600 have even in theory had the opportunity to learn to read and write. (Dissanayake, 1995, p.204)

She continues, using an evolutionary perspective that says that the competency to learn how to speak, just as the capacity to make images and to form social relationships, appears to be encoded in our genes,

> …and our brain has evolved to function with oral communication and in oral culture. But this is not the case for reading and writing, which many children find difficult to learn, requiring a disembedding from context that is quite unnatural to the spontaneous way the mind seems to work. (Dissanayake, 1995, p.204)

It is this disembedding from context and the aspect of detachment that potentially fosters dissociation and isolation. In the age of modernity and postmodernity, human development has become marked with detachment, dissociation, and isolation. These may be part of the price paid for the sweeping advances made through technology and the language of the sciences. This dissociation and fragmentation is powerful. If we do not find ways to reintegrate the domains of our soul and spirit and our interior, subjective worlds with our moral, social, and cultural spheres, we may lose our ability to be informed and replenished by them. This will have a potentially negative effect on how we feel, think, dream, behave, and function as humans in this world.

Dissanayake (1995), in her discussion on how art can be restored so that it once again plays its vital role as an important, human, life-sustaining behavior, states the following:

> Regarding art as a *behavior* – an instant of "making special" – shifts the emphasis from the modernist's view of art as object or quality or the postmodernist's view of it as a text or commodity to the *activity* itself (the making or doing and appreciating), which is what it is in many premodern societies where the object is essentially an occasion for or an accoutrement to ceremonial participation. (p.223)

Within the context of this book, images were not looked at as objects. Instead, the activity of working with the images through a continuous, dialogical process and also of working with the different functions of the images allowed the process of art toward healing to unfold within the microcosm of art therapy. Interpretative quilting, with its emphasis on lived experience and on the image-making process within a community context, is an attempt to break down the dissociation between the different domains and to stay closely grounded in lived experience.

Wilber (1995) presented an interesting view on dissociation that was in a broader sense than the dissociation experienced by the subjects in this book. However, his view opens many possibilities and reveals many implications for the exploration of the subject of dissociation. In his theory on holons, he put forward the idea that there are many natural hierarchies that we need to be aware of and respect. These hierarchies are different from artificial ego-driven hierarchies.

> *Holons emerge.* Owing to the self-transcendent capacity of holons, new holons emerge. First subatomic particles, then atoms, then molecules, then polymers, then cells, and so on. The emergent holons are in some sense novel; they possess properties and qualities that cannot be strictly and totally deduced from their components; and therefore they, and their

> descriptions, cannot be reduced without remainder to their component parts. (Wilber, 1995, pp.46–47)

If we destroy the lower level, for example on a molecular level, we will destroy all higher levels such as plant life, animals, and human beings. He describes two main ways in which the normal balance can become disrupted. He writes:

> ...normal hierarchy, or the *holism between levels*, goes pathological when there is a breakdown between levels and a particular holon assumes a repressive, oppressive, arrogant role of dominance over other holons (whether in individual or social development). On the other hand, *normal* heterarchy, which is holism *within* any level, goes *pathological* when there is a blurring or fusion of that level with its environment: a particular holon doesn't stand out too much, it blends in too much; ...it loses itself in others – and all distinctions, of value or identity, are lost. (Wilber, 1995, p.23)

There is another aspect to finding a healthy balance, boundaries, and a distinction between part/whole relationships. This aspect is awareness. It involves functioning with the whole without disappearing into it or dissociating from it. When looking at the knowledge that has been made available to us through the physical sciences, social sciences, medical science, philosophy, psychology, aesthetics, the arts, and the many other specializations within the various fields, it becomes apparent how readily we can access this knowledge if we choose to. However, it also becomes apparent that it would be very difficult to integrate this vast knowledge for a number of reasons. So how can we prevent dissociation from knowledge systems and fragmentation from lived experience from occurring and why should that be a goal?

Within a clinical context we can observe the phenomenon of dissociation in cases of complex Post Traumatic Stress Disorders and Dissociative Identity Disorder (DID) where individuals are able to function, in some cases quite highly, in certain areas of life through dissociation from other parts, yet in the long run this way of functioning is not sustainable. It leads to the overall breakdown of the whole system and individuals eventually seek treatment in order to re-establish communication, awareness, and an internal equilibrium in which all the different, dissociated parts can start to work together and function as a whole in an authentic way within a community context. Art therapy for these clients appears to be particularly helpful (Cohen, 1996; Cohen, Giller and Lynn, 1991). According to Cohen (1996), there are many parallels between the dissociative reality and the art reality. This, he argues, is why therapists who can capitalize on this affinity will be able to provide more effective treatment than those who use verbal therapy alone. Perhaps we can learn from this clinical picture.

Within the Healing-Flow Model, energy flow is conceptualized in terms of a force that connects all things (i.e., matter, body, mind, spirit, and soul) and that is a vital part of the transformative part of evolution and the continuous reorganization and balance of part/whole relationships. The working with the healing flow and the process of art toward healing connects with what Levine (1995) has called *tending the fire.* In her writing she describes how she is able to work with this primal energy in her work as a therapist. She states: "The fire of creativity is built right away, as soon as we enter the world; and it is lit as soon as we begin to relate to others" (Levine, 1995, p.68). She gives examples of how this primal energy can be disrupted and how one, as a therapist, can help through the language of the arts to rekindle the fire of creative energy and promote its expression in the world.

Looking at the process of art toward healing within a clinical setting makes the dynamics just discussed quite visible. Many of the subjects who contributed to this work through their images and their dialogical processes were struggling with finding their own voice and their authentic identity within a community context. By looking at art dissociation and fragmentation and at the dialogical process between lived experience, images, and text within this microcosm, we may be able to see a parallel with the issues raised in this chapter and with what was made visible through the Interpretative Quilt. It appears that the image-making process using the dialogical image/word approach seemed to facilitate a process for individuals to reconnect and integrate their mind, body, and spirit within a social context in a more primal, intuitive way. The individuals' struggles represented in this book through images, metaphors, and fictionalized text and the issue of finding healthy, sustainable boundaries that go beyond the objectification of the body can be seen as a parallel process. This process becomes visible between the dissociation and fragmentation with which many patients have struggled and the cultural fragmentation and dissociation that are visible in the arts, literature, popular culture, and postmodern thought. One aspect of most therapies is that they attempt to "heal the split between the conscious and unconscious aspects of the psyche so that a person is put in touch with 'all of his mind'" (Wilber, 1979, p.10). This is an important aspect of psychotherapy but Wilber (1995, 1996, 1997) writes in his later works that we need to go beyond that and that we need also to include a process that helps to put us in touch with our whole being (mind, body, and soul/spirit).

Looking at the evolutionary role of the image-making process, art, and human history, Dissanayake (1995, 2000) reminds us that the arts play a vital function in human evolution. The dialogical image/word approach is an attempt to reintegrate lived experience through images and text in a way that they are grounded in perceptions guided by our senses (visual, sensory motor, auditory, emotional, intuitive, and intellectual) and our whole being. The flow of energy can only be experienced and become visible through the whole body's actions. As described in Lusebrink's (1990) work, the external images are grounded in the kinesthetic and sensory level, the perceptual and affective level, and the cognitive and symbolic level. Creativity is present at all levels and connects with the most inner core of being and the spiritual dimension that are then played out within a social/cultural dimension. As long as the energy flow, the body, and the externalizations are in harmony, the being is not aware of its internal functioning. Only when the flow becomes unbalanced, by either being slowed through blockages or through flowing too quickly, does the system become unstable or pathology occur. As already stated, the balance of the part/whole relationships of all things can become interrupted. There are many ways in which the systems will adapt to the imbalance and many may be part of the general ebb and flow that is part of evolution, as Wilber's (1995, 1996, 1997) writings have already explored. Systems imbalances, regressions, or dissociation on a pathological level can occur on all levels of being either along the different holons or on a molecular level reaching up into the larger system of community/society.

On a cultural level, art can provide a similar space for reflection and reintegration, provided that it is placed in a context where the viewers are able to authentically resonate with and reflect with the work. The plight of modernity, with its emptiness that cannot be filled with facts provided by scientific advances, illustrates how we need to be nourished through arts that set off a resonance that ripples through the social fabric of our communities and beyond. The soul or spirit, as conceptualized in this work, is closely linked with creative forces that provide another essential energy for the process of art toward healing.

> The idea of a subtle life energy is close to universal. Most of the world's religious and healing systems, now and throughout history, acknowledge such a concept. Only Western biomedicine, it seems, rejects the idea of a

> spiritual energy or force that heals disease or helps to maintain health and wellness. (Levin, 2001, p.172)

In Oriental philosophy, the concept of "Ki" or "Chi" has been associated with health and well-being. In Oriental medicine, the flow, or interruptions in the flow, of "Ki" or "Chi" have been associated with many different illnesses. In the regulating and re-establishing of the flow of this vital energy, many practices and remedies have evolved over the centuries. These practices are rooted in a larger belief system that incorporates a view of the world that includes the transcendental, spiritual, or metaphysical realm.

> *Subtle energies* research has postulated, and in some cases apparently confirmed, that there exists subtler types of bioenergies beyond the four recognized forces of physics (strong and weak nuclear, electromagnetic, gravitational), and that these subtler energies play an intrinsic role in consciousness and its activity. Known in the traditions by such terms as prana, ki, and chi – and held to be responsible for the effectiveness of acupuncture, to give only one example – these energies are often held to be the 'missing link' between intentional mind and physical body. For the Great Chain theorists, both East and West, this bioenergy acts as a two-way conveyor belt, transferring the impact of matter to the mind and imposing the intentionality of the mind on matter. (Wilber, 1997, p.272)

Throughout history, the arts and creativity have been closely linked to the church and spiritual matters. In tribal societies, the arts, shamanism, and rituals have been very closely linked with healing and spiritual-meaning systems. In our society, technological and scientific thinking predominates and provides us with many "truths" about our way of being in this world. In our culture, the medical and helping professions mediate important events such as birth and death. What once were matters for the church and the spiritual realm are now in the realm of medicine, science, and technology. In this shift, what has happened to the soul and what can the process of art toward healing offer us?

The edited book by Farrelly-Hansen (2001) is devoted to matters related to spirituality and art therapy and many of the chapters of the book support the important connection between spirituality, arts, meditation, and being a therapist. In this book, I cannot prove this important connection in an empirical sense but it can be explicated through images and words and the dialogical image/word process. I further hope that I can make it visible through the Interpretative Quilt that was created here. I cannot prove that creative energy and the spiritual dimension exist by using an empirical methodology but I can make their effects visible through the Interpretative Quilt, with its imagistic pauses, and through other writings dealing with this area.

> The research findings summarized in this book herald a new era in medicine and biomedical science – a post psychosomatic era. Studies in the epidemiology of religion, coupled with the results of experimental trials of prayer and spiritual intercession, signal that the "bio-psychosocial" perspective on health and healing does not go far enough. (Levin, 2001, p.219)

Therefore, Levin (2001) proposes a shift toward a model of theosomatic medicine for the future that includes body, mind, and spirit. This book, with its explication of the process of art toward healing, is an attempt to move in this direction.

> Our world as healers is that of the contemporary shaman, the artist mystic, the contemplative art therapist. The arts are very much about exploring the edges of convention, where habits of mind and collective mindsets are tampered with, inviting perceptions that often confound our usual way of holding ourselves together. (Marek, 2001, p.73)

Marek's (2001) experience with being an art therapist and with Buddhist psychology is that both can gently challenge old beliefs and help us with "relaxing our usual modes of perceptions, opening our senses, and dropping our habitual frames of reference..." (pp.73–74). When working with grief and expanding its energy, Marek confirms my understanding of the transformative process that can transpire through working with images. Marek writes that:

> Before we name it there is just sensation. The challenge is to experience and express grief and its rawness. Too often we want to expel it or stuff it away rather than simply be with it. When we have the desire to expel it, we reject our own experience; when we stuff it, we constrict the flow of energy. (p.58)

The need to honor our lived experience in a socially connected manner and to allow energy flow to move through the transformative cycles is an essential part of the Healing-Flow Model. The dialogical image/word approach described in this book has offered opportunities to individuals within different art therapy groups to work with traumatic experiences and grief related issues. Marek (2001), in his work with patients with psychiatric and medical difficulties, has also found that "the arts can be deeply transformative, emotionally and spiritually" (p.57). He also, like myself and many others in the field of art therapy such as E. Levine (1995), S.K. Levine (1992), and McNiff (1992), has questioned how we can bring back the soul and our spiritual connection into the work of healing and therapy.

The Healing-Flow Model with its dialogical image/word approach may be a way to integrate and utilize the spiritual dimension. In the story of the water dream at the beginning of this book, the sea represented the unconscious and the universal energy symbolized the creative process. The woman represented the vessel through which the creative energy was able to come to consciousness and the painting was the medium. There is a risk involved when engaging in the process if it is not bound in structure and limits. A guide or conceptual structure is needed and a cosmology is essential in order to utilize the creative energy in a healthy and safe manner.

In his discussion on "exoteric" and "esoteric" religion and what functions they may have in our health and well-being Levin (2001) writes:

> We have seen how religious affiliation, attendance, worship, beliefs, and faith contribute to preventing illness and promoting health and well-being. Each defines or reflects participation in the outer path of spiritual traditions – what scholars call "exoteric" religion. The exoteric features include organized denominations, religious services, officially sanctioned prayers and beliefs, and accepted ways to channel one's faith. Research has shown that the exoteric features involve behaviors, social relationships, emotions, beliefs, and thoughts that are strongly health-related. (Levin, 2001, p.154)

Esoteric religions on the other hand are more personal and less externally controlled and they "may be nurtured through contemplative or mystical activities" (Levin, 2001, p.155). Individuals who practice esoteric religion may have encounters of a deeply personal nature with the divine or the sacred which could be reached through "meditation, personal growth activities, creative arts, bodywork, or just being with loved ones or in nature" (Levin, 2001, p.155). Research in this area indicates that "exoteric, institutional religion apparently discourages or depresses the experience of mystical states of consciousness" (Levin, 2001, p.157). He indicates that the health benefits of esoteric religion are not as well researched as they are for the exoteric, institutional religion and that some research would suggest that deeply personal or mystical experiences could be positive, neutral in nature, or very distressing as in the case of diabolical types of mystical experiences.

> This seems to agree with the personal accounts of many people who have been through life-altering events that defy conventional explanation: near-death experiences, out-of-body journeys, moments of clairvoyance or clairsentience, brief states of feeling united with God or with all living beings. After such experiences, for many people life is never the same. (p.160)

At this point, I would like to make a distinction between mystical experiences described here, images that emerge through spontaneous engagement with the creative process, and those images that are produced through psychosis. Rothenberg (1990) indicates through his research on creativity that there are particular, specific thought processes used by creative people during the process of creation that are present in all disciplines and are independent from the media used. In reference to the relationship between the creative process and psychosis, Rothenberg describes how the creative processes seem to involve unusual types of conceptualizing and that these "processes transcend usual modes of ordinary logical thought" (Rothenberg, 1990, p.11). He further postulates that the creative process involves consciousness and logical awareness which are, by their very nature, "highly adaptive and healthy in their psychological function" (Rothenberg, 1990, p.12). He admits that there is a superficial similarity between creative thinking and psychotic modes of thinking.

By looking at artists who have suffered from psychosis or other mental illnesses, one may see these processes as connected. However, according to Rothenberg (1990), the person who suffers from these illnesses is actually shifting between these processes. He believes that during the time that person is engaged in the creative process that individual is thinking healthily. He further points out that:

> Unlike psychotic episodes, in which bizarre thinking develops because of the person's inability to tolerate extreme anxiety and that thinking also seems to serve a defensive function, the creative process requires an ability to tolerate high levels of anxiety and a relative lack of defensiveness in order to proceed. (Rothenberg, 1990, p.36)

His conclusions about the creative process are similar to that of Dissanayake (1988, 1995, 2000) in that both see the creative process as an adaptive and healthy one and one that is separate from pathology.

> The creative person's emotional energy is not directed toward himself, as in psychosis, and he knowingly formulates unusual conceptions in order to improve on reality and to create. He is able to take mental risks and formulate the seemingly illogical and incredible because he is relatively free of anxiety and can assess reality well. (Rothenberg, 1990, p.36)

He continues by stating that although unconscious feelings and unresolved conflicts of the artists may influence the themes and contents of their work, this does not make the underlying process pathological in nature. What is important to look at here is how the creative process is externalized and what functions it has for the individual and the community as a whole.

Working with people who have been severely traumatized by life experiences and especially working with them within the context of the image-oriented psychotherapy group allowed me to come to the understanding that there are many aspects of human existence that are almost impossible to express in words. Within the therapy context, the image-making process, with its dialogical features, appears to open possibilities for giving form to experiences, memories, and dreams, while at the same time providing opportunities to connect with the creative process in a supportive and reality-oriented environment.

As in the water dream at the beginning of this book, we cannot live in the sea for any great length of time because we, as humans, are creatures who belong on land. In our connections with the creative process we need to respect the limits of our "being." The shaman, or what today in some cases is a therapist, is essential to the development of the soul, as the therapist treats the whole being. A spirit guide can take many forms and is always necessary. So, much like in the dream, we could be swept away by the sea of creative energy if we lose the sense of our individual being in this world. We can dissolve dangerously into the whole. We can experience the beauty of images and resonate with their vital force but we need to respect our limitations and boundaries. We need to maintain the balance between the part/whole relationships (Wilber, 1995, 1996, 1997). Yet, if we do not allow ourselves to resonate in some way with this vital force, and if we do not have a belief system that allows us to expand beyond ourselves as separate, alone, and isolated individuals who are disembodied of a soul or a spirit, we run the risk of becoming ill through fragmentation, dissociation, and the disruption of the continuous flow of energy.

In terms of representing my lived experience of the process of art toward healing, I knew from a very early point that images played a vital role. The limitations of using words led me to develop the Interpretative Quilt, with its dialogical image/word process, as a way of representing these unusual experiences with the creative process in a more integrated manner. Levin (2001) goes on to suggest that energies or associated forces that could be released during these experiences are difficult to assess and research. These experiences are only accepted by some scientists and are rejected by many who perhaps see them as dilutions. The question then arises as to whether it is possible to truthfully examine and communicate authentically these intrinsically non-verbal, powerful experiences. As mentioned at the beginning of this book, the metaphor of the water dream and the creation of an Interpretative Quilt were an attempt to study the phenomenon of the process of art toward healing by using a representational style that can be understood by others in the field of psychology, art therapy, and other related fields.

References

Achterberg, J., Dossey, B. and Kolkmeier, L. (eds) (1994) *Rituals of Healing: Using Imagery for Healing, and Wellness.* New York: Bantam Books.

Adamson, E. (1990) *Art as Healing.* Boston: Conenture, LTD.

Assagioli, R. (1971) *Psychosynthesis: A Manual of Principles and Techniques.* New York: Penguin Books.

Bachelard, G. (1969) [1958] *The Poetics of Space* (M. Jolas, trans.). New York: The Orion Press. (Original work published 1958)

Ball, H.K. (1999) *Quilts as Social Text.* Unpublished doctoral dissertation, Wilfrid Laurier University, Waterloo.

Barthes, R. (1981) [1980] *Camera Lucida: Reflections on Photography* (R. Howard, trans.). New York: Hill and Wang. (Original work published 1980)

Berger, J. and Mohr, J. (1982) *Another Way of Telling.* New York: Pantheon Books.

Bloom, S. (1997) *Creating Sanctuary: Toward an Evolution of Scene Societies.* New York: Routledge.

Bollas, C. (1987) *The Shadow of the Object: Psychoanalysis of the Unthought Known.* New York: Columbia University Press.

Boltin, L. and Newton, D. (1978) *The Nelson A. Rockefeller Collection: Masterpieces of Primitive Art* (first edition). New York: Alfred A. Knopf.

Brazelton, B.T. and Cramer, B.G. (1990) *The Earliest Relationship.* New York: Merloyd Lawrence Books.

Bry, D. and Callaway, N. (1989) *Georgia O'Keefe: In the West.* New York: Alfred A. Knopf in association with Callaway.

Cahill, J. and Skira, A. (1977) *Treasures of Asia: Chinese Painting.* New York: Rizzoli International Publications, Inc.

Caiserman-Roth, G. and Cohen, R. (1993) *Insights, Discoveries, Surprises: Drawing from the Model.* Montreal and Kingston: McGill – Queen's University Press.

Cameron, J. (1992) *The Artist's Way: A Spiritual Path to Higher Creativity.* New York: G.P. Putnam's Sons.

Cohen, B.M. (1996) 'Art and the dissociative paracosm: uncommon realities.' In L.K. Michelson (eds) *Handbook of Dissociation: Theoretical, Empirical and Clinical Perspectives.* New York: Plenum Press.

Cohen, B.M., Giller, E. and Lynn, W. (eds) (1991) *Multiple Personality Disorder from the Inside Out.* Baltimore: The Sidran Press.

Colilli, P. (1993) *Signs of the Hermetic Imagination.* Toronto: Toronto Semiotic Circle.

Courtney, R. (1982) *Re-Play: Studies of Human Drama in Education.* Toronto: The Ontario Institute for Studies in Education Press.

Courtney, R. (1987) *The Quest: Research and Inquiry in Arts Education.* Lanham, MD: University Press of America.

Darroch, V. (1984) *Voice of Hearing.* Victoria: Sono Nis.

Darroch-Lozowski, V. (1989) 'Initiation in hermeneutics: An illustration through the mother and daughter archetype.' *Human Studies: A Journal for Philosophy and the Social Sciences 13*, 237–251.

Darroch-Lozowski, V. (1993) 'Immemorial images through chronological time.' *Create: Journal of Creative and Expressive Arts Therapy Exchange 3*, 25–28.

Darroch-Lozowski, V. (1999) *Uncoded World.* New York: Peter Lang Publishers.

Darroch-Lozowski, V. and Silvers R.J. (1982) *Interpretive Human Studies.* Lanham, MD: University Press of America.

Darroch-Lozowski, V., Crawford, L.A. and Ponti-Sgargi, L. (1997) *Not One But Many: On the Centennial of the Women's Institute (1897–1997).* Manitoulin Island: Ice Lake Press.

Dissanayake, E. (1988) *What is Art For?* London: University of Washington Press.

Dissanayake, E. (1995) *Homo Aestheticus: Where Art Comes from and Why.* London: University of Washington Press.

Dissanayake, E. (2000) *Art and Intimacy: How the Arts Began.* London: University of Washington Press.

Farrelly-Hansen, M. (2001) *Spirituality and Art Therapy: Living the Connection.* London: Jessica Kingsley Publishers.

Figley, C.F. (ed) (1995) *Compassion Fatigue: Coping with Secondary Traumatic Stress Disorder in Those who Treat the Traumatized.* New York: Brunner/Mazel.

Gablik, S. (1995) *Conversations Before the End of Time.* New York: Thames and Hudson.

Gadamer, H.G. (1985) *Truth and Method* (second edition) (J. Weinheimer and D.G. Marshal, trans.). New York: Crossroad.

Gadamer, H.G. (1986) *The Relevance of the Beautiful and Other Essays* (N. Walfer, trans.; R. Bernasconi, ed). New York: Cambridge University Press. (Original work published 1986)

Grosch, W.N. and Olsen, D.C. (1994) *When Helping Starts to Hurt: A New Look at Burnout among Psychotherapists.* New York: Norton.

Hacking, I. (1995) *Rewriting the Soul: Multiple Personality and the Sciences of Memory.* Princeton, NJ: Princeton University Press.

Harris, P. (1993) *A Child's Story: Recovering Through Creativity.* St. Louis: Cracom Corporation.

Heidegger, M. (1977) *Basic Writings from Being and Time (1927) to the Task of Thinking (1964)* (D. Krell, ed). New York: Penguin Books.

Hudnall Stamm, H. (ed) (1995) *Secondary Traumatic Stress: Self-Care Issues for Clinicians, Researchers, and Educators.* Lutherville, MD: Sidran Press.

Hupka, R. (1979) *Michelangelo Pietà.* New York: Crown Publisher, Inc.

Irving, M. (1996) *The Survivors Monument Project: Share the Dream.* Toronto. Contact 274 Rhodes Avenue, M4L 3A3 or Tel. 416 469 4764 for copies.

Johnson, M. (1991) 'The imaginative basis of meaning and cognition.' In S. Küchler and W. Melion (eds) *Images of Memory: On Remembering and Representation.* Washington: Smithsonian Institution Press.

Krakow, B., Hollifield, M., Johnston, L., Koss, M. *et al.* (2001) 'Imagery rehearsal therapy for chronic nightmares in sexual assault survivors with posttraumatic stress disorder.' *The Journal of the American Medical Association 286*, 5, 537–545.

Küchler, S. and Melion, W. (eds) (1991) *Images of Memory: On Remembering and Representation.* Washington: Smithsonian Institution Press.

Larsen, S. (1988) *The Shaman's Doorway.* New York: Station Hill Press.

LeBoeuf, M. (1980) *Imagineering: How to Profit from Your Creative Powers.* New York: Berkley Books.

Levin, J. (2001) *God, Faith, and Health: Exploring the Spirituality–Healing Connection.* New York: John Wiley and Sons, Inc.

Levine, E. (1995) *Tending the Fire: Studies in Art, Therapy and Creativity.* Toronto: Palmerston Press.

Levine, S.K. (1992) *Poiesis: The Language of Psychology and Speech of the Soul.* Toronto: Palmerston Press.

Lusebrink, V.B. (1990) *Imagery and Visual Expression in Therapy.* New York: Plenum Press.

Marek, B. (2001) 'Each time a new breath: buddhism, art, and healing.' In M. Farrelly-Hansen (ed) *Spirituality and Art Therapy: Living the Connection.* London: Jessica Kingsley Publishers.

McNiff, S. (1981) *The Arts and Psychotherapy.* Springfield, IL: Charles C. Thomas Publisher.

McNiff, S. (1989) *Depth Psychotherapy of Art.* Springfield, IL: Charles C. Thomas Publishers.

McNiff, S. (1992) *Art as Medicine: Creating a Therapy of the Imagination.* Boston: Shambhala.

McNiff, S. (1998) *Art-Based Research.* London: Jessica Kingsley Publishers.

Meekums, B. (1993) 'Research as an act of creation.' In H. Payne (ed) *Handbook of Inquiry in the Arts Therapies.* London: Jessica Kingsley Publishers.

Montgomery-Whicher, R. (1996, August) 'Drawing from life: the practices of art and research.' Paper presented at the Fifteenth International Human Science Research Conference, Halifax, Nova Scotia.

Mook, B. (1996) 'Transformation through imaginative play in child psychotherapy: a phenomenological hermeneutic approach.' Paper presented at the fifteenth International Human Science Research Conference, Halifax, Nova Scotia.

Nachmanovitch, S. (1990) *Free Play: The Power of Improvisation in Life and Arts.* Los Angeles: Jeremy P. Tarcher, Inc.

Payne, H. (ed) (1993) *Handbook of Inquiry in the Arts Therapies.* London: Jessica Kingsley Publishers.

Pearce, J.C. (1992) *Evolution's End: Claiming the Potential of our Intelligence.* New York: Harper San Francisco.

Peavy, R.V. (1996) 'Sociodynamic counselling™ beyond twentieth century forms of helping.' Paper presented at the fifteenth International Human Science Research Conference, Halifax, Nova Scotia.

Pritzker, P. and Dopagne, J. (1975) *Ernst.* New York: Leon Amiel Publisher.

Random House Webster's Dictionary. (1991) Computer software. Orem, UT: WordPerfect Corporation.

Rothenberg, A. (1990) *Creativity and Madness: New Findings and Old Stereotypes.* Baltimore: The Johns Hopkins University Press.

Rubin, W. (ed) (1980) *Pablo Picasso: A Retrospective.* New York: The Museum of Modern Art.

Schaufeli, W. and Enzmann, D. (1998) *The Burnout Companion to Study and Practice: A Critical Analysis.* London and Philadelphia, PA: Taylor & Francis.

Schaverien, J. (1992) *The Revealing Image: Analytical Art Psychotherapy in Theory and Practice.* New York: Tavistock/Routledge.

Schnetz, M. (1990) *The Process of Art Toward Healing.* Unpublished Master's thesis, University of Toronto, Toronto.

Schnetz, M. (2003) *The Healing Flow: Artistic Expression in Therapy.* Unpublished doctoral dissertation, University of Toronto, Toronto.

Shapiro, M.J. (1985–86) 'Metaphor in the philosophy of social sciences.' *Cultural Critique 2*, 191–214.

Silvers, R. (1988) *A Pause on the Path.* Philadelphia: Temple University Press.

Silvers, R. (1993a) *Once Upon a Time.* Manitoulin Island: Ronald Silvers.

Silvers, R. (1993b) 'Manitoulin Island Summer 1992.' *Create: Journal of Creative and Expressive Arts Therapy Exchange 3*, 63–66.

Sirén, O. (1963) *The Chinese on the Art of Painting.* New York: Schocken Books.

Skovholt, T.M. (2001) *The Resilient Practitioner: Burnout Prevention and Self-Care Strategies for Counselors, Therapists, Teachers, and Health Professionals.* Boston and London: Allyn and Bacon.

Spiegelberg, H. (1971) *The Phenomenological Movement* (second edition, Vol. 2). The Hague, Netherlands: Martinus Nijhoff.

Stachelhaus, H. (1987) *Joseph Beuys.* Düsseldorf: claassen Verlag GmbH Düsseldorf.

Stein, S.A. (ed) (1986) *Van Gogh: A Retrospective.* New York: Wings Books.

Stern, D.N. (1985) *The Interpersonal World of the Infant.* New York: Basic Books.

Stern, D.N. (1995) *The Motherhood Constellation: A Unified View of Parent–Infant Psychotherapy.* New York: Basic Books.

Storr, A. (1988) *Solitude: A Return to Self.* New York: Free Press.

Talbot, M. (1991) *The Holographic Universe.* New York: HarperCollins.

Van der Kolk, B.A. (1989) 'The compulsion to repeat the trauma.' *Psychiatric Clinics of North America 12*, 2, 389–411.

Van Manen, M. (1990) *Researching Lived Experience: Pedagogy.* New York: State University of New York Press.

West, A. (1993) *Poetic Formation: The Curator and the Open, Artistic Work.* Unpublished doctoral dissertation, University of Toronto, Toronto.

Wilber, K. (1979) *No Boundary: Eastern and Western Approaches to Person Growth.* Boston: Shambhala.

Wilber, K. (1995) *Sex, Ecology, Spirituality: The Spirit of Evolution.* Boston: Shambhala.

Wilber, K. (1996) *A Brief History of Everything.* Boston: Shambhala.

Wilber, K. (1997) *The Eye of the Spirit: An Integral Vision for a World Gone Slightly Mad.* Boston: Shambhala.

Winner, E. (1982) *Invented Worlds: The Psychology of Arts.* Cambridge: Harvard University Press.

Wisechild, L.M. (ed) (1991) *She Who Was Lost Is Remembered: Healing from Incest through Creativity.* Vancouver: The Seal Press.

Wolf, F.A. (1994) *The Dreaming Universe: A Mind-Expanding Journey into the Realm where Psyche and Physics Meet.* New York: Simon and Schuster.

Wright, J. (1996) 'Image-oriented psychotherapy using drawing as a feedback mechansim.' In D.L. Nathanson (ed) *Knowing Feelings: Affect, Script, and Psychotherapy.* New York: W.W. Norton and Company.

Subject Index

Author Index